155.64
S

B&T   12/09
TS

Mean Mothers

Mean Mothers

OVERCOMING
THE LEGACY OF HURT

Peg Streep

Foreword by
Rachel Harris, Ph.D.

WILLIAM MORROW
An Imprint of HarperCollins*Publishers*

Library of Congress Cataloging-in-Publication Data

Streep, Peg.
  Mean mothers : overcoming the legacy of hurt / Peg Streep ; foreword by Rachel Harris.
     p. cm.
  Includes bibliographical references.
  ISBN 978-0-06-165136-6
1. Mothers and daughters. 2. Love, Maternal. I. Title.
  HQ755.85.S77 2009
  155.6'463—dc22

                                             2009013160

09 10 11 12 13 OV/RRD 10 9 8 7 6 5 4 3 2

For my daughter, Alexandra Emily Israel,
and for daughters everywhere

Contents

Foreword
by Rachel Harris, Ph.D.

PSYCHOTHERAPISTS MAY DISAGREE, EVEN VEHEMENTLY, ABOUT THE-
ory or practice, but we all agree on the mother's central importance in
a woman's life. From day one, or even before as some perinatal psychologists believe, the mother's capacity to be empathic and responsive to her
baby will shape the very architecture of her daughter's developing brain.
This is just the beginning of the mother's impact on a daughter's life.

After almost forty years of private practice, I still listen for the most
important clue in a new client's history — *Did she feel loved as a child?*
I never ask this question directly because it's too difficult to admit that
"No, my mother didn't love me." Even adults who were abused as children
may feel that they were loved, although during the course of therapy they
may come to reconsider their answer, while others who didn't feel loved
may eventually appreciate that their mothers were too damaged to be able
to love anyone. Ultimately, this seemingly simple question is more complex
than it might appear.

Mean Mothers asks the very same question and explores the lives of
women who are able to say that they were not loved well enough or even

that their mothers were mean. How these women understand their mothers' impact on their lives will enlighten all of us, no matter how we perceive our mothers.

Peg Streep weaves the latest psychological research into her exploration of mean mothers within the context of the whole family—the mean mother's relationship with her mother, the role of the father, and how other siblings were treated. There are no simple answers here. Family dynamics are such a complex mix of personality, genetics, and environment that it is impossible to define the impact of a mean mother in simple terms. Streep uses personal stories from many women to deepen our understanding of mean mothers and to arrive at a place of hope, if not reconciliation. Hope resides ultimately in the daughter and how she chooses to live her life, and not in her relationship with her mother.

Along the way, Streep shares her own experiences with a mean mother and how she grew to understand that she is both worthy of being loved and capable of being a loving mother. It is perhaps by becoming a loving mother that Streep both frees herself from her own mother and surpasses her in this ultimate challenge. It requires persistent courage and hard work for an unloved girl to grow up to become a loving mother, and it's not an easy journey. Yet it is the greatest life task to have the awareness and compassion not to pass on the legacy of familial dysfunction to the next generation. This is the achievement of the author and the book.

The opportunity for the reader is, first of all, to learn that she is not alone if she has had a mother who's been less than loving. If she has the courage to explore the possibility of *Mean Mothers,* she will find good company in the many intimate examples of other women struggling with their legacy of hurt. Knowing that there are others who share a similar history will help the reader to trust her own feelings, and give validity to her experience.

This is extremely important, since most people consider the very phrase "mean mothers" to be an oxymoron because mothering and meanness are incompatible by definition. Sadly, after years in practice, I have to report that there are more mean mothers than most of us would like to admit. There's a continuum from horribly abusive mothers to motherly saints, but there are plenty of mothers in the middle range who are unable to love or who say mean things to their daughters. And many of these mothers see themselves as good mothers. Trust me, I've asked them about their relationships with their daughters and have been rendered speechless in reaction to their denial and accompanying conviction that they've been loving mothers.

Both the mothers' denial of their responsibility and the cultural taboo against acknowledging the possibility of mean mothers serve to keep unloved daughters trapped in self-blame. *Mean Mothers* can help free the reader from these myths and provide hope that adult daughters may be able to reclaim themselves and their own life stories. It's quite a personal journey to break through the cultural myth of motherhood to discover that one's own mother was just plain mean.

Another opportunity for the reader is to learn how other women have dealt with the internalized voice of their mean mothers. Each of us hears her mother's voice inside her head, but those with a mean mother have a more difficult time preventing that voice from continuing to hurt them. This book presents a variety of personal stories describing how different women have dealt with the internal legacy of a mean mother and found greater self-worth.

No matter what kind of mother we might have had, we all have to find a way to accept and transcend our mothers' limitations in order to become the kind of women and mothers we want to be. This book can help us to deepen our understanding of ourselves and our mothers and to make more conscious choices about how we mother our daughters.

Mean Mothers

· One ·

The Myth of Mother Love

I WAS NO OLDER THAN THREE OR FOUR WHEN I KNEW MY MOTHER didn't love me. Of course, the way in which I knew this was different from how I would know and understand it at other times in my life, but I knew it nonetheless. I knew it first by the way she stiffened when I tried to sit in her lap or touch her arm and how she turned her face away when I kissed her. She wasn't like the people who loved me—my father, my grandfather, my great-aunt, or even my teachers—whose faces softened with pleasure when I drew near.

Later, I knew that who I was—a round-faced, curly-haired girl full of energy and curiosity—was enough to irritate or infuriate her. "Stop skipping!" she'd say when we walked together, dropping my hand in punishment, as though my joy was an affront to her. I would slow down, chastened by her sharp voice, instantly lonely but reassured by the clatter of her high heels on the pavement that she was still there. She was the bullet I couldn't dodge, and the gunfire could come from anywhere and nowhere. It might be a stranger telling her she had a pretty child, inadvertently setting off a tirade as sudden and violent as a summer storm. She would begin with a defense of her own beauty that would build into a hurricane of complaints, gathering energy as it went, each new thought more saturated with anger than the one before, all directed at me. The seeds of her rage and disappointment could blossom in a bewildering instant.

I knew, more than anything, that her power was enormous and that the light of her sun was what I needed. But that light could burn, flicker, or disappear for any or no reason. Yet, as a small child, I loved and needed her, and wanted desperately to please her, as much as I feared her.

When I was a little girl, I learned to tiptoe through her shadows and find sunshine in the real world and that of my imagination. Before he died, my father was a safe haven, since she largely hid both her anger and meanness toward me when he was home. I hoarded the attention I got from my teachers, my babysitter, the woman who cleaned our apartment, the mothers of my friends, and tucked it away, deep inside.

I drew the stories in books up around my shoulders for comfort, my thumb in my mouth. I called myself Eloise and was happiest living vicariously in the blissfully motherless Plaza Hotel, with a loving nanny, a turtle, and a dog named Weenie. I pretended that I was Jo March with a mother named Marmie, and the boy who owned Ole Yeller and the girl who rode Flicka. I saw myself living in that little house on the prairie, all safe and warm, with the pumpkins big enough to sit on in the dry cellar. I mothered my dolls the way I longed to be mothered; I told them stories, cuddled them, and made sure they were safe.

I mothered myself by imagining that I'd been handed to the wrong mother at the hospital somehow and that the mother to whom I really belonged would come and find me—knowing all along that the mother I had was the one I'd been born to. I could see my mother's reflection in my face just as easily as I could see, standing on a chair in the bathroom, the red outlines her hands left on my back when her anger left her speechless.

As I got older, my mother's menace diminished, though not her meanness or the mystery of her rage. With the birth of my brother when I was nine, I saw that my mother could love a child who wasn't me. Try as I might, I couldn't puzzle it out; what was it about me that made her so angry? Why didn't she love me? When I asked her just that, as I would time and again over the course of many years, her answer was always the same and maddeningly indirect: "Every mother loves her child, Peggy." I knew it to be a lie, but I didn't yet see that she lied to protect herself, not me.

There was no reconciling the mother I knew—the one who literally shook with fury and missed no opportunity to wound or criticize me—with the charming and beautiful woman who went out into the world in the highest of heels, shining jewelry on her hands and neck, not a hair out of place. She flirted with everyone—even my girlfriends and later my boyfriends—and they pronounced her delightful. Her secret—and mine—was closely held; who would believe me if I told? And so I didn't. But she was all I had left when I was fifteen and the two men who had loved me—my father and my grandfather—died within three months of each other.

By then, the struggle between us took a different shape. She could still hurt me—I never forgot the moment she told the first boy I loved that despite my pretty outside, I was rotten inside—but she couldn't scare me. I watched how she acted with her own mother, a dance set to a melody of jealousy and competition. Slowly—very slowly—I had my first inkling that how she treated me might have nothing at all to do with who I was.

I was younger, smarter, better educated than she, and I began to realize that she was afraid of me and the truths I told. By the time I was a sophomore in high school, I had a countdown of the days before college—it was more than a thousand—and that made my life trapped under her roof seem almost temporary and gave me the illusion of imminent freedom.

But I still wanted her love as much as I wanted to be able to answer the question I couldn't answer as a child: Why didn't she love me?

I know the answer now, and that knowledge absolutely coexists with a terrible longing for the mother love I never had and never will have.

GROWING UP, I THOUGHT I was alone—the only girl born on the planet whose mother didn't love her. Mothers in books were nothing like mine, and the moms on television—it was the late 1950s and early 1960s—were women who wore aprons and served dinner with smiles on their faces and love in their hearts. I envied my friends for the mothers they had. I wanted to be Lynne, whose mother was both thoughtful and attentive and bought Lynne her first kitten heels as a surprise when we were in sixth grade, or Beth, whose mother told funny stories and let us make messy cupcakes in her kitchen. Even Roz's mother, who was born in Europe like mine and more formal than the born-in-America moms, was kind and loving. It happened over forty years ago, but I still remember how she stroked Roz's hair, absentmindedly and contentedly, as they stood side by side in their hallway, saying good-bye to me after a study date.

I watched strangers—daughters and mothers in the supermarket aisles or taking a walk together—and was all the more bewildered. What made my mother and me so different? Why didn't my mother love me the way she was supposed to? Whose fault was it? Hers or mine?

My mother's physical control waned as I grew taller, but she had power nonetheless. I still couldn't understand what it was about me that made me, in her eyes at least, so eminently unlovable. I wavered between thinking I had done nothing to deserve her treatment and not being quite so sure—a testament, I now know but didn't then, to nothing more than the centrality of the mother sun to a daughter's world. The parent of a child, as Deborah Tannen has written, has the power not only to create the world the child lives in but the ability to dictate how that world is to be interpreted. Seen from that point of view, one of the lasting and important legacies of a mean mother is a wellspring of self-doubt. The other, explained by adaptive behavior, is a need to replicate the relationship she has to her mother with other people, regardless of how unhappy it makes her.

When I was sixteen, I read Erich Fromm's *The Art of Loving.* I stopped dead in my tracks when I saw what he had to say about a mother's love: "Mother's love is bliss, is peace, it need not be acquired, it need not be deserved." I read on, astonished that the simple act of giving birth should be enough to spark a love truer than any other.

Unconditional love: I finally had the words for what I was missing.

It took me many years to understand that for the unloving mother and unloved daughter alike, our idea of unconditional love is a two-edged sword.

STORIES OF MEAN MOTHERS make women uncomfortable.

I understand this with greater clarity when I tell people what I'm working on. "Was *your* mother mean?" my hair colorist asks me. She's twenty-eight, a child of divorce, and fiercely loyal to the mother who raised her alone, whom she counts among her best friends. I often talk about my own daughter, who's off at college, but this is the first time I've ever mentioned my project or my mother. After I've answered, her response is downright hostile: "Why would you want to dig all that up now? She must have done something right, because you turned out okay, didn't you?" From the other end of the spectrum, a friend—a psychologist who specializes in mother-daughter relationships and is herself the divorced mother of a twenty-three-year-old daughter—sends me an e-mail that's more like a cheer than anything else: "Good for you—this is courageous. You're telling the story no one else wants to tell. It's about time."

Women's reactions betray the power of cultural taboos. I give a small dinner party in my new home in Vermont, and one of my guests, a fellow baby boomer who raised three children and is now a doting grandmother, looks frankly skeptical when I tell her about the book and responds, slowly and deliberately: "I don't think it's fair to talk about those things. My mother did what she could." My other guest is a woman in her early seventies who raised four now-grown children and is long divorced. She seems delighted to be able to talk about her mother, who she says categorically "was the most unloving and critical person I ever met. She never missed an opportunity to make me feel bad about myself, no matter how kind or loving I tried to be." When I ask her whether she ever confronted her mother, she looks at me nonplussed: "Of course not. She was my mother, after all."

Mother love is a sacred concept in our culture, and like all things sacred it has a mythology of its own. There isn't any room in our ideal of "mother"—that essential multitasker and nurturer, the one made up in equal parts of a pastel-tinted Madonna cradling her baby, the smell of freshly baked cookies in the oven, self-sacrifice, and Hallmark verse—for the mother who doesn't love her child. As Western fairy tales make clear, cruel or uncaring mothers are never biological mothers but interlopers or stepmothers instead. "Real" mothers neither hate nor envy; it's Rapunzel's jealous stepmother who locks her in the tower, just as Cinderella's rapacious one would consign her to a life of servitude.

Today, we prefer to think of mothering as instinctual and automatic— even though mothering, for our species at least, is very much learned behavior, and definitions of what constitutes good mothering are no more than cultural constructs. Our insistence on maternal instinct flies in the face of both human history and the history of child-rearing practices. It doesn't take into account the extraordinarily widespread practice of abandoning children, from the time of the Greeks right up through the Renaissance; the hundreds of thousands of foundlings left in hospitals established for that very purpose throughout the "civilized" world; or the practice of wet-nursing, which resulted in the deaths of literally millions of infants, for example.

We talk about mother love as though it were a universal and absolute truth, and perhaps this has nothing to do with motherhood at all. If Erich Fromm's idealized if wishful thinking about unconditional, instinctual love is a shorthand summary of what we hold to be the truth about motherhood, it probably also testifies to our deep psychological need for a love without strings or complications.

We want desperately to believe that every mother falls in love with her baby at first sight and that the complexity of relationships, so evident elsewhere as part of the human condition, is totally absent from the connection between mother and child. This ideal is so ingrained in our culture that, until relatively recently, even science held that pregnancy and childbearing were a protection against maternal unhappiness or depression—rather than potential causes of them. In 2005 Brooke Shields's frank depiction of her struggle with postpartum depression—after years of trying to conceive a child—was newsworthy for that very reason: how could a famously beautiful mother with an equally beautiful daughter possibly be made so miserable by motherhood?

Our culture understands motherhood to be one of the most fulfilling roles of a woman's life, if not the apex of fulfillment. Of all the roles we play, parenting is considered to be the one that promises the greatest personal and social rewards. There's little scientific evidence, however, to support this cultural trope; in fact, the preponderance of the evidence absolutely negates it. A major study reported in 2005 by Ranae J. Evenson and Robin W. Simon confirmed what other studies had found before: Unlike other adult roles such as marriage and employment, parenthood did not appear to confer any mental health advantage. On the contrary, childless adults were far less likely to suffer from depression than their peers with children. In addition, mothers with minor children were the group most likely to be depressed, a finding the researchers attributed to the emotional benefits of parenting being "canceled or exceeded" by the emotional costs associated with the role. Not surprisingly, single parents were more likely to be depressed than their married peers, because of decreased economic and social resources. Fathers were less likely to be depressed than mothers, unless another factor was added in, such as unemployment. Most important, the incidence of depression increased depending on the mother's experience of parenting, which the researchers categorized in the following way: the demands and normative expectations associated with the role; the perception of her ability to satisfy the role expectation; her self-evaluation as a parent; the quality of her relationship to her child or children; the stressfulness of the role; the availability of social and economic resources; the emotional gratification and sense of purpose and meaning derived from motherhood. It's extraordinary that of the seven measures of the experience of parenthood, only one—social and economic resources—_doesn't_ have to do with the _idea_ of motherhood.

Unlike all the other relationships each and every one of us has in our lives—sometimes messy, fractious, or in need of "work"—the mother-child relationship is supposed to be both beatific and instant. The concept of "bonding"—despite its lack of scientific basis—has become a contemporary cornerstone of good mothering, a way of guaranteeing that every single supposed seed of instinctual nurturance in the new mother will burst into flower. What would accomplish this miracle of nature? Just some quiet moments right after birth—the so-called critical moments—with the infant pressed against her mother's flesh.

Popular books on parenting and, even more specifically, mothering have given further ballast to the idea of "instinctual" mother love while reinforcing the notion that the mother's ability to "bond" instantly with her child at birth is a reliable predictor of both the child's future ability to thrive and the mother's ability to parent. No less an authority than Dr. Spock, who presided over the rules of parenting beginning at the end of World War II, began to promote the idea of instant "bonding" by the mid-1970s. "Rooming-in" as well as breast-feeding became obligatory for any women who aspired to be a good mother.

There is no room in our contemporary ideal for ambivalence or emotional discomfort; our insistence on the breadth and depth of absolute mother love is itself absolute, except perhaps in the contemporary chat rooms of the Internet, where the mothers of newborns and small children, cloaked in anonymity, express their frustrations to total strangers. Even loving mothers sometimes find themselves hobbled by the burden unconditional love imposes. As Lila confided, speaking of her sixteen-year-old daughter, "I feel guilty when Sarah disappoints or angers me because, at those moments—and just for the briefest moment—I do love her less and it makes me feel awful."

It's been proposed, in fact, that our cultural enthronement of idealized mothering combined with an intolerance for any maternal ambivalence becomes a problem for every mother, whether she is loving or not. Psychotherapist Rozsika Parker has suggested that in denying those experiences in motherhood that inevitably evoke maternal ambivalence, we also miss the possibility that feelings of ambivalence can be a creative source for the mother to attain new understanding of her child. It is, as she writes, "the troubling co-existence of love and hate that propels a mother into thinking about what goes on between herself and her child." It's probably not an accident that Adrienne Rich's groundbreaking book, *Of Woman Born,* begins with a reflection of that ambivalence which every woman feels at one point or another in her life as a mother but is forced to deny, because of guilt or anxiety: "My children cause me the most exquisite suffering of which I have any experience. It is the suffering of ambivalence: the murderous alternation between bitter resentment and raw-edged nerves, and blissful gratification and tenderness." As Anne Roiphe writes in *Fruitful,* "Every mother knows, even if she cannot consciously admit it, that she doesn't always love her child and the desire to be free of the baby rises, hardly acknowledged, there at the edge of the mind, in the bad dream, the excessive anxiety, the overprotectiveness that disguises angry wishes."

Mother love is also assumed to arc seamlessly through all the stages of life the child and the mother experience—denying that the parenting skills required for a toddler and a teenager are indeed very different. Our dependence on "the instinct" of mother love refuses to take into account communication skills or personality, even though what experts call "goodness of fit" is a component in every mother-child relationship (and every father-child relationship as well).

There's no room in this view for conflict. Yet, as Laurence Steinberg has written, the coincidence of certain life stages—a daughter's adolescence and her mother's entry into midlife, for example—can often provoke a crisis for the mother, one with deep and far-reaching implications. Similarly, the potential conflict between an adult daughter's choices and those her mother made is rarely addressed. Our ideal of motherhood steadfastly denies competition or jealousy, despite evidence to the contrary.

Even researchers are taken aback when their findings subvert some of our most cherished notions about mothers and daughters. Carol Ryff, Pamela Schmutte, and Young Hyang Lee looked at how parents were affected by their adult children's achievements and success. To their astonishment, the researchers discovered that mothers who perceived their daughters' achievements as surpassing their own reported *lower* well-being; to indicate their surprise, the researchers put the word *lower* in italics! Simply put, their daughters' successes made them feel lousy about themselves. Most notably, this was not true of fathers—with either sons or daughters—or for that matter of mothers when the more successful child was a son.

Cultural expectations set up a dynamic that, by refusing to allow maternal ambivalence, effectively traps the mother who has difficulty connecting to or loving the daughter she has borne. For a mother to concede that she doesn't love the child she brought into the world unconditionally or at all is to admit to the greatest of failures as a woman and a person; it is both unthinkable and "unnatural" at once. Nancy Friday, in *My Mother/My Self,* astutely observed that the myth that mothers *always* love their children is so controlling that the woman who can be honest about everything else will not be able to admit that she does not love or like her daughter.

In a similar vein, Harriet Lerner, Ph.D., author of *The Mother Dance,* recounts how, after reading Rozsika Parker's book *Mother Love, Mother Hate,* she discusses the possibility of mother hate with her husband, a therapist, who states categorically that she needs to delete the word from her book, since in all his years of practice he's never heard a mother talk about hating her children. Lerner herself ends up waxing mystical, if illogical, in the face of all she knows about mother hate and love, writing, "Still, beneath whatever negative emotions or distance we feel, the bond between the mother and child is so deep and mysterious that even hate cannot permanently dismantle it." Her words betray the myth at work.

But not all mothers love, unconditionally or otherwise. For the

mother who doesn't, the cultural myths of unconditional love and maternal instinct require her to hide and deny her feelings at all costs, even if
she cannot always keep herself from expressing them in words or gestures.
There's no room in the mother myth for the mother who resents all the
attention her infant or toddler needs, or who chafes at the necessary loss
of freedom and self-focus the transition into motherhood usually entails.
In her book *You're Wearing That?,* an examination of mothers and adult
daughters, Deborah Tannen rightly observes that "love gives and it takes
away; it makes you more than you were before but it also makes you less."
Acknowledging that motherhood, like all adult choices, is a trade-off, Tannen writes, "In reality, though, many women, even those who genuinely
want the children they have, may not foresee, or may not be all that happy
about, the ways their children will limit them."

What may be a temporary period of unhappiness for a loving mother
can become a virtual prison sentence for an unloving one. She may find
herself envying her daughter—for her looks, for her choices, for the future
ahead of her. Her own insecurities and inadequacies may be magnified
by what she sees in her child, during both the daughter's childhood and
adulthood. The denial made necessary by the myth makes resolution of
the conflict virtually impossible.

Since the myths of motherhood are cultural constructs—and evolve
along with culture's mores—the burden they place on the unloving mother
may vary from generation to generation. It's probably not an accident that
many of the adult daughters interviewed for this book were the children
of women who gave birth in the years following World War II—the 1950s
and early 1960s—when the popular wisdom pertaining to the good mother
and motherhood had a specificity of its own. Experts of the time—echoed
in popular magazines and doctors' advice—saw motherhood as a fulfillment of biological and personal destiny. A "healthy" woman had children;
a "happy" and "fulfilled" woman was a mother.

Out of these decades came the vision of Mother as above all empathic,
catering to all her child's needs with consummate care. The flip side—a
much darker one—was that if anything were to go awry with her child,

none other than Mother was to blame, a view promulgated both in books and the popular press. Psychoanalyst René Spitz actually went so far as to categorize the "psycho-toxic diseases of infancy," maintaining that each and every problem associated with childhood had its origin in a maternal disorder. According to Spitz, even colic was caused by a mother's "primary anxious over-permissiveness." That says it all.

The model of the good mother as the sacrificial mother who denies her own needs and desires for the sake of her children came out of the same wellspring.

Then as now, the chokehold of the mother myths results in denial, both conscious and not. It's not just mothers who deny the dynamic; other family members, including fathers, feel the same pressure. Some mothers will simply deny what they've said to or about their daughters, even in the presence of witnesses, or insist that the punishment, whether it is verbal or physical, was deserved. Others will plead that their words and gestures have been misunderstood or that they acted as they did for their daughters' "good." Hypercriticality or even cruelty is explained away in terms of behavior or example.

In the cultural house of mirrors, there are many ways of avoiding the truth, and almost universally the truth stays a tightly held secret. A mother who is mean to her daughter may be able to be loving to a son—who doesn't pose the same kind of threat to her sense of self—or to another one of her own daughters who doesn't seem to be a competitor in the same way or whose personality is simply a better fit. The dynamic is complicated and fearsome, most particularly for the daughter who is singled out. In an entirely different sense, it is fearsome for the mother as well.

The conflict can spread out from the mother-daughter dyad to envelop the husband and father. Some fathers will become rescuers—the knight in shining armor the daughter needs to hold her own against her mother—while others will become complicit, either ignoring or denying the mother-daughter dynamic. In other families, particularly those in which the burden of child rearing is assumed to be the mother's, a father will simply defer to his wife's assessment of their daughter. Divorce further complicates matters for the mother who already has a weak or nonexistent foundation of love for her child.

The power of the mother-love myth affects daughters in myriad ways, one of which is reflected in the reluctance of the daughters of mean mothers to come forward and talk. One woman, the mother of ten-year-old twins, declined to talk about her mother, from whom she is long estranged, for fear it would make her sound whiny or self-indulgent. Another was afraid to talk outside of a therapeutic environment, fearing the pain she knew she would experience. One woman pulled out after we spoke because she felt guilty, while another was convinced by her older sister that it was "unseemly" for her to talk about their mother, even though they shared the same vision of her as withheld and self-absorbed.

With one exception, all the women I interviewed requested that I give them pseudonyms and change details of their lives to further assure that they couldn't be recognized, for fear that family, friends, acquaintances, and colleagues would think less of them. In some cases, to further disguise them, I have given a single woman more than one name so that the thread of her story in these pages won't reveal her identity. A girlfriend who is also a writer sent me a list of her close friends who might possibly agree to be interviewed and then, just a few hours later, e-mailed back: "On reflection, I don't think you should approach these women, because I'm not sure they actually recognize that their mothers are mean to them. I've witnessed some pretty awful stuff first-hand but that doesn't mean they see it that way."

The myth of mother love requires a daughter to maintain her silence.

Diane, a married woman who chose not to have children, sums it up this way: "I don't feel good talking about my mother, because I'm afraid people will think I'm exaggerating the things she said to me and still says, for that matter. The few times I've tried talking to a girlfriend about her, I felt that somehow that friend ended up thinking less of me because of how I criticized her. Besides, my mother is very careful about what she says to me in front of other people, so complaining makes me sound crazy or worse. I swear it took my husband a few years to catch on to what was really going on. He adores his mother, so it was natural for him to make excuses for mine, at the beginning at least. He knows now, and he's totally with me on that. But other people? Well, no."

Many daughters of mean mothers struggle with balancing societal expectations against their need to protect themselves from maternal hurt. The obligation of filial piety—part and parcel of sacred mother love— can render a daughter speechless and filled with guilt. The vitriol heaped on Christina Crawford for her filial disloyalty when *Mommie Dearest* was published is simply the same theme writ large. Cultural pressures become even more complicated when the daughter becomes a mother herself and has to choose whether she wants to include her mother in her life as her child's grandmother—or not.

Not even therapy makes it easy to untangle what the culture tells us a daughter *should* feel for her mother from what she does feel. One woman confided, "I have more insight into how her life influenced who she is, and I am able to understand that she has to own it or not because it's not mine to own. What gets in my way is that I can understand all the dynamics on an intellectual level, but it's a long way to owning it on an emotional level because of the damage the past has done to my spirit. It very much feels like I am stuck in a developmental stage. I am seeing lots of improvement with therapy, but the old wounds bleed when I am fatigued."

Protecting herself from maternal hurt may be further complicated by the taboos associated with cutting off ties to her mother. This is both a cultural stance and a therapeutic one.

I know this firsthand because I've seen it in the eyes of strangers: the surprise on the face of the cochair of the PTA committee when, in answer to her question, I told her that my daughter had never met my mother, or the way a doctor reassessed me after he questioned me about my mother's medical history and I answered that I didn't know, adding that I hadn't seen or spoken to her in more than fifteen years.

Cathy works as a bookkeeper in a small company and is the mother of an eight-year-old girl whom she is raising with her second husband. She went fourteen years without speaking to her mother and only recently began to renew their relationship. Her disappointment is palpable when she tells me her story: "I was one of three girls, and the only one who had any problem with our mother. It's funny because I've always been the most successful of all of us—good at school and all that stuff as well as popular. From the time I was little, she would tell me that she was sure that the hospital had sent home the wrong baby, that they'd gotten the bracelets mixed up. She never had a nice thing to say about me, and finally, when I went off to college in another state—and I was the first person in my family to go to college—I made the break."

Cathy pauses, then continues, her voice low: "She never once called me in those years—not even when my daughter was born. I finally buckled to the family's pressure to let my mother back into my life, and all I can say is that it's all too depressingly familiar. Nothing has changed. She criticizes everything about me just as she always did, except now it includes how I mother my child, treat my husband, and decorate my house. I thought the reconciliation would be mutual, but it's clear to me now that I am not and never was important to her."

Cathy has not decided what do to about their relationship, but she is clear about one thing: "This has nothing to do with me. I didn't really get that when I was a child, but now, looking past the hurt, I realize that I have done nothing to deserve her or her treatment. It's her problem."

Therapists, it should be said, generally also adhere to seeing maternal cut-off as the choice of last resort. Many therapists believe that resolution or healthy attachment needs to be accomplished within the mother-daughter relationship, not outside of it. While some therapists will advise their patients to go on a temporary break, few will ever initiate the recommendation that a patient break with her mother. Even self-help books tend to advocate that daughters be "fair" in their assessment of their mothers; as one writer puts it, "The danger lies in tipping too far, either toward blaming the mother or toward dismissing the daughter's suffering. An important task of a wounded daughter is to see the mother-child relationship from *both* sides."

But for some daughters—myself included—"divorcing" my mother was the only way I could move forward into a healthy future.

Most daughters who've broken with their mothers acknowledge that this is less a "solution" than a lifesaving strategy that only offers partial healing. Whether the separation from a mother's ability to hurt and inability to love occurs because of "divorce" or death, the result falls very short of being perfect. Terri's mother died when she was eighteen, ending what had been a reign of terror and emotional deprivation. But even the abrupt ending wasn't really an ending at all. Her voice low but insistent, Terri tells me, "There is always a hole in me that needs to be filled, and can't be. Not the love of my four kids or my husband of twenty-odd years or my friends fills it. It's always there, like a tear or a hole in fabric. You can put threads in to repair the weave—the threads of other relationships—but the hole is still there."

I know precisely what she means: I will go to my grave still grieving the mother love I never had and wishing just as hard that I had been born to someone else.

THE DAUGHTER WHO IS an only child has a special burden since she lacks a sibling to help her test her vision of emotional reality. She's more likely to feel that she's at fault or responsible for her mother's behavior. As one woman told me, "I do think I would have been different if I'd had a sibling because I would have had a buffer who might have helped me either by sharing our experience and talking about it or distracting from the all-consuming effect my mother had on me." Another only child is Sarah, fifty-two, an artist and writer who now lives in Wisconsin with her husband, two thousand miles away from where she grew up. She left home at the age of eighteen when she went off to college, and she's never gone back. "I had an exit strategy," she says dryly, "from the time I was little." She has no children, explaining, "I promised myself as a preteen that I'd never have kids until I could figure out how to raise them better than my mom raised me." Her early experiences sound nothing if not claustrophobic: her mother was smothering, controlling, and at the same time impossible to please. Both of her parents were the youngest of twelve siblings, and her mother was raised largely by an older brother and sister because her own mother ignored her.

Most of Sarah's earliest memories are of being controlled and restricted—being made to sit in a chair while her mother cooked and prepared dinner and being told not to talk so as not to disturb her mother or "get in her way." Her mother didn't want her helping and, on the rare occasions when she did, would criticize whatever Sarah did. "I felt as though I was always being observed," Sarah says. If she didn't "clean her plate" at dinner, the plate went into the refrigerator where it would become Sarah's breakfast, or lunch if necessary. "I felt as though I didn't really exist and I grew comfortable living under the radar," she tells me. "I had a rich fantasy life—complete with imaginary siblings, friends, and animal companions. When I was five, we moved to a new house and my mother threw out all my stuffed animals. I replaced them with imaginary ones and, later, with imaginary scenarios about how my parents weren't really my parents and that my real parents would come and get me someday." As she got older, she was often forbidden to play with other children and join in activities. This was explained, she tells me, as a way of protecting her, of making sure "she didn't get into trouble," as were all the restrictions and controls placed on her when she got older.

Reading became a source of comfort and escape at an early age and continued through her adolescence when she discovered science fiction and fantasy. But Sarah's father encouraged her to excel at school, and that, she says, "saved me. I don't think my father was really aware of how my mother treated me—the house was her domain and having a job was his—but he did give me the support and inspiration that ultimately got me a scholarship to a great college and out of the house." Most confusing was how her mother was with others, in the outside world: "She could be flirtatious and outgoing, not at all like who she was with me, and it was very confusing. How could she be so nice in public and then so mean to me? It made me feel crazy. I remember once having someone over and my mother baked cookies—something she never did—and the way it all seemed so normal, as if she did this every day the way another mother might, made it even crazier."

Sarah's father died when she was in her first year of college, and she has, as she puts it, "moved on to an intentionally chosen family." When I ask her how her relationship to her mother shaped her, her thoughtful answer underscores how childhood experiences shape all of us in both obvious and subtle ways: "Looking back, when I grew up, some of my childhood ways of coping stayed with me, if sometimes in disguised form. When I was involved with the theater, I worked on lighting, illuminating others but staying behind the scenes, out of the spotlight, under the radar myself. As an artist, I'm mainly an observer even now, separated from the world by a camera lens. But the rich interior dialogue I used to survive my childhood has still served me well."

Sometimes a sibling who shares a daughter's experience can be a source of comfort and validation. In her book *The Sister Knot,* Terri Apter writes: "The quarrels we each had, in very different ways, with our mother threatened to crush us; but together, taking these to each other, sharing our information, they became bearable. We could name our confusions." Distinguishing the talk between girlfriends and sisters, Apter notes, "For all the family complaints swapped between girlfriends, there are things one often isn't allowed to say. With my sister we could talk and complain, without ever worrying that we were being outrageously disloyal. . . . I knew I was safe from social exposure. My sister would never say to someone else, in mockery or disdain, 'She has the most awful mother.'"

But sibling relationships can also be shaped by the dynamic between the unloving mother and her daughter, most particularly when a mother differentiates between her children, being loving and attentive to one but not to another. In many families, the dynamic will weaken sibling bonds. In other families, though, particularly when there is an age gap between siblings and an absence of mother love, a sibling may step into the breach and serve as both a safe haven and a touchstone for her sister's emotional development. Research confirms, in fact, that some of the most intense sibling bonds may be formed when a mother or father or both parents are consistently unavailable or unloving.

Mean mothers are often the daughters of mean or highly ambivalent mothers, as my own mother was—a negative bond passed on from generation to generation, without acknowledgment or analysis. Over the past forty years, attachment theory—which started with the observation of monkey mothers and their offspring and then expanded to human mothers and infants—has offered a reliable explanation for why some families engender a mother line of pain. "Ghosts in the nursery" was the phrase Dr. Selma Fraiberg coined in the 1970s to describe how generation after generation of women were bound to repeat the same patterns of maternal behavior, no matter how sincerely they wanted to mother their children differently from the way their mothers had. As Fraiberg wrote, "While none has been issued an invitation, the ghosts take up residence and conduct the rehearsal of a family tragedy from a tattered script."

Patterns of relationship in families are tenacious precisely because they are established on both a behavioral and a physical level. Research on the development of the brain and the formation of the self during infancy and childhood has confirmed the basic tenets of attachment theory and expanded its implications. By studying infant interactions with their mothers in a tightly controlled laboratory setting, Mary Ainsworth was able to categorize the type of relationship a child enjoyed with her mother or primary caregiver as either "securely attached" or "insecurely attached." The model used, the so-called Strange Situation, was relatively simple, and her results have been duplicated in hundreds of studies since. The mother and infant arrive in the lab together. Within a short period of time, the mother departs, leaving the baby with an adult who, while caring, is nonetheless a stranger to the child. What happened when the mother returned was the focus of Ainsworth's study.

As she expected, the majority of children acted like the baby monkeys she'd studied; they were distressed by their mothers' absence and were immediately comforted when they returned. These children rushed to their mothers, literally flung themselves into their mothers' arms, and

looked into their eyes, reestablishing both physical and psychological contact. But to Ainsworth's surprise, some children didn't behave in this way.
Some seemed uncomfortable when their mothers were with them, showed
little distress when their mothers left, and derived no comfort when they
returned. Others showed no emotion when their mothers left and, upon
their return, avoided all contact with them.

The first group of children were those Ainsworth labeled "securely
attached." Their mothers were women who were attuned to their children's
needs and were capable of responding to those emotional and physical
needs on a consistent basis. Seen through the lens of brain development,
Daniel J. Siegel, M.D., and Mary Hartzell, M.Ed., explain that attachment
is a system of the inner brain that evolved to keep human children safe
because of the length of time it takes to reach maturity. Attachment has
three effects: first, it enables the child to seek proximity to the parent;
second, to go to the parent for comfort in times of distress; and third,
to internalize the relationship with the mother as an internal model of a
secure base. It is this "secure base" that will serve as a template for friendships and relationships in adult life.

The other group of children—those who didn't exhibit the kind of
behavior expected—were categorized as "insecurely attached." Insecure
attachments can be avoidant, ambivalent, or disorganized in nature. Children of mothers who are repeatedly unavailable or repeatedly rejecting
adapt by avoiding physical and emotional closeness with them. Children of
mothers who are only sometimes available and who aren't reliably attuned
adapt by being ambivalently attached. Because they don't know what to
expect—is she going to be the nice mommy or the yelling one?—these
children develop anxiety and insecurity about the maternal relationship
and, as adults, a sense of all relationships as being essentially unreliable.

The last category of insecure attachment is the most problematic.
When a child's needs are unmet and she finds her mother's behavior
frightening or chaotic, she may develop a disorganized attachment. Disorganized attachment is most closely associated with parents who are physically or emotionally abusive. It is the type of attachment that engenders

the most conflict within the child and is most destructive to the formation of self. As Daniel Siegel writes, "In this situation, the child is 'stuck' because there is an impulse to turn toward the very source of terror from which he or she is attempting to escape." This impulse explains those horrible instances of child abuse when a child is injured by his or her mother but, in pain, still calls out for "Mommy."

Mary Ainsworth's work was expanded by her student Mary Main, whose research confirmed *why* there were ghosts in the nursery. Using the Adult Attachment Interview, she found that an adult's recollection of how she was treated during childhood accurately predicted how she would relate to her own children. The way parents made sense of their own early childhood experiences, revealed both in the content of their answers and the coherence of *their* life narratives, was the factor that most accurately predicted their children's security of attachment. Without intervention—through either therapy or a relationship in which new patterns of emotional connection could be established—insecurely attached children would grow up to be insecurely attached adults who would, in turn, end up raising insecurely attached children themselves. The patterns continued, despite differences in temperament and other personality factors.

The securely attached daughter will become a securely attached woman who is emotionally available, perceptive, and responsive. The insecure-avoidant daughter will become an emotionally unavailable adult, unperceptive, unresponsive, and rejecting. The insecure-ambivalent daughter will become an unreliable mother—sometimes there for her child, sometimes not. She will be unlikely to recognize her child's boundaries, and her behavior will often be felt as intrusive by her child. Children with disorganized attachment—who have incorporated what one researcher called "fright without resolution"—are likely to parent in the same way.

The daughters of mean mothers whom I've interviewed all describe relationships that fall within the continuum of insecure attachments; all of them confirm that their mothers' mothers as well were, to one degree or another, incapable of consistent and attuned mothering.

One woman, Ella, explains how this works in her family: "My mother doesn't intend to be mean, but she seems to be without the ability to empathize. Because the mother love she received was so limited, she never learned to be loving." Ella's mother was intimidated by her daughter's strong sense of self and retaliated with a critical parenting style that continues to this day.

"I have spent years," Ella tells me, "trying to get my mother's voice out of my head—the voice that told me I was too fat when I was a teenager, the voice that tells me today that I am a lousy housekeeper, the voice that always reminds me that nothing about me or my life is perfect." Her mother's lack of emotional availability was largely hidden in her relationships with her two other children, each of whom had problems she could tend to and manage. In those relationships—with a daughter who showed early signs of bipolar disorder and a son who suffered from severe allergies—her role as a caretaker gave her a sense of comfort and confidence while masking her deficiencies. With healthy, smart, and ambitious Ella, her mother was always critical and often cruel and insensitive.

Even so, throughout Ella's childhood and much of her early adulthood, her craving for her mother's attention never abated: "When I was a kid, I would fake being sick just to get the kind of love my mother was capable of. Even as an adult, I needed her love as much as I always had as a child, and I did just about anything to please her. I'd try to ignore all the thoughtless and often mean comments she would make—that's how much I needed her. Only now—as my own daughters reach the end of their teens—am I learning, with the help of a therapist, to set healthy boundaries with my mother."

Cultural norms—backed up by the Judeo-Christian tradition—require us to honor our mothers and fathers and above all speak no ill of them. These cultural strictures affect *all* daughters, including those raised by essentially loving, if occasionally imperfect, mothers. They can get in the way of the work a daughter needs to do when she moves from one stage of her development to another—from adolescence to young adulthood and then into adulthood and motherhood, for example—and must confront the task of seeing her mother wholly and realistically. Our cultural unwillingness to challenge the idealization of motherhood, combined with the injunction against criticizing our own mothers, can leave any daughter unable to take the next necessary step in her evolving relationship to her mother. As Christina Robb notes in *This Changes Everything,* "Mothers and daughters in good relationships learn to see, hear, and love each other as they are, and not as approximations of an ideal or stereotype, negative or positive."

For the daughters of mean mothers, the concept of mother love—instinctual, inviolable, sacred, unconditional—has a different kind of chokehold.

I learned early on that discussing my mother frankly could be an uncomfortable experience for me and whoever was listening. I remember a college friend insisting that my mother *couldn't* have meant all the things she said to me, simply because she had given birth to me. Other daughters of mean mothers, some of whom stay in contact with their mothers and others who have broken all ties with them, have had similar experiences.

The myth of mother love makes it harder for daughters to confront their histories, even when the line between meanness and abuse is crossed. Terri, now the mother of four, had a mother who was both mean and unstable and abused her emotionally and physically. Terri tells me that coming home from school was always fraught: which mother would greet her—the smiling one or the angry, crazy one? One day, when she was five or six, after serving her lunch, her mother came in and yanked her comfort blanket from her hands. Big scissors in her hands, her mother taunted her: "Big girls aren't scared to sleep without a blankie. How can you be a big girl with a blankie?" Terri's blanket was her solace; her place of safety. Slowly her mother cut her blanket in two and threw one piece into the trash, saying, "I'll show you what a big girl is. A big girl watches me cut up her blankie and doesn't cry. A big girl thanks her mother for helping her grow up."

Each day, Terri came home to a smaller and smaller piece of the blanket until it was finally gone.

Years later—long after she had four children of her own—Terri told

the story to a friend, the mother of three children. The friend insisted that
Terri was making too much of the incident and that there was no malice
on her mother's part. Her mother *must* simply have been trying to make
Terri more independent. Her friend just didn't get it, because her assumptions about mothers and the unconditional love they bear their children
overrode her common sense.

In the court of mother-daughter conflict, it's usually the daughter
who's on trial.

The cultural myth of absolute mother love combined with the real-
world power of a mother to inform her child's universe often create a
terrible conflict within the daughter herself. Precisely because a child is
dependent on her mother not just for her physical needs but for the emotional cues that inform her sense of self, the pain caused by her mother's
ambivalence or meanness coexists with her need for her mother's love and
attention. In a loving, securely attached relationship between a mother and
child, power isn't an issue. With insecure attachment—whether avoidant,
ambivalent, or disorganized—the mother always has the advantage, and
there is ample opportunity for the abuse of maternal power. Barraged by
constant and cruel criticism, a daughter may actually become more dependent on her mother, precisely because her mother's words communicate a
single lesson: you are not good enough to survive without me. Others, like
myself, may find themselves asking a single question: What's wrong with
me that my mother doesn't love me?

Some daughters internalize their mothers' words and actions and,
long after childhood, seek out other relationships—with friends and lovers
alike—that echo the maternal one, no matter how much pain it has caused.
"I see now," Sheila confided, "that all the relationships I had with men during my twenties and thirties were all about my mother. I backed away from
her but filled the hole she left in me with the same kind of cruelty and uncaring. It took years of therapy to understand why I was choosing the men I
did. When I finally understood, I was able to make new choices—and, par-
enthetically, broke off all relations with her." For many daughters of mean
mothers, myself included, this is a familiar story, if a confusing one.

Why would daughters of unloving mothers seek out relationships in later life that replicate the pain of their childhood experiences? This paradox is explained by Thomas Lewis, M.D., and his coauthors in their book, *A General Theory of Love*. The developing human brain is actively shaped by the quality of attachment and relatedness we experience during infancy and childhood. They write: "Love and the lack of it change the young brain forever. The central nervous system was once thought to unfold into maturity in accordance with the instructions in its DNA. . . . But as we now know, most of the nervous system (including the limbic brain) needs exposure to crucial experiences to drive its growth. . . . The lack of an attuned mother is a nonevent for a reptile and a shattering injury to the fragile limbic brain of a mammal."

We learn about love not because we are told about it but because we experience it on a neurological level. The infant or child's experiences with her mother (and father) forge connections among the cells in the higher brain. The human brain is designed to be adaptive, and it wires itself to adapt best to the environment in which it finds itself. This biological adaptability—which affects both the brain's structure and its chemical systems—can work for or against a child's well-being. With secure attachment to a parent or parents, we learn that "love means protection, caretaking, loyalty," and we know this because our brain "automatically narrows crowded confusion into a few regular prototypes." With insecure attachments, "a child unwittingly memorizes the precise lesson of that troubled relationship: that love is suffocation, that anger is terrifying, that dependence is humiliating, or one of a million crippling variations." Put more simply, if a child has a bullying parent, she unconsciously adapts to living in a bullying world and adopts behaviors appropriate to it. This unconscious knowledge propels daughters to seek out the familiar negative later in life, and for these daughters this unhealthy comfort zone will make disengaging from the destructive maternal legacy even harder to accomplish.

A few daughters recount that, even as children, they were able to understand they'd done nothing to elicit their mother's behavior. While this understanding insulates these daughters to a degree, it still does little to assuage their feelings of emotional loss and deprivation or to help them forge healthy connections later in life. Seen from the vantage point of relational psychology—which echoes the findings of other scientific approaches but with a different vocabulary—what a daughter learns from this primary relationship will stream out into her future life and relationships. As Irene Stiver observed, when a child's expressions of thoughts and feelings aren't heard or responded to, when she feels that who she is has no impact on the important people in her life, when she is powerless to change these relationships, when there is no one to share her pain, there are profound and potentially lasting consequences. Most important, Stiver writes, "Growing up in dysfunctional families, children learn how to *stay out of relationships* while behaving *as if* they are *in* relationships."

Ellen was the only biological child in her family, with an adopted older brother and sister. Her father was loving but detached, and while he knew about his wife's cruelty to Ellen, he did little to stop it. Now the mother of a young daughter and son herself, she says, "I understood from a young age that there was nothing I could do to satisfy my mother. She was totally self-absorbed, a narcissist, and she was never able to see me as anything but a projection of herself. And the anger, meanness, and disappointment which began inside of her simply radiated out toward me. She herself was the daughter of a hypercritical and dominating father and a docile mother who did little to protect her from her father's cruelty. She was different with my adopted siblings precisely because they didn't reflect on her in the same way. In my case, the biological tie was a negative." But, Ellen adds, "Knowing what was going on didn't stop me from hurting. It took me years to achieve any sense of emotional balance and connection."

Some daughters will wrestle with how, among siblings, they alone are singled out. Gillian was the eldest child, the only girl among three brothers. But her mother identified her most closely with her father, a man who had abandoned his wife and children. Her mother's anger at her ex-husband focused on Gillian, and her own disappointments were fueled by the bright future she foresaw for her academically gifted daughter.

THE DAUGHTERS OF MEAN MOTHERS tell me of experiences very different from those of women whose mothers were merely unable to parent with grace, ease, or any kind of sureness. Recent memoirs by adult daughters, such as Jeannette Walls's *The Glass Castle* and Alexandra Fuller's *Don't Let's Go to the Dogs Tonight,* testify in abundance that mothers who appear to fail every conventional test of motherhood but who lack cruelty or mean intention can, in fact, be loving mothers despite their obvious shortcomings.

Unlike their mean counterparts, less than perfect mothers can sometimes face what they lack with both grace and intelligence. When I ask my friend Jane, the daughter of actor Bert Lahr and the mother of an adult daughter herself, whether her own mother—a former Ziegfeld Follies girl who, given her self-absorption and love of social life, was probably as unsuited to motherhood by her nature and personality as any woman could be—was mean, Jane's answer is categorical: "Absolutely not."

Her mother, Mildred, came from a background that might have hobbled anyone less ambitious and insistent: she was one of four children abandoned by their father when she was two, by her mother at four, and, after she failed to be adopted, raised by her grandparents. "What was extraordinary about Mom," Jane tells me, "is that she knew both that nurturing was important and that she couldn't nurture. But if she couldn't nurture, what she could do was manage, and manage she did. She created a household full of people—the nanny, the cook, the cleaning lady—who were kind and loving and who supported me and my brother. She knew education was important and she sent us to schools, camps, and lessons that cultivated our individuality." Even if Mildred's own childhood had lacked love and nurturing, she knew what her children needed and, as a mother, did what she could to make up the difference.

Unfortunately, not every mother with an emotionally deficient childhood will have that amount of insight into the problem.

DURING ALL OF MY twenties and some of my thirties, my relationship with my mother was like a wound that wouldn't heal. I continued to struggle with it, even with therapy—breaking off all contact for weeks, months, or years and then going back to the well one more time, peeling off whatever scab had managed to form. It didn't occur to me until years later that never once did my mother initiate a reconciliation, and I now understand why: she was relieved by my absence. From her point of view, I was the mirror that reflected her greatest fear and failure: her own unloving nature as my mother. Keeping that secret was, I believe, more important to her than I was.

What I wanted from her is easier to see: I still wanted her love, but by then I wanted, in equal measure, her admission that she was wrong not to love me. In the end, neither would be forthcoming.

My struggle was hardly unique. Other women confirm behaviors that testify to the depth of the hunger for mother love when it is withheld or absent. As a denizen of a culture dominated by the mother myths, the child within each and every one of us longs for that perfect mother, the one who is *always* available, understanding, and supportive. But the securely attached daughter of a loving mother can regain her foothold after her mother's occasional misstep; the insecurely attached daughter can't. Ambivalence reigns supreme. Mixed in with the anger and the hurt is almost always a measure of hopefulness that her mother will become the mother she longs for and needs.

The journey of the daughter of a mean or unloving mother is different in kind from that of the daughter who from the very beginning has understood and grown from her connection to her mother. The influence of any mother on her daughter during the formative years of childhood through early adulthood can hardly be overstated, and perhaps the influence of the unloving mother is more powerfully destructive than that of a loving mother is constructive.

The mother's relationship to her daughter not only forms the earliest, if not the primary, foundation for how the daughter formulates her sense of self, but is the basic template for her understanding of how relationships work in the world. In this sense, each individual's definition of love and emotional connection is learned during infancy and childhood. Adaptive behavior learned in childhood—dealing with an emotionally unreliable mother, for example—will carry over into adulthood unless there is intervention in the form of either therapy or some other relationship that offers a daughter (or a son) "earned" security or another way of connecting. As we've already seen, for many daughters, this will lead them to seek out relationships with other partners that echo the maternal one.

Aside from relationship, the question that looms largest is "Can I mother differently than my mother?" Nearly all daughters I interviewed viewed the choice of whether or not to have children with caution, if not real hesitation.

If, as Hope Edelman has so eloquently observed, daughters who lose their mothers early in their lives may experience a new upsurge of grief when they become mothers and may have difficulty mothering without a maternal guide, then daughters of mean mothers face a task that in some ways is even more difficult. If motherless daughters face the task of mothering without a map, then the daughters of mean mothers are both motherless and mother-burdened at once. They must consciously discard the maternal model as well as the behaviors they learned and internalized in their childhoods. They must learn how to mother from scratch. And only some of them will fully succeed.

Ella married the man who would become the father of her daughters at the age of twenty-two but waited more than a decade to have children: "We both had difficult childhoods and knew we needed to make some conscious changes so as not to repeat the mistakes we felt our parents had made. I felt very strongly about it—I knew I could handle the baby phase because I adored babies and, as a young girl, had used babysitting as an escape and a chance to shine in the eyes of others who appreciated me. But my mother's controlling way of parenting was so ingrained in me that I knew I would need help raising my own children. I knew what I wanted to accomplish—the values I wanted to instill—but I just didn't know how to do it on a daily basis."

Ella and her husband joined a local group that taught parenting classes and in time they became class leaders themselves until they thought they were ready: "When each of my daughters was born, I instinctively knew each was a gift passing through me. I did not own them, nor did they reflect on me. I made mistakes along the way as I raised them but, unlike my mother, I made a conscious decision to apologize when I was wrong. I learned what my mother never learned: that the real power was in giving up control, in encouraging, not criticizing. I learned that if I gave my children love that wasn't dependent on outcomes, they would feel safe and confident enough to learn and to make mistakes." But even as Ella evolved as a mother, her mother's relationship to her remained mired in the same patterns; Ella's new psychological growth continued to coexist with old conflicts.

For a few women, their mothers' behavior provided the template for everything they would *never* do to their own daughters, without providing them with a model for what they *should* give them.

Lynne writes me in an e-mail, "I deliberately focused on every need in me that my mother left unmet, and concentrated on how I could meet that need in my own child. With the help of a therapist over many years, I understood how my sense of self had been abraded by my mother's refusal to listen to me or to consider my observations valuable. I have always honored my daughter as an individual in her own right, separate from me— something my mother could never accomplish." Another woman, whose mother was emotionally absent during her childhood and adolescence and who is now the mother to two daughters ages twenty-one and twenty-three, describes how close she and her daughters are and how different it is from her relationship to her own mother and goes on to say, "But my parenting skills came naturally. It is not something I worked at, read about, consciously worked on. I liked my daughters, I respected them, and I wanted to be with them more than anyone else."

I too felt that my experience as a child gave me an inner compass as a mother; I knew what not to do. And because my mother had never listened to me, I became, with my daughter at least, an attuned and attentive listener.

Yet not every story is a success story, as Barbara confides: "My mother did nothing for me, and so I did everything for my daughter so that her childhood, unlike mine, would be 'perfect.' I didn't realize that in my effort to give her everything I needed when I was a child and didn't get, I completely lost sight of her. I was controlling and smothering her. It took the crisis of her adolescence and her full-fledged rebellion to make me realize I needed help in mothering her."

These stories are particularly important because they permit us to look past the myths of mother love, with their simplistic formulas for this most complicated and important relationship. The stories of mean mothers aren't always the most uplifting of narratives, but they have lessons to teach all of us nonetheless. In their own way, they cast a new and important light on the topography of the mother-daughter relationship.

THAT TATTERED SCRIPT

When Hollywood tackles the mother-daughter relationship, even a difficult one, a happy ending is never out of sight. Even troubled mother-daughter stories—think *Terms of Endearment, Postcards from the Edge, Anywhere but Here, Tumbleweeds*—always end on bright notes of love and reconciliation. In real life, it doesn't always happen that way, but even so it's damn hard to give up on that idea of unconditional love, that bit of leftover paradise in an otherwise uncertain world.

One morning in February of 2001, my phone rang. I picked up to hear my brother's voice. "Mom is dying," he said. "I thought you might want to come see her." At that point I hadn't seen or spoken to my mother for over ten years; in fact, I didn't even know she'd been ill.

"Has she asked for me?" I asked. There was silence, and then he cleared his throat. "No," he said, "she hasn't." "Has she ever mentioned me in the last months or years?" I asked. There was another pause and then the word "No." There was another pause and then he said, "I thought you might want to come to see her anyway. She's floating in and out of consciousness and it doesn't look like she's going to be able to hang on much longer." I thanked him for his call, wished him luck, and told him I'd get back to him.

I called friends, relatives, and my therapist and the verdict was unanimous: I should go. I owed it to her, the logic went, because she'd given me life, and besides, seeing her again and saying good-bye would give me "closure." My therapist—a woman I genuinely admired—was categorical, telling me I might never forgive myself if I didn't go. Closure, she said, was too important. The possible scene she described—one of final reconciliation and declarations of mutual love—brought me to tears in her office, even though back in cool winter air on the way to my car it seemed more like theater than anything else.

My closest friends stressed that by performing this last act of filial duty, I would feel good about myself. Even if my mother had behaved badly through the years, through this gesture I would prove once and for all that, in the most important ways, I was nothing like her.

Everyone was helpful, kind, and said what they did because they wanted me to be happy with my choice. I know each of them meant well. But not one of them had had a childhood or a parent like mine, and in the end I understood that they didn't understand at all.

The scene I saw in my mind's eye was not what Hollywood or even my therapist envisioned. I saw myself standing by her bed talking, and just as in every other conversation I had ever had with her she would be incapable of hearing me. Perhaps this time she wouldn't hear me for a different reason, but the scene would be painfully familiar nonetheless. I would stand there, tears in my eyes, and ask her that same question she'd never been able to answer—"Why didn't you love me?"—and this time her silence would stretch out into eternity. And the little girl in me once again would be there, hoping and praying with all her heart that this time Mommy *would* love me.

I didn't go, and I have never regretted it. I ignored everyone's advice and chose for myself with full understanding of the implications and the costs.

This is, I know, a story no one wants to hear. But it is a story that needs to be heard along with the stories of forgiveness and reconciliation and others that lie somewhere in between. Each of these stories, in its own way, testifies to what can happen when a mother can't love her daughter in the way she needs to be loved.

THE MYTH OF MOTHER love pervades our thinking about family and other relationships in ways both simple and complex. It's not a single myth but one that is more like the largest of those nesting dolls, each of which, when pulled apart, reveals a smaller doll within it. It's a fitting metaphor, since those Russian dolls are called *matryoshkas*, or "mothers," and symbolize motherhood as all-embracing; the smiling face on the largest doll tells us that motherhood brings only satisfaction and joy. Within the largest doll is the myth of absolute love, free of all and any emotional ambivalence, which in turn holds the myth of mother as fully empathic, sacrificial, and without needs of her own. Within that myth is yet another that tells us that mothering is instinctual and that all females are nurturing, which implies that every woman should be a mother and can be a good one while marginalizing the anxiety and guilt even a loving mother feels when she doesn't feel up to the challenge that mothering presents. Nestled in that doll is a still smaller one that denies the complexity and difficulty of mothering across the life stages—both those of the mother herself and her daughter as well. Hidden within the smallest doll is a myth with a specific power and poison of its own that can shape-shift the landscape of the family as a whole and the sibling relationships within it. This is the myth that tells us that every mother loves each of her children equally and in the same way, denying the impact of personality, goodness of fit, and where a woman finds herself in life when her daughter is born.

These myths shape all mothers, loving or not. They get in the way of gaining a fuller understanding of how a mother's behaviors can help or hurt, as well as imposing a nearly impossible standard of perfection on every mother. Equally, these myths prevent the daughters of unloving mothers from giving voice to their experiences without feeling ashamed or guilty, making their journeys as women all the more difficult. Taken together, these myths are the foundation for one of our most potent cultural taboos and stand in the way of an open discussion of what happens when a mother doesn't or can't love the daughter she has borne and brought into the world.

It's my hope that this book will help change all that. The point of view presented in these pages is that of daughters, not their mothers. And while the book is deliberately one-sided, so that stories of daughters can occupy center stage and their experiences can be illuminated in fullness, I've also tried hard not to demonize the women who were unloving or mean, and I hope I've succeeded. Calling a mother "mean," as I sometimes have in these pages, is obviously not a clinical description but underscores the mother's refusal to acknowledge or accept responsibility for her treatment of her child and to change her behavior, even if confronted. By not responding to her daughter's complaints and observations, a mother undermines both the reality of her child's experience and her sense of self. In most cases, I've deliberately excluded stories of mothers who seemed to suffer from a definable mental illness.

It's worth noting that I am neither a psychotherapist nor a social researcher, so the stories in this book occupy a different place than they would if I were either. They don't constitute a survey or a scientific sample but are meant to illustrate, by way of story, what science tells us about this most important relationship.

Almost every woman I've spoken to or interviewed has asked me the same question: Would I write this book if my mother were still alive? The answer is yes, because there is nothing in these pages I wouldn't have said to her face. But at the same time, it's important to remember that these mothers, including mine, were daughters too. As Adrienne Rich so acutely observed, "It is hard to write about my own mother. Whatever I do write, it is my story I am telling, my version of the past. If she were to tell her own story, other landscapes would be revealed. But in my landscape or hers, there would be old, smoldering patches of deep-burning anger."

· *Two* ·
My Mother and Her Mother Before Her:
Patterns Old and New

THE INTENSITY AND INFLUENCE OF A MOTHER'S RELATIONSHIP TO her daughter remain in both the presence and absence of emotional connection. When mother and daughter are finely attuned, their connection can be an enormous source of pleasure, sustenance, and satisfaction that enriches the lives of both. But when the connection is inconsistent, damaged, or absent, the relationship nonetheless continues to influence the daughter in ways large and small, unconscious and conscious, realized and not.

The link between these two generations of women—whether it is the forged bond of love strengthened by shared experience or a thin twisted strand shaped by biology and a tincture of withheld love, anger, or envy— is permanent, even if the literal relationship between them is later severed. The mother-daughter relationship has a psychological depth and import that sets it apart from the relationship between a mother and son and perhaps from every other relationship a woman experiences. As Barbara Zax and Stephan Poulter note, "For each woman, the early relationship with her mother is the foundation upon which she will build *all* of her future relationships." Its complexity and power belie the nature of the facts, which appear to be simple only on the surface: that every mother is herself the daughter of a mother.

No matter what the myths of mother love and womanhood tell us, a woman's capacity to love isn't inborn but learned or, perhaps better put, cultivated. And just as a garden reflects the gardener's caring, spirit, and rigor, so too a woman's inner self and her ability to love reflect the quality of the care and attention she's received from her parents. What she has learned about love from her mother (and her father) will inform not only how she loves herself, her siblings, and her partner or husband, but even more particularly how she mothers and loves her daughter.

Leah, fifty-six and the mother of two daughters now young adults, describes the common thread in the last two generations of her mother line: "My grandmother was very critical and bossy. She was tall and beautiful and talented—she painted on fabric long before it was a trend and was an entrepreneur selling cosmetics—but she was emotionally distant. She and my mother didn't get along, and my mother moved away from her as soon as she was accepted to college. So it's not surprising that my mother is emotionally distant too. She was never taught to hug, and even today if I or my kids hug her, we have to hug her first. Like her mother, my mother is hypercritical; everything has to be done her way or not at all. With my grandmother, we all knew that whatever was hers was hers for life, whether she gave it away or not. As a teen, I quit accepting things from her. The memory that takes the cake in my mind is that of one Christmas when I opened a gift and she looked at it and said, 'Oh, I always wished I had one of those.' I remember thinking, 'What am I supposed to do . . . give it to her?'" Leah pauses and then adds, "So it's really not surprising that my mother is critical in the ways her own mother was, and I sometimes wonder whether if my mother had seen having children as a real choice, if she'd been born today, whether she would have had any at all."

Eleanor, now a fifty-nine-year-old therapist, grew up on the West Coast. Her parents were both factory workers, working different shifts during her childhood, so that one took care of her while the other worked. Her father and mother couldn't have been more different. Eleanor tells me, "My father thought I was the best thing that ever happened to him. He was happy and lighthearted, and even though he could be a strict disciplinarian and held me to high standards of achievement, I always knew that he loved me, cared about me." Her mother, though, was another story: "Growing up, my mother was indifferent to my emotional needs and sometimes even to my physical needs. She literally didn't listen to me or hear me. If I told her I wasn't hungry, she'd just put food out anyway, as if I hadn't said anything at all. I remember feeling, even as a young child, that it was almost as if I weren't there. When we were home alone together, she never spoke to me, unless it was something functional like 'Are you ready to go to your dance lesson?' The only question she asked me when I got home from school each day was 'What did you have for lunch?'—never anything about me personally. The predominant feeling between us was emptiness, which made me feel that I didn't really matter or, worse, that I didn't really exist." Eleanor pauses and then adds, "As a child, her indifference made me feel unlovable. At the same time, I still tried to please her through my achievements. I assumed I had to be responsible for her treatment of me."

On the surface and to the outside world, Eleanor's mother seemed to be everything a mother should be—a hardworking woman with a high-achieving daughter and a nicely maintained home, a good and thoughtful neighbor, a person guided by her strong sense of faith and active in her church. All of this served to isolate Eleanor even more: "I was alone in trying to understand my sadness as a child. You see, no one knew—not even my father. When I became an adolescent, she remained indifferent on some level but intruded into my life on another. When she felt needy, she would try to use me to make herself feel loved. She would want to hug me, and I would get angry because I felt she wasn't responding to me but to her own need to feel loved."

Her mother's inability to be emotionally attuned to her on any kind of consistent basis affected Eleanor in many ways: "I used to be easily controlled by other people's perceptions of me. And I emerged into young adulthood not really understanding interpersonal boundaries. I would either be withdrawn from others or overwhelmingly attached—there was no in-between. It took me a while to understand where I leave off and others begin." Both therapy and a long, strong marriage to a man who was, by Eleanor's admission, "crazy about me" and who came from a big family full of love, helped her move away from her own history and become a loving mother to a son and a daughter to whom she is now close. "I didn't know how to be a mother," Eleanor confides. "I just knew how *not* to be her."

Sometimes intergenerational patterns can be shaped by the pain of a mother's own childhood loss. Georgia, now fifty-two and the mother of a twenty-year-old daughter and fifteen-year-old son, tells about her mother: "My mother isn't really mean, but she is deeply wounded. She never met her mother, who died right after she was born; she had a stepmother who was right out of *Cinderella*. She was terrified, lonely, scared of the world, and disoriented. When she became a mother herself, her incredible instincts saved her and her strong creative nature gave her what it took to become a mother to her own three daughters. I am the youngest. Clearly, she drew a great sense of strength, capacity, and self-confidence in taking care of us, in doing a lot of things right, in being sweet and fun. But she drew her own sense of connectedness from our relationship and so, instead of giving to us, she took from us. Not in mean and cruel ways but in remaining the center of everything, in taking credit for everything we did. She wanted to be seen, loved, told she was great, important, talented, beautiful, intelligent, capable, and so she didn't give those words or qualities to us. That left me, the youngest one—the last one able to make her feel important—undernourished, without healthy and normal validation by my mother. I was there for her but, in a deep energetic sense, she wasn't there for me."

She tells me an anecdote that captures the psychological exchange between mother and child in her family: "I was about ten years old and we were in the kitchen. I was angry with her because she kept telling me to do my homework in nagging ways. She was washing the dishes and, in response to my anger, she began to cry and said, 'I want to go, I want to die. . . .' It was scary, and this is how she would respond every time I challenged her. I couldn't express anything challenging to her without feeling responsible for her happiness and for her being alive."

Georgia goes on to explain that what was "a dark abyss in my mother became a gap in me, and I go around waiting for someone to tell me I'm great, talented, beautiful, intelligent, sexy. My need for that validation often fogs up any legitimate flow of exchange." Now, as an adult and after years of therapy, her connection to her mother is strong, but the effects of her childhood remain. She bears a scar, she says, "one which still holds pain at times and which feels healed at other moments."

In another family, the patterns of two generations or more continue until they are finally rewritten by an unloved daughter who finds a way to forgive and to restore. Eliza is thirty-eight and the mother of a nine-year-old girl. She grew up in Oregon, the only child of a contractor and a secretary who divorced when she was four. She lived with her mother for two years after the divorce but moved in with her father by the time she was six because "he was in a better situation at the time to raise me." She doesn't remember her mother being around while she was growing up and, as she tells it, "I could never understand why my mom didn't want to be around. I felt a huge part was missing in my life that only my mom could fill." Eliza's mother herself had a mother who'd been cruel and distant to her as a child, and while they maintained contact, it was a love-hate relationship and her mother still felt a great deal of unresolved pain about it. During Eliza's adolescence, things got even harder when her mother remarried and had two other children and her father became an alcoholic: "My mother tried being in my life more, but I often shut her out. I wasn't happy about her new life and I harbored a lot of resentment. She is close to her other two children—she has a good relationship with them, I would say—and they are closer to her than I ever was. Growing up, I felt very left out because they were the family I never got to have."

Eliza married, had a daughter, and, ironically, divorced when her daughter was four, the same age she had been: "But it was all different. I had decided that I was going to be the mother to my daughter I never had growing up. I decided early on that I was going to be more affectionate, emotionally available, and closely connected to my daughter. When my ex-husband and I separated, I vowed to be there for her, and he and I maintain a good relationship so that we can coparent our child together." Most important, Eliza and her mother have healed their relationship through therapy, beginning when she was a young adult: "In therapy, we had many long, painful conversations about our relationship—how she treated me and how I treated her, how I felt and she felt. I learned a lot of truths I did not know. For example, I never realized that my father, in many ways, was sabotaging my relationship with my mom by telling me all the things he hated about her. She welcomes the time she has with me now, and I feel that she is finally there for me unconditionally and happy to be there. She truly wants a relationship with me and my family."

Both patterns of relationship and coping mechanisms for dealing with relationships can be transmitted across generations of women, as exemplified in a case treated by family therapist Betty Carter. The family she describes is one in which at least three generations of women—perhaps more, in fact—had battled with their mothers throughout their lifetimes. In each generation, the father was seen as a warm and idealized person for whom the daughter had great sympathy (because he'd been burdened by marrying such a dreadful woman) and as an ally against the mother. For three generations, the "solution" to the mother-daughter stress was a cutoff of the mother-daughter relationship, among others. Carter notes that in each successive generation, the cutoff was used more and more often to manage the anxiety of these relationships. Carter's own patient, then a thirty-year-old doctoral candidate, had cut off her mother, as well as other relationships, as had her mother and grandmother before her.

Both the science of brain development and attachment theory reveal why, in many cases—though not all—mean, emotionally unavailable, or unloving mothers are themselves the daughters of women who were unable to be attuned to their needs. We learn how to love and indeed whom to love from our first teachers, our parents, in ways that are more specific than not.

While each baby is born with all she or he needs—the basic hardware and wiring—to learn about love and connection, a baby cannot use it or begin to sense and incorporate the emotional world without a consistent guide. Seen from this point of view, the small gestures of mothering have unexpectedly great import and the absence of consistent, attuned mothering even greater impact. Looking into a baby's eyes and having her look back, touching and stroking her, cooing and gurgling back and forth are not just gestures of maternal affection but a key part of what is actually a "life-shaping process," the jump start the limbic system of the brain needs to learn about love. As Thomas Lewis and his colleagues write, "If a parent can sense her child well—if she can tune into his wordless inner states and know what he feels —then he too will become skilled in reading the emotional world." Conversely, with a parent incapable of tuning into or resonating with her infant, the result is very different.

Much of what a baby learns about what she feels, she learns second-hand through observation of her mother's face and her emotional reactions, as Thomas Lewis and his coauthors explain. His example, adapted here, will be familiar to anyone who's ever had close contact with a toddler or sat in a playground on a summer day. The toddler tumbles and then, in that split second before she reacts to her fall—provided, of course, that she hasn't really been hurt—she'll check her mother's face. If her mother registers nervousness or worry, the baby will cry; if she smiles at the baby, then the baby's smile will ensue. A mother's resonance is essential to a baby's first recognition of her own feelings; paradoxically, a human being's first inkling of emotional experience begins as derivative.

How necessary this limbic resonance is to a baby's physiological and emotional development is demonstrated by what happens when it is absent or unreliable. Limbic communication actually stabilizes the neural rhythms of the baby; as a result, the heart rhythms of securely attached babies are steadier than those with insecure attachments, while the infants of depressed mothers are four times more likely to die of

SIDS than their counterparts with healthy mothers. When very young infants are deprived of parental stimulation for long periods of time, the result can actually be fatal as the not yet fully developed nervous system "devolves into chaos."

During the first years of life, an infant garners emotional knowledge— "an impression of what love feels like"—before forming memories of events. These impressions—one by one—work by a process of accretion; over accumulated experience, neural memory compresses these impressions, each of them "featherweight," into what Lewis and his coauthors call a "dense imprint." As they explain: "That concentrated knowledge whispers to a child beneath the veil of consciousness, telling him what relationships *are,* how they function, what to anticipate, how to conduct them." When a parent is attuned to her child—what Lewis calls "loving in the healthiest way—wherein his needs are paramount, mistakes are forgiven, patience is plentiful, and hurts are soothed as best they can be"—then that is how the child will relate to him or herself and to others. This is secure attachment. Conversely, if those neural impressions impart another lesson—that "his needs don't matter, or where love is suffocating or autonomy intolerable"—that is how the child will relate to him or herself and to others. These are attachments that may be avoidant, ambivalent, or disorganized in nature.

Mutuality and attunement are key, research suggests, and provide the answer to the question posed by Edward Z. Tronick in one paper: "How is that some children become sad, withdrawn, and lacking in self-esteem, whereas others become angry, unfocused, and bitterly self-assertive, while still others become happy, curious, affectionate, and self-confident?" What is meant by *attunement*—and the corresponding level of secure infant-mother attachment—is demonstrated by a homely but revealing example in Tronick's study, as is its counterpart, lack of attunement and insecure attachment.

Imagine a game of peek-a-boo between an infant and mother. Assume as well that how the mother and infant interact during this game is prototypical of the way they usually interact. In the first example, an infant-

mother dyad play until the "peek" moment of intensity, at which point
the baby turns away, sucks her thumb, and stares into space. The attuned
mother understands that the baby is overly excited and is trying to comfort
herself. The mother stops playing, sits back, and watches quietly. In seconds, the child turns back to her and looks up with an interested expression, provoking the mother to move closer, smile, and say something like
"Hi, sweetie, you're back." The baby smiles in response and coos back.
Once again the baby puts her thumb in her mouth, looks away, and the
mother waits. After a few seconds, the infant once again turns back to her
mother and they both smile.

Tronick describes this scenario as attuned behavior in which the
mother correctly reads the message the baby is sending her—that she
needs to calm down and regulate her emotional state. The affective communication between child and mother—the one signaling to the other
that there's a need for a break and the other understanding that signal—is
attuned behavior.

But in another infant-mother dyad playing the same game, the mother's responses are markedly different, even though the baby is sending the
same signals. Once again the assumption is that the mother's behavior
is typical of her interactions with her child. This time, when the baby
turns away from her mother, she doesn't turn back. The mother leans over
the baby, puts her face near the baby's face, and clicks her tongue to get
the baby's attention. The infant continues to ignore her mother, and in
response the mother moves her face even closer to the baby. The baby
grimaces and begins to fuss and starts pushing at her mother's face. Then
she turns away from her mother and starts sucking her thumb. As Tronick
explains, this mother actively disregards her infant's message—despite the
baby's clear signal that the mother should change what she's doing—and
as a result the infant becomes more affectively negative as she tries to cope
with her mother's intrusiveness.

Extrapolating from this and other situations, Tronick suggests that
the infant in the first example will look at her mother more often, exhibit
more positive affects, and experience less distress when she's stressed.

The second infant, in contrast, will be more withdrawn than the first and exhibit more sadness.

For better or worse, human infants are designed to be exquisitely sensitive to the emotions of their mothers or caregivers. In a famous study, researchers had nondepressed mothers pretend to be depressed as they interacted with their three-month-old infants. The mothers assumed a monotone voice, moved farther away from their babies than they usually would, expressed little or no facial affect, and didn't touch their children. A mere three minutes of this simulation was enough for an infant to become distressed, look away from the mother, and display wariness and disengagement while intermittently trying to reengage the mother to make her resume her usual affect. Even after the mother "returned to normal"—smiling and touching as she usually did—the baby continued to be distressed. The implications for the daughters of depressed or detached mothers are clear, as they are for daughters of anxious or panicked mothers (and, it should be said, for their sons).

What may be even more surprising is that the infant isn't passive during these interactions with her mother, not even in the first months of life. Studies have shown that when a mother is fully attuned, the connection between mother and child is truly dyadic, indeed relational, as early as three months of age. Jeffrey F. Cohn and Edward Z. Tronick found that in the conversation-like pattern of mother-infant interactions in which each partner appears to be responsive to the other, the mother and the infant were both equally influential in directing the interaction

A mother's facial expressions, her voice, her touch—all the areas of communication between mother and infant—teach her child much more than the lesson of "I love you." The mother communicates all manner of information about the world and the baby's place in it, including whether the world is safe or dangerous. In one classic study, researchers placed one-year-old infants on a visual cliff. Their mothers were then instructed to make their facial expressions communicate either happiness or fear. An astonishing 74 percent of infants whose mothers communicated happiness—the "It's okay, sweetie" signal—"went over" the visual cliff; not one infant whose mother's face communicated fear—the "Don't go there" or "Stop" signal—did. As Edward Tronick notes, what is remarkable is that infants "actively seek out affective information from another person not only to supplement their information about the event *but even to override their own appreciation of the event.*" I've added the emphasis to Tronick's statement because it really alerts us to the power of a mother's ability to inform her child's sense of the world.

Because the maternal and paternal behaviors described by attachment theory are encoded on a neural level in the infant's brain, providing the basis for both how she perceives the world of relationship and responds to it, the daughters of unloving and unattuned mothers are likely to become unloving and unattuned mothers themselves. Why is that? Because the coping mechanisms or strategies they have developed from infancy through childhood in response to relationship—dealing with an intrusive mother, an emotionally absent one, or even a malevolent one—will carry over into their adult behaviors and relationships, including the maternal one, unless they are able to adapt to a new model of understanding and relating.

The Adult Attachment Interview (AAI) provides a way of analyzing an adult's attachment status by looking not only at the *content* of the child-hood story but, more important, at *how* that story is told and understood. Securely attached adults tell coherent stories of childhood; they are able to put events into meaningful contexts and to reflect on those experiences, even if some of them were negative. It is the coherence and density of the narrative that matters, and the way in which specific events are put into meaningful contexts and function as a story of the self. Relationships are viewed as valuable.

In contrast, the narrative of an avoidantly attached adult will be "dismissive" in nature; many of these adults insist that they don't remember any specific childhood experiences, offer little detail, and have no sense of how the past has contributed to the present. In these bare-bones narratives, the self is often viewed as being outside of relationships. The narratives of ambivalently attached adults tend to be "preoccupied" or "entangled" in nature; these narratives reveal that the issues of childhood remain largely unresolved, and impinge or intrude into the emotional present. Finally, the narratives of disorganized attached adults—those who have had frightening or abusive connections to a parent—show that the trauma or terror of childhood remains unresolved, and display a profound sense of disconnection.

What's truly astonishing about the AAI findings is that they remain highly predictive (with 85 percent accuracy) of how any individual will mother or father, no matter the age of the infant of the interviewed parent; in fact, the interview remains predictive even if the parent is interviewed during pregnancy, before the child is born. What this means, as Dr. Siegel notes, is that "The parents' narratives are not merely some reaction to the infant's temperamental characteristics or a function of the parent-child relationship."

Relational psychology, which asserts that girls and women rely on relation and connection to define the self, yields a slightly different view of the mother's effect on her daughter. Looking through both the lens of brain development and that of relational theory, it becomes clearer why the absence of maternal attunement can deal a devastating blow to a daughter that can reverberate not just through her relational life in general but can impact her ability to mother. If a daughter's mother is the first mirror in which she catches a glimpse of herself, then the wound to the daughter who has a mother who is unattuned during her infancy and childhood and, later in her life, emotionally withheld or even hostile, will be a deep one.

Lydia, now forty-six, remembers her childhood as "overwhelming." Her mother—the daughter of a mother who could be both distant and volatile by turns—was, she tells me, "very authoritarian, very erratic, and unpredictable. It was a lot of 'do as I say, not as I do.' So sometimes she was lots of fun and sometimes a tyrant. It was like living in a war zone; I was constantly walking on eggshells, waiting for the other shoe to drop."

Anne Roiphe, writing about her own mother, captures both the desperate urgency a daughter feels when a mother doesn't or can't love and the essence of what she learns from the experience: "I have written it many times. I can't seem to stop. I come back to it in novels, in stories, in articles. I started writing my first novel with the picture of a child waiting outside a closed door. The child was me. I would lie on the carpet outside her room, my face pressed to the crack under the door through which I could see the blankets on her bed rising and falling. I didn't play. I didn't move. I waited, my back pressed to the wall so nothing could grab me. She was there but I couldn't reach her. . . . In the dark corridor a child was learning that all love is not requited, at least not in equal amounts."

There is probably no lesson more painful.

A SAVING GRACE: EARNED SECURE ATTACHMENT

While the "tattered script" of family relationships, as Selma Fraiberg called it, can be highly reliable, it isn't, thankfully, the *only* script. There is another category of secure attachment called "earned secure attachment," which explains how daughters of mean mothers can become loving and attuned mothers themselves, breaking the patterns of previous generations. Contrary to what science once thought about the development of the brain, recently it's been suggested that the learning acquired during the critical periods of brain development (infancy to two years) can actually be unlearned; in fact, the brain is far more plastic than previously thought, and there's evidence that people can literally "change their minds."

What is *earned secure attachment* precisely? It means that by making sense of childhood experiences and understanding how those experiences affected her development, a woman can actually move from an "insecure" to a "secure" functioning of the mind. How does this work?

Secure close relationships, whether therapeutic or personal, are responsible for earned secure attachment. The personal growth that these close relationships offers can both "heal old wounds and transform defensive approaches to intimacy." Even though the narratives of individuals with earned secure attachment may recount incidents that were clearly negative or harsh (and the result of what can be politely called "suboptimal" parenting) and thus are usually associated with insecure attachments, the narratives themselves are coherent and make sense of the past in the same ways that the narratives of securely attached adults do.

Most important, a daughter with earned secure attachment can go on to parent in ways that are no different from those of a daughter who was securely attached during infancy and childhood. While adults with earned secure attachments are at greater risk for depressive symptoms than their counterparts who were securely attached from infancy onward, there are few other meaningful differences between them.

With a few notable exceptions, none of the mothers discussed in this book who were themselves the daughters of unattuned mothers ever underwent therapy, nor did they appear to have relationships that might have helped them develop new ways of connecting. Many of their daughters also described their mothers as incapable of introspection, but it's clear that cultural taboos associated with a mother's ambivalence or negativity toward her child would also hinder any impulse toward introspection. After all, you can't reflect on something you can't admit. In contrast, *all* of the daughters interviewed have been in therapy at one point or another in their lives. While a later chapter discusses in detail how the daughters of mean mothers have accomplished cutting the "mother line," the ability to engage in meaningful self-reflection and to make sense of past experiences is a very large part of the task.

Leah explained in an e-mail how she was able to mother differently from her hypercritical mother and grandmother and at the same time earn her own secure attachment by putting her childhood experiences into a meaningful context: "At one point, therapy helped me to begin the journey of separation. I thought—in my twenties and thirties—that I was independent of my mother, only to find out later that I was very much attached to what she thought of me, just as I was in my childhood. Therapy helped me understand that her behavior belonged to her, and I was encouraged to find a way not to take her actions personally. The tools that helped me flip the core belief were awareness and acceptance: awareness of the situation as it is happening and acceptance of who she is. I tell myself over and over again that what Mom says comes from her experience, not mine."

While earned secure attachment explains how the chain between generations can be broken, the rest of this chapter is devoted to seeing how the chain gets established in the first place.

BEYOND THE MOTHER MYTHS: REAL WOMEN

What emerges from the stories daughters tell about their mothers is how truly *personal* each story is in the most profound of senses, regardless of the broad themes that may unite them. Not one is ever precisely the same. The word *personal* seems an odd one to use, but it does capture the essence of each and every story. Contrary to what our cultural myths assert, every mother reacts to her daughter not in the abstract, not as an idealized stereotype of a mother, but as a singular person with her own history, experiences, and emotions.

And for her daughter, her mother's reactions become personal in another sense, since they shape, in no small measure, the person she will become. Most important, the stories daughters tell about their mothers— whether they were loving or not—are always stories about the wellspring of the self. The daughters of mothers who are attuned to them report memories of childhood that are very different in kind from those told by the daughters of unloving mothers.

If we turn off the music of the cultural myths and actually listen to the stories of daughters whose mothers were attuned to them, we can begin to realize that attunement doesn't describe maternal perfection or sacrifice, nor does it necessarily mean a mother whose only focus is her daughter. Mary Ellen was the only daughter in a family of four children; she had two older brothers—separated from her by four and two years—and a younger brother born four years after her. She tells me several stories, the first of which is one of her earliest memories of her mother: "I was about five years old, I think, and it was late at night, and I couldn't sleep. My mother brought crackers with jelly up to me in bed and I was delighted and surprised. She usually didn't have time for focused, individual attention—I have three brothers—and I thought it was so kind. Years later, I asked her what might have prompted her gesture and she said she thought I might have been hungry or in need of comfort if I were up so late. The second memory is on my ninth birthday amid a horde of relatives not really there for me but to see our new house. I was a little lost in the crowd. I caught her eye from across the room and she winked and smiled at me. Again, it was about that special, specific recognition, personal and private."

Imagine, for a moment, the variety of responses these two situations might have evoked in a less attuned mother who discovered that one of her four children was still awake at the end of a long day after she'd gotten her infant son and her two other boys to bed and *finally* had a moment to herself. Or how easy it would have been for a mother in full hostess mode surrounded by guests after the house has been cleaned within an inch of its life to simply look past the little girl who looked a bit lonely in the crowd. Thinking about these possible scenarios—imagine an annoyed or angry mother berating or yelling at a sleepless little girl or one who simply ignores the sounds she hears coming from her daughter's bedroom, or any number of variations on the theme—tells us precisely what is meant by attunement.

The idealized portrait of motherhood the culture encourages us to carry in our hearts and heads—awash with the soft pastels of a Renoir or the exquisite tenderness of a Mary Cassatt painting of a mother and child—certainly captures *some* of what many women experience at least *some* of the time, but not *all* of the time.

On the bookshelves in my bedroom, there's a snapshot of me with my then five-day-old daughter in my arms taken over twenty-one years ago; our eyes are locked in mutual adoration and she is smiling up at my beaming face. But as either of us would tell you today—she at twenty-one and I at sixty—despite the unalterable love each of us feels for the other, the photograph doesn't tell the whole story. *That* would require a veritable collage of images—perhaps one of the two of us with our arms around each other, watching a comfort chick flick or shopping, right next to one of the two of us screaming at each other as we walk down the street. We'd need a picture of her holding her own as she challenges me, muttering *"Never mind!"* with all the insolence a young adult can muster up, and one of me, holding on for dear life to the love I feel for her while she is totally driving me crazy. We'd need a picture of how she sometimes feels that my achievements are like a shadow cast over her by a giant skyscraper and one of my intense pride in what a splendid and thoroughly original human being she is and how glad I am that she has her own strengths and that she isn't just like me.

What makes the mother-daughter relationship so intense, so important, is that it involves sometimes contradictory goals and inevitable frictions and requires the equipoise of a highly skilled acrobat. Even the mother who begins attuned to an infant daughter must learn later to stay attuned to a toddler intent on exploring the world, and then later, a pre-schooler who will talk back and act out. The balancing act of mother and daughter during the years of adolescence—involving the contradictory acts of permitting a child to begin to chart her own course while staying connected—requires a completely different set of skills. Later, an attuned mother must stay connected to her now young adult daughter while permitting her to move away, physically and symbolically, to make her own choices and her own mistakes. Sometimes that will include her daughter's moving away from the examples she has set, the behavior she's modeled, the life and career she has chosen. The daughter has an acrobatic challenge of her own.

Even in an essentially caring relationship between a mother and a daughter, the combination of a mother's controlling manner and her inability to be fully attuned to her daughter may leave her daughter feeling that she's not the daughter her mother wanted or that her mother doesn't really know her. Jane is forty-one, an architect and the mother of a four-year-old daughter and a seven-year-old son. She was adopted at birth and has a brother who was born to her parents four years after she was adopted. She grew up in a small midwestern city in a traditional family, with a stay-at-home mother and a father who was an architect. "Both of my parents were loving and fairly involved," Jane tells me, "but they were, and still are, very concerned with appearances—looking good to others matters a great deal to them. My mother took good care of me when I was young and she was loving, but even then I remember her as being very controlling. I remember having to take naps when I wasn't tired and being made to wear clothing she thought would make me 'the best-dressed kid in school.' Instead, I stood out among all the other kids in their casual shirts and Levis, and was the subject of their ridicule."

The way her mother mothered only intensified in adolescence: "She tried to control every aspect of how I looked—my wardrobe, my haircuts, and even how my bedroom was decorated. I didn't have much self-confidence and I lacked a sense of self. She even got me my first job when I was sixteen without consulting me. Mind you, it was a fine job, but I would have liked to be part of the process."

Things became more tense between them as Jane began more and more to make her own choices, which were different in kind from the choices her mother might have made herself or approved of. "I went to graduate school on the East Coast instead of choosing the kind of career she had in mind for me—say a legal secretary or a dental hygienist. In the end, I think she would have preferred me to marry an architect rather than be one myself. My mother called the day I got engaged 'the worst day of her life,' for no other reason than that the man I was engaged to and later married didn't fit into her vision precisely. I think her ideal would have been to have a daughter with a part-time career who loved shopping and wore makeup and nail polish and whose husband was the primary breadwinner, athletic, and comfortable at the country club."

Jane talks to her mother once a week and visits her as often as she can. She appreciates the fact that her mother is good with her children and supportive of them, but she also tells me: "She's still not understanding of me or respecting of me, who I am and the choices I make. She continues to criticize me one way or another. When I was working full-time, she criticized me for that; now that I have cut back to spend more time with my kids, she takes issue with that too. Living independently, my professional training and success, and parenting my children have resolved the self-confidence and sense-of-self issues. But it's still frustrating at times when I hear of my mother's feelings—either from her directly or from my brother—that she still doesn't understand or appreciate me for who I am."

The need to be known by her mother—to be seen, appreciated, and understood for who she is—is a common thread that runs through almost every story a daughter tells about her mother, whether she was loving or not. In her book *Altered Loves,* Terri Apter has suggested that the intensity of the mother-daughter relationship during the years of adolescence and young adulthood—the period of mother-daughter life when the tension is often highest—has more to do with being known than needing to separate or individuate. She writes of the process: "Daughters worked deliberately upon their mothers to get recognition and acknowledgment of the newly forming adult self. They offered a hundred reminders each day that the habitual ways of viewing them were not right. Mothers responded to their daughter's efforts, but themselves offered reminders . . . of what the daughter should be doing, thinking, feeling, or becoming." Apter asserts that at this stage communication between daughter and mother is "a type of argument about self-definition and self-justification." And while those arguments can be more or less hostile, filled with love or anger, Apter maintains that "the aim of the argument was never to separate; it was always characterized by the underlying demand, 'See me as I am, and love me for what I am.'"

Not being "known" by her mother can make a daughter feel essentially fraudulent and at risk of being found out. When the mother-daughter relationship lacks mutuality, it isn't relational in the deepest sense, when it lacks "the mutual desire to understand—to know the other and to feel understood and known by the other—to see and be seen in the moment and over time," as Janet Surrey puts it. Catherine, now fifty-seven, was the eldest of four daughters and was born when her mother was twenty-one; her mother was not yet twenty-five when Catherine's youngest sister was born. Catherine tells me, "My mother wasn't emotionally capable of taking care of all of us, so I became her helper. I needed to please her more than anything else and so I became the 'perfect' child, which helped to insulate me from her anger. I got good grades, helped her around the house, and took care of my sisters. But as a child and through my young adulthood, I had no sense of self-worth or self-esteem. My mother's vision of me was of a smart, talented, good girl because I helped her out and didn't give her any trouble. But I didn't feel smart, talented, or particularly good, so I had a constant battle raging inside me about what would happen when people found out I wasn't what I seemed." Relational disconnection is created when there is an absence of "mutual authenticity, . . . when either the daughter's voice or the mother's voice is dominant or silenced." As Louis Cozolino, Ph.D., observes, "A consistent theme of adult psychotherapy clients is that they had parents who were not curious about who they were but, instead, told them who they should be." What happens, Cozolino explains, is that the child creates a "persona" for her parents but doesn't learn to know herself. What happens is that "the authentic self"—the part of us that is open to feelings, experiences, and intimacy—"remains undeveloped."

The configuration of the mother-daughter relationship may evolve over the life cycle of the two women but it never loses its complexity, not even when both the mother and the daughter consider the relationship close and rewarding. In her study of midlife daughters and aging mothers—subtitled *Mixed Emotions, Enduring Bonds*—Karen L. Fingerman notes that even in caring and evolving relationships between mothers and daughters there are inherent, perhaps inevitable, tensions. It's worth noting that Fingerman's sample of mother–adult daughter dyads was defined by specific relationship characteristics that most of us would readily acknowledge as close: the mothers and daughters lived near to each other and were in frequent contact, some 90 percent of them reporting at least one weekly phone call and at least one visit every two weeks. Even so, while mothers consistently reported fewer tensions than their daughters did, Fingerman was struck by how the relationships were characterized by both strong positive *and* strong negative emotions.

Not surprisingly, mothers and daughters not only saw the tensions and conflicts differently but also didn't necessarily agree on the stage in the daughter's life—the teenage years, young adulthood, or after the age of twenty-five—during which their relationship had been most difficult. Even in these close mother-daughter relationships, there were times of conflict, although conflict at earlier periods of life did not predict conflicts later in adulthood. Fingerman notes that this runs counter to the cultural belief that earlier relationships shape later ones.

Even in a loving relationship the mother-daughter tie changes over time, with variances in both closeness and conflict. Fingerman offers several explanations for the surprising news that a conflict-free beginning may not necessarily ordain a conflict-free relationship between an aging mother and her adult daughter and that conflicts earlier in life are not necessarily predictive of the relationship later in life. First, she proposes that a close mother-daughter relationship that doesn't evolve either in childhood or in adolescence may become troubled when the daughter begins to individuate in adulthood and to make her own choices. It's also possible, she writes, that mothers and daughters who "experience conflicts in the early years of life may develop means of negotiating their differences so that by the adult years, their relationships are relatively problem-free." Finally, she admits, these findings may reflect something else entirely, such as distortions of memory: "Mothers and daughters who experienced many difficulties while the daughter was growing up may see more recent years as better, whereas mothers and daughters who view the present as tension-laden may remember the early years fondly."

Writing as a daughter, not as the mother of three sons, Adrienne Rich tried to capture the essence of it, writing, "Probably there is nothing in human nature more resonant with charges than the flow of energy between two biologically alike bodies, one of which has lain in amniotic bliss inside the other, one of which has labored to give birth to the other.

The materials are here for the deepest mutuality and the most painful estrangement."

The stories that follow are not those of "deepest mutuality" but those where the connection may approach "painful estrangement." They are presented so that we can better understand how it is that some mothers aren't capable of giving their daughters the love and attunement they so crucially need.

WE ALL DREAM OUR CHILDREN long before we have them, beginning in childhood and throughout our adulthood; daydreaming about ourselves as parents and as members of a family other than the one we grew up in is part of the developmental process. We dream both the child herself—her looks and personality, her likes and dislikes, the possibilities her life and future hold for her—and our relationship to her. Contained within that dream is a comparison of the relationship we had with our own mother and the one we will have with the child we've dreamed.

For a securely attached daughter, the dream will include re-creating the intimacy and mutuality she's already experienced. Leslie's mother died when she was fifteen; even today, some forty years later, she remembers her mother as a presence—a feeling of safety, love, and, in the context of her earliest memories, joy. These memories are part and parcel of how she mothers her own daughter, Lily, now sixteen: "One of my earliest memories, maybe my earliest, is of picnicking on those big rocks in New York's Central Park with my mother when I was about three, I guess. Another is of having lunch with her outside in the Central Park Zoo café. There were pansies in the window boxes all around us; it must have been spring. I'm very happy in both memories; it's interesting that they both involve my mother, food, and Central Park. And while they don't sound very significant, they were a significant template for motherhood, if you will. When Lily was born, I couldn't wait to take her to the zoo and to those rocks, which I did many times during her childhood. They still remain some of my happiest memories of her as a child. Just talking about this makes me feel happy."

For a daughter who is insecurely or avoidantly attached to her mother and who has no earned secure attachment to change her ability to connect to her child, even the dreamed relationship can be more problematic. When that daughter herself becomes a mother, her expectations as a parent, her perceptions, and her behavior will be shaped by the mental model of attachment she has.

For all of us—women and men alike—these dreams and expectations take a more precise shape at the moment when we learn we are pregnant, even before we can actually feel that we are, and continue to refine themselves up until the moment of birth, when we finally meet the child we have dreamed so long. If there are other children in the family, parental fantasies will extend to the sibling relationship as well.

The experience of pregnancy too will factor into how a mother feels about the child she is carrying and, in some cases, may continue to influence her feelings long after birth. A calm and relatively uneventful pregnancy may make a mother feel, from the beginning, that her child is an unadulterated source of joy, while a difficult pregnancy, birth, or infancy may do the opposite. As Stephen P. Bank and Michael D. Kahn note, "By attributing certain characteristics to the new baby who 'is giving me trouble' or 'is making me tired' these women can react to the changes in themselves caused by the pregnancy. Unconscious resentments and satisfactions about being pregnant are also elements in this critical period in which the identity of a child can be imposed."

While we like to think of parenting as being blind to gender, there's plenty of evidence that it isn't. For sixty-six years—since right before the bombing of Pearl Harbor in 1941, in fact—the Gallup Poll has been asking Americans the same question: "Suppose you could only have one child: would you prefer a girl or a boy?" While 35 percent of Americans say they have no preference, in 2007, 37 percent preferred to have a boy, while 28 percent wanted a girl. The 2007 results are amazingly similar to those of 1941—despite the enormous cultural shifts America has undergone in the intervening years. There's never been an overall preference for a girl, it should be said; in fact, in two years—1947 and 2000—the preference for a male child was 15 percent greater than that for a female. The results are attributable to the strong preference men have for male children (based on an assumed closer connection between men and boys, carrying on the family name, and the assumption that boys are easier to raise and less expensive than girls to clothe), while women, since 1941, have not shown a correspondingly strong preference for girls.

No woman mothers in a cultural vacuum, and every generation of women comes to the task with a series of assumptions, both cultural and personal, about gender. These too will shape how she mothers a daughter or son in different ways. Gender stereotypes can affect how a woman mothers a girl or a boy, in ways both subtle and not. For example, researchers have noted that while mothers appear to model roughly the same expressions to daughters and sons in the first six months of life, there are subtle differences nonetheless. Mothers tend to match their sons' expressions more closely and smile at sons more as they grow older, while they decrease both matching expressions and smiling with daughters the same age. At the same time, mothers tend to be more expressive with their daughters. Some researchers have suggested that because male infants tend to be less regulated and more expressive than their female counterparts, a mother's interaction with a son may be more about containing the son's affect. When interacting with their daughters, on the other hand, mothers express their feelings more openly, thus exposing girl babies to more emotional displays than their male counterparts. Overall, mothers tend to interact with boys and girls differently. One possible reason is gender stereotypes: mothers relate to their daughters differently because of the assumptions they make about female nature. This pattern becomes even clearer after infancy, when research shows that parents talk more to girls about emotion and, when telling a story to a girl, are more likely to encourage her empathy. Similarly, mothers of children just under three "spoke more to their daughters than their sons about sadness and its causes" and, in contrast, "spoke for longer periods about anger with sons and showed more acceptance of their sons' expressions of anger."

A woman comes to the experience of motherhood shaped by her experiences as a daughter *and* as a woman, and her feelings, both positive and negative, may be heightened if her first child is a daughter. Since the late 1970s, feminist studies have focused on how mothering a girl is shaped by personal experience. For example, it's been suggested that for some women, having a daughter will involve projection, which from the daughter's point of view can be intrusive and make her feel as though her mother doesn't know or see her. Having a son will not raise this problem because, as Luise Eichenbaum and Susie Orbach noted, "Mother can see her son as 'other,' as different; the gender difference provides a clear-cut boundary between them." With a daughter who shares the same biology, that boundary isn't present. Eichenbaum and Orbach suggest that throughout "the many phases of her daughter's life, a mother watches and is continually reminded of her own girlhood, her own childhood wishes and desires, as well as the restrictions she experienced. Images of her own childhood insinuate themselves into the interactions between her and her daughter."

In a similar vein, Jane Flax, a feminist and therapist, has suggested that because mothers "identify more with their girl babies," "more internal conflict is likely to be stimulated by their own role as mother." Flax writes too that some women chose to become mothers so that they can "regain a sense of being mothered themselves" when their daughters are older, and says that sometimes the relationship between mother and daughter will include a confusion of who is the mother and who is the child. The conflicts a mother feels may be conflicts about being female, which in turn create even more conflict within the mother who both wants and doesn't want her daughter to be just like her. Flax asserts that these conflicts make it difficult for a mother to be as emotionally available to her infant daughter as her daughter needs her to be.

Lillian, thirty-four, was the eldest of three children, just two and a half years older than her brother and three and a half years older than her sister. This is how she remembers her early childhood in an agrarian part of the South: "We were very poor for the first five or six years of my life.

My mother stayed home and my father was often out of work. My mother, while essentially loving, seemed unhappy and needy when I was little, and I became more of a mother's helper than a child she tended to. By the time I was five, I was learning how to cook and do laundry and clean the house. I liked the praise I received from both of my parents for doing such a good job. My brother and sister got more attention from my parents. Later, when my dad made more money and we moved, life got easier and Mom was able to give more to them because her life was more stable. When I was an adolescent, she seemed busy and overwhelmed."

Even though the children in the family weren't separated by many years, Lillian, as the eldest, experienced the family differently than her siblings did. Today, even though her mother tries to be loving to her, she never seems—as she didn't when Lillian was small—to be attuned to her: "When I was a young adult, my mother seemed concerned, sometimes overly concerned, about my choices. She didn't want me to make the same mistakes she had. As a result, I was unable to have authentic conversations with her about my life. Now, I'd say our relationship has changed and it's better now than ever. But it seems I am never okay for her. Now the focus has changed from her disapproval of my living with boyfriends to her dismay that I don't have one at all. Now my obligation to marry and have a family in the near future is of utmost importance, never mind my other goals. She doesn't seem to understand my desire to have a life of my own before entering a marriage relationship or having children."

The tension between the life a mother has lived and the one her daughter envisions for herself continues the dynamic. After all, by the time Lillian's mother was thirty-four—Lillian's age now—she had three children, the eldest of whom was seven, and she'd been married for a decade.

For some women, having a daughter will push buttons that having a son did not. Gwen—whose mother always called her the more formal Gwendolyn—is a sixty-three-year-old landscape architect in California and the mother of a daughter to whom she is very close. She paints a picture of an empty marriage and a mother who "probably shouldn't have had a daughter at all." Her mother married late, after an improbably long (eleven-year) courtship. Her goal was to marry the handsomest man in town and have a boy, a girl, and a white clapboard house. And that she did. But theirs was a relationship lacking in affection and balance—the outgoing wife with a strong personality who loved attention and devoted herself to volunteer work, bridge, and gardening and the quiet and retiring man who worked and was content to nap and to read four newspapers a day on his days off—and Gwen grew up understanding that her parents weren't happy. "There was no love, no touching in our household, just tension," she recalls.

Her brother is just a bit over two years older, and early in her life Gwen began to understand that her mother's relationship to her brother was different. "I was a very pretty little girl and, while I don't remember ever being hugged, I do remember my mother fussing over my long, curly hair, making sure that my white shoes were always beautifully polished. My earliest memory of her, when I was about three or so, was in our basement, where she put polish onto my shoes, using an applicator and a bottle that came out of a box with a picture of a nurse on it. She took pride in me, as something she'd made, a reflection of herself. Then, when my hair got dark and my teeth got wonky, she was embarrassed. She was manipulative and controlling. In time, I became pretty again and my mother, who was never beautiful, became jealous of the attention I got. She dwelled on what I couldn't do—I was dyslexic, even though it wasn't diagnosed back then—and had trouble in school with reading and math until I went off to college. As I grew into a person who could challenge her, she couldn't handle it except to tell me that I 'couldn't do anything.' She never really talked to me or even asked about my work."

Gwen's older brother, though, could do no wrong. He did everything his mother asked and always sought out her advice. Gwen laughs a bit when she tells me that her brother actually became an accountant because their mother thought it was a steady profession and he'd make a lot of money. While her mother showed no interest in her work or her life except to criticize her, she relished every detail of her son's success.

Gwen pauses for a moment and then continues: "When my mother was ninety-nine and in a nursing home, I came to visit and she introduced me to another little old lady who was so wonderful and my mother said, 'This is my daughter Gwendolyn—her hair always looks terrible.' The other poor woman just didn't know what to say. My mother always liked to be the belle of the ball. She could be that with my brother but she couldn't with me. She wasn't, all in all, a terrible person and she certainly had a gift for making people laugh. She adored her own mother and was close to all her sisters. But she could never ask me about the good things I'd achieved in my life; she just never thought about it, even though she did ask about my daughter and her children because she loved them. "

I am struck by how nuanced Gwen's understanding of her mother manages to be even though the pain of the experience still echoes in her voice. And then she tells me one more thing: "At the end of her life, my mother turned to me and told me she loved me, just as I was leaving her room. I was so taken aback—my mother never hugged me nor did she ever really talk to me—that I turned and, without thinking or censoring myself, said, 'Excuse me?' She looked at me and said, 'Your brother told me I was supposed to say that.' "

ALL IN THE FAMILY

Our cultural myths about family tend to emphasize connection and similarity rather than differences, as anyone who's ever visited a new mother in the hospital or at home can attest to. We lean over the crib to identify not how the newborn is unique or different but how she reflects the familiar: "She has your eyes," says one smiling visitor, turning to the mother, "and your nose," to the father. Like the myth of unconditional love, our myths about family speak to our human need for connection, continuity, and sense of belonging. We look to heredity to explain the similarities between us and our firstborn children and, later, the similarities between siblings.

But, in fact, heredity is also responsible for the ways in which our children are different from each other, and indeed, most siblings are more different from a genetic point of view than they are alike. All children inherit half of their genetic makeup from their mother and half from their father, and, on average, siblings have only one-half of what they inherit from their parents in common.

Seen through the prism of family relationships, the differences between and among siblings can become even more marked, so much so that siblings growing up in the same family may not even share the same experience of growing up in that family. This sounds counterintuitive— after all, siblings have the same mother and father, live in the same house, eat the same food, participate in the same family routines, and may even go to the same schools—but it is true nonetheless. Why is this? The first reason is that parents treat their children differently, and even if parental treatment seems to be similar, each sibling may experience that treatment differently because of her or his temperament and personality.

Most important, despite strong social taboos against parental favoritism and differential treatment *and* a social norm that insists that mothers (and fathers) love and discipline their children equally, they don't. In their book *Separate Lives: Why Siblings Are So Different,* Judy Dunn and Robert Plomin cite two separate studies, one conducted in Colorado and the other in Cambridge, England, that showed startlingly similar results. Only one-third of the American mothers reported "a similar intensity and extent of affection" for both of their children, and only one-third said they gave similar attention to both. That, of course, leaves two-thirds of the mothers loving their children in different and unequal amounts. (Some 52 percent of the mothers reported being more affectionate to their younger children, while 13 percent reported being more affectionate to their older ones.)

Another one of Dunn and Plomin's findings both surprised and enlightened them. Given that mothers reported differentiating between their children, the authors expected that mothers would treat the same child differentially throughout every stage of development. Instead, what they found was that the mother who was particularly affectionate and responsive to her twelve-month-old child wasn't particularly affectionate or responsive to that same child a year or two later but that she would be relatively affectionate to a subsequent child at the same developmental stage of twelve months. Recognizing that the stage of development had a profound effect on a mother's behavior, Dunn and Plomin were then able to look at what happened to older siblings when they observed their mother's responsiveness to a younger one, and it led them to posit a new vision of family dynamics and a different answer to the question of why siblings are so different. Noting that all children closely monitor their mother's responses to other siblings, Dunn and Plomin asserted that "witnessing *differential* treatment to self and other children may be more important than similar experiences of *direct* interaction with parents." Put another way: "Seeing your mother's evident affection for your sibling may override any amount of affection you in fact receive." Those siblings who perceived differential treatment were less confident and had lower self-esteem. What this means to the stories daughters tell is this: it may not simply be about how their mothers treated them but about how they treated them differently from their siblings.

In addition, while we like to think of families—especially intact families—as stable and unchanging, in fact, every family changes over time. If we were to look at any family the way the ruins of an ancient, half-buried city are examined, we'd find layer after layer of archaeological detail, year by year, decade by decade. We'd see that a firstborn child might have grown up in a more financially stressed household with a still inexperienced new mother but that she had the benefit of a still-vibrant relationship between her mother and father. The next layer, some five years later, might record the birth of a younger sister who has grown up in a now more economically prosperous household with a mother more confident in her parenting skills but also one in which strains in her parents' marriage have already developed. The final layer might record the birth of a son some seven years after the firstborn. The family now lives in a big house on a suburban road but, within a year or two of that son's birth, the mother has returned to the workforce after a decade of staying at home, and her relationship to her husband has become even more distant. Needless to

say, the ways in which these siblings experience what is, from the outside
at least, the "same stable family" will be very different. In addition, any
individual's experience will also be shaped by large gaps in age between
siblings and intervening events, such as illness, death, or divorce.

Lisa, now sixty, is the youngest of three daughters whose sisters were
nine and eleven years older than she. Her mother was thirty-six when she
was born and, as she tells it: "By the time I came along, my mother had
really finished parenting. She had been much more involved with my two
older sisters—leading a Brownie troop and the like—and although she
wasn't truly loving to any of us, I don't remember her ever being really caring toward me. By the time I was four, I knew my mother was unloving. I
went to a nursery school where my aunt, whom I adored, was the teacher.
She was eighteen years younger than my mother, glamorous, and incredibly loving. After nap time, I would pretend to stay asleep so that I could
go home with her instead of to my own house."

"Even at a very young age," Lisa says, "I knew my mother wanted
little to do with me. She sent me to preschool very young—in those days
most kids stayed home until kindergarten—and away to sleepaway camp
at six or seven. Instead of the usual two weeks, I stayed for the entire
summer. She wanted me to be away from her, and I acted out as much as I
could." Lisa's eldest sister became a surrogate mother of sorts, even when
Lisa was a baby. "I know she felt a responsibility to shield me from our
mother," she says. Her sister's own battles with their mother made her an
ally and protective of her little sister, but her presence couldn't entirely fill
the void left by her mother's lack of attunement and attention. Lisa's anger
and despair only grew as she approached adolescence: "I really felt like
I was alone in the world. Since my mother had my father and my sisters
had their husbands, I felt that the thing I really wanted in life was to be
the most important person in the world to someone. A part of me is still
looking for that. I was very depressed but didn't and couldn't talk to my
mother about it. She denied emotions and emotional subjects; nothing was
ever explained and everything was waved away. My family never talked,
never discussed. I was extremely angry, particularly toward my mother,
and expressed it openly."

The crisis finally culminated with Lisa's nervous breakdown in the tenth grade. For Lisa, it was a life-changing event: "I checked out of childhood and, in a real sense, out of the family. My mother's response to what I'd done was all self-referential; she kept saying, 'What did I do wrong to deserve this?' While I was sent to a therapist and my parents saw a counselor, nothing really changed, except that perhaps they became nervous about how to respond to me. My mother never, ever talked to my older sister about it, even though she was profoundly shaken. After I went off to college, I was pretty emotionally removed from my parents. When I came home from college on vacation, I stayed at my sister's, not my parents' house, and they never even asked about my choice or mentioned it."

After going to medical school, Lisa moved away from California and headed for Vermont, where she married and went on to have two daughters of her own. She tells me one more story with great resonance: "Because my sisters were so much older, I like to say that they had different parents while having the same parents. In a real way, that's true. Who I was in this family is revealed by the following story. After my father died, I was on the phone with my mother, who told me that because 'the girls'—my two sisters—had been back in our hometown, she'd had the unveiling of his gravestone. She didn't seem to notice or recognize that I had the same blood relationship and was every bit as much her daughter and his as they were."

Every story a woman tells is *personal* in the deepest sense, perhaps because, as Judy Dunn and Robert Plomin write, "Children's perceptions of events . . . are probably more important to their development than are the 'actual' events themselves." Those different perceptions of the environment both within and outside the family shape their personalities, their behavior, and their relationships in important ways and are another source of the profound differences among siblings raised in the "same" families. This may explain why a memoir written by one family member may be hotly disputed by another member of the same family. This point is underscored by Susanna Sonnenberg's searing memoir of her mother, *Her Last Death,* in which she gives pseudonyms to all the members of her family save her father and herself, to emphasize that her "memoir" is hers alone.

By Sonnenberg's account at least, "Daphne" is the hands-down winner of the most unsuitable and awful mother award. She's a compulsive liar, manipulator, thief, poseur, and, perhaps, a sexual predator, not to mention sexually promiscuous, drug-addicted, and thoroughly amoral. The book opens at the moment when Sonnenberg must choose whether to go to her mother's bedside; she is apparently near death. This moment threatens what Sonnenberg calls the "uneasy" truce between her and her younger sister "Penelope" on the subject of their mother; as Sonnenberg notes, "We don't want to fight, so we don't mention her." Underlying that truce, though, is something much larger, as Sonnenberg admits at the start: "She doesn't see what I see and I can't infuse her with my history. My sister, having lived the same years in the same rooms, lived them differently."

As surprising as this might seem, it isn't at all unusual.

MIRROR, MIRROR: THE TRUTH ABOUT SNOW WHITE

Raised on Walt Disney, most of us hear the phrase "Mirror, mirror, on the wall, who's the fairest of them all?" and the first image that pops into our heads is that of the evil stepmother with her stark white face and red lips in the animated film and book spin-offs of *Snow White*. But like other folktales collected by the Brothers Grimm, their original source—and indeed their first version of the story, published in 1812—wasn't about an evil stepmother but a mother-daughter pair, and it was Snow White's own mother who was her envious antagonist. In the original version, the beautiful queen who pricks her finger while sewing and wishes for a child "as white as snow, as red as blood, and as black as the sewing frame" gives birth to Snow White. It is Snow White's own mother who, obsessed with her own beauty, checks her magic mirror when Snow White is seven only to hear that her daughter, not she, is "the fairest of them all." It is Snow White's mother who tries her best to have her daughter killed throughout the rest of the story until innocence trumps maternal envy in the end. By

1819, the Grimm Brothers had banished to the cupboard of taboos the psychological truth mirrored in the original folktale—of the potential rivalry between a mother and daughter, or maternal envy—by having the "real" mother die after giving birth and a sinister stepmother take her place.

Almost three hundred years later, maternal envy remains taboo but hardly nonexistent. Writing in the *Times* of London in 2007, journalist Charlotte Phillips tackled the subject in a piece called "When the Green-Eyed Monster Is Mum." Phillips begins with a telling anecdote: In an unguarded moment, having coffee with friends, she confides that "I'd have to swallow a mouthful of unmaternal gall if my eldest daughter succeeded in her long-term ambition to write a bestseller." The response from the other women was swift—"The collective intake of breath from the other mothers was strong enough to suck the foam off my cappuccino." Oops.

But more interesting than the piece itself were the responses from women from all over the world, some thirty of them posted on the paper's website, almost every one of them grateful for the airing of the subject. Many of these women wrote not just about their mothers' jealousy or envy but about how their mothers' diminishment of who they were—their achievements, personalities, or looks—coexisted with their need to gain their mothers' approval. One woman wrote: "I grew up with an insanely jealous mother who reveled in my failures that she deliberately engineered. She actually stole clothes from my wardrobe that flattered me and bad-mouthed me to as many people as she could. I STILL wanted her to like me." Yet another commented: "I had the same experience with a jealous mother. As a child I sensed her dislike so tried really hard to gain her approval. When I won straight A's and scholarships as a result, she disliked me more and more. I interpreted that as me not being good enough and the cycle went on and on. . . . A few years ago I realized that mothers should be proud of their children no matter what their achievements and whatever my mum's feeling toward me wasn't my fault. Sadly, I still crave her approval and am so jealous of other people's relationships with their mums."

Writing about her own mother, feminist writer Phyllis Chesler suggests that an envious mother diminishes her daughter to save herself from feeling diminished: "Once, long ago, I must have been my mother's little girl, someone she dressed, whose hair she braided—but then she left me, and I left her, and we kept leaving each other. No matter what I did to try to gain her love or approval, it was never enough, because all she wanted was me for herself, me, merged, me as her shadow, me, devoured. She loved me, but in this primitive way. I failed this love." Chesler recounts that her mother simply wanted her to be more like her—to make the choices she had, as a woman who had always put her family, not herself, first.

What Chesler intuits, psychologists confirm by explaining how envy and jealousy reflect the self—not the object of envy or jealousy. As Peter Salovey and Alexander Rothman explain, jealousy and envy are highly personal. (Yes, there's that word again.) They write: "We are not envious of just anyone's random attributes that we have not attained ourselves. Nor are we invariably jealous when our lovers flirt with random others. Rather, envy and jealousy are most likely to be felt in domains that are especially important to how we define ourselves—that 'hit us where we live.' " Similarly, we are most likely to feel jealous when an important relationship is threatened not just by anyone but by someone we feel inferior to in "some domain that's especially important to us." Those domains are those central to an individual's self-esteem and self-definition.

In my mother's family, those domains were physical beauty and material possessions. A portrait of my mother painted when she was seventeen hung over the sideboard in my grandparents' apartment in Amsterdam, in plain view of the dining room table. I always thought that the artist must have been more than a little in love with her, because her features had been softened, her demeanor idealized. She was all sweetness and light. I remember sitting at the table with my grandmother when I was six or so and, in an unguarded moment, looking up at the portrait and saying, "Mommy was so beautiful then." My grandmother pushed back from the table without saying a word and left. I sat there, wondering what I'd done. After what seemed a long while, she came back with a box of photographs, which she emptied out onto the table.

There were pictures of my grandmother I'd never seen before—sepia-toned studio portraits taken when she was a young woman. To my child's eyes, these images bore no resemblance to the heavyset woman in her late fifties who sat next to me, with her coiffed gray hair, a stiff corset to make her look thinner, and a look of perpetual dissatisfaction on her face. Not even the jewelry she wore day and night—the pearls she slept in to maintain their luster, the stacks of gold bracelets that she never took off, the diamonds that sparkled on her fingers— could soften her. No, this young woman with the long wavy hair piled up on her head, in a long dress with a sailor collar, with a beautiful smile and soft dimples must be someone else. "You see?" my grandmother said with an air of triumph. "I was much more beautiful than your mother ever was. That's why your grandfather married me—I was the prettiest girl he'd ever seen."

Perhaps what was most extraordinary about the rivalry between my mother and her mother was both how fully it was expressed—an intricate pas de deux they engaged in whenever they were together, in full view for all to see—and how completely it was denied at the same time. Most amazingly, neither of them ever acknowledged that dance. Each of them was bound by the myths that hold women tight: of unconditional mother love and filial duty. Even so, their rivalry dominated their interactions, and they fought like trained gladiators, each fixing on the other's weaknesses to wound and hurt.

Our word *rivalry* comes from the Latin, meaning "rights to the same stream," and in their case, the historical stream was my grandfather's love and attention.

Their dance was tightly scripted, its themes highly reliable. Each was envious of the other in matters large and small, and by the time I was a small child, they'd danced so long that the smallest thing—a pretty new shawl belonging to the one but not the other or some other trinket of no real import—could set them in motion.

It was inevitable, I suppose, that my mother would come to see me just as her mother had seen her: as a potential competitor for the attention and love she needed from not just her father and my father but everyone else who came into our little world. With my father's death, when I was fifteen and she a forty-one-year-old widow with a teenage daughter and a six-year-old son, what happened next had all the inevitability of a Greek tragedy. When she began to date a few years later, her heart was set on a more glamorous and financially prosperous life than the one she'd lived with my father, and she banked on her beauty and charm to make it happen. She turned down the older men who might have been willing to take on an instant family and turned her attention to the younger ones, still single or fresh from a divorce—never seeing that there wasn't room for an aging beauty and her two kids in the sleek two-seater sports cars they drove. She got older and so did I, and it wasn't long before her would-be suitors began flirting with me when I came home from college. And in the end, my then fresh-faced beauty became a rebuke of another kind, and her cruelty took on another, even sadder, aspect.

The crossroads at which my mother and I found ourselves—as she entered middle age and I young womanhood— simply intensified the patterns that had long been part of our relationship. As we look at how unloving mothers are different from their loving counterparts, it's important to remember that even loving mothers may experience feelings of envy or competitiveness at certain stages of the mother-daughter relationship. In his study on how a child's entry into adolescence may trigger a parental midlife crisis, Laurence Steinberg notes that while the majority of mothers enjoy their daughters' blossoming into womanhood and achievements, there are others for whom their daughters' metamorphoses will heighten their sense of dissatisfaction, lost opportunities, and aging.

Because the mother myths have hidden the kernel of psychological truth once contained in the original version of *Snow White,* even loving mothers find it harder to confront, admit, and manage their feelings at these cusp moments in time.

TWO PARTS OF THE DYAD: GOODNESS OF FIT

While a mother is certainly in control of the relationship with her daughter during infancy and childhood, the child is nonetheless an active participant, because her inborn temperament will influence and shape the connection between her mother and herself, positively or not. Psychiatrists Stella Chess and Alexander Thomas called the interplay between parental expectations and personality and the temperament and personality of the infant "goodness of fit." Simply put, a high-strung mother might find it easier to relate to a docile, low-affect baby rather than a fussy one who triggered her own excitability, and vice versa. The closer the match of mother and child, the easier the job of mothering. This doesn't, of course, excuse a mother's lack of empathy for her daughter, but it does explain yet another aspect of it.

Jennifer, now fifty, is the mother of four children, three of them daughters (ages twenty-six, twenty-three, and seventeen) and all of them different. Her explanation of the way "goodness of fit" shaped how she mothered each of her daughters illuminates another aspect of the mother-daughter dyad in every relationship, both loving and not. Her first daughter, Sarah, and she weren't innately a good fit: "Sarah was a strong-willed and fit-throwing child who didn't share easily. From day one, she was one of those people who has no margin in her tolerance levels. When she was hungry, it was *right then, right now*—no waiting even a second—with huge emotional ramifications. On the other hand, I'm strong-willed but fairly detached from the drama of things, so I didn't play into her tantrums. We are polar opposites in our basic natures—she lives from the center of her emotions but has a hard time not being swept away by them, while I live contemplating things from the outside and then acting, and have a hard time getting into my core emotions. The result was a nice balance: I honored her basic nature while honoring my own, and I worked hard to teach her where the middle ground was."

From the beginning, her second daughter, Lizzie, was what Jennifer calls "a perfect fit at most times. We were always in sync. She withdraws sometimes when she wants more space and I understand that. With Lizzie, it was like mothering myself. She was intuitive, empathic, emotionally sensitive, wildly mobile, and had learning disabilities, and it was never an issue."

Her youngest daughter, Abby, was essentially a good fit but was more challenging to parent. "I was glad I was her mom because another mother might not have been able to handle her force, and that could have wrecked her. She was *so* powerful and she needed a strong, loving container and someone who wasn't afraid of fire. She got that from me. She would fight to death for something, and without the kind of fortitude I had, she might have won, when all she was really looking for was the edge of her container."

In his remarkable book *The Neuroscience of Human Relationships,* Louis Cozolino, Ph.D., writes that "the brain is primed to grow in conditions of safety, positive excitement, shared openness, and exploration." These conditions—which we've seen called "secure attachment" and "attunement"—allow parents to adapt to their children, on the one hand, and help children, on the other, to discover "their inner worlds." He notes that most adult psychological distress has its roots either in having parents whose picture of a child doesn't match the child or in lack of fit between the temperaments and personalities of parents and children.

Some, though not all stories of unloving mothers are indeed narratives about the lack of "fit."

While a mother has an extraordinary power to shape a daughter's world and her sense of self, she is not alone. There is another figure in a daughter's world: her mother's husband and her own father.

· *Three* ·
In the House of the Father:
Heroes and Coconspirators

BEFORE THERE IS A CHILD, THERE IS A RELATIONSHIP BETWEEN A woman and a man, whether it's a casual encounter or a fully committed marriage of some duration, the relationship on which this chapter focuses. Every child is born into an existing relationship between her two parents; her presence will change that relationship as much as her parents' relationship, histories, and personalities will shape her. As children, who our parents were before we were born and how they related to each other then is the stuff of myth and family lore, made real only by photographs in an album and the stories we are told. As children, it's inconceivable to imagine the world without us in it—just as it's impossible to imagine our parents being anything other than our parents. But the influence of the child on the parental dyad with the influence of the dyad on the child is always a bidirectional process, even if not consciously perceived.

While the culture mythologizes the act of "starting a family," assuming that it will strengthen the bonds among the individuals within it, that assumption is far from a universal truth. In stark contrast to the idea that a child always reflects the love and commitment spouses feel for each other and is thus necessarily a source of mutual satisfaction and pleasure, research actually confirms that "children's presence and marital quality tend to be inversely related." Studies also show that the gender of the child affects the quality of the marriage and the level of marital satisfaction; in fact, for couples with a single child, the risk of divorce rises by 9 percent if the child is a girl. In families with two children, the patterns stay the same: at highest risk are those with two daughters; at lowest risk are those with two sons.

Like all other cultural myths, myths about family contribute to and shape the behavior of the adults within any given family in different degrees; while many of these myths remain stable from one generation to another, still others evolve and change over time. For example, the preponderance of adult daughters interviewed for this book were born in the 1940s, 1950s, and 1960s, before the shift sometimes referred to as "the divorce culture" took place. Although a number of these daughters have been divorced themselves and a few did have divorced parents, most of their mothers and fathers stayed married. (The rise in divorces involving children began in the late 1960s, peaked in the 1980s, and has stayed relatively stable since. This more relaxed societal tolerance of divorce yielded, it's been argued, a new vision of the relative importance of the traditional obligation of parents to provide a stable familial environment for their children, on the one hand, and the right of the individual parent to seek out personal happiness and satisfaction, on the other.)

Perhaps more important, the mothers of these daughters born from the 1940s through the 1960s and early 1970s weren't likely to have become mothers with any conscious examination of whether they were suited to mothering, or any active sense of choice, since married women, according to society's norms, were expected to have children unless they were physically unable to. (I remember my parents discussing the rare childless couple they knew in hushed, somber tones and a sense of pity, and they certainly weren't alone.) The success of these social norms during these decades is underscored by the fact that voluntary childlessness was at a historical low for the entire century and wouldn't increase until the early to mid-1970s. Additionally, the cultural pressure to have more than one child was equally effective, since a single child implied, in the absence of physical impediments, a lack of full commitment to motherhood on a woman's part.

The cultural coercion may have made it harder for those women who came to mothering with an already tattered script—as the daughters of unloving or distant mothers—to function in the ways they were supposed to, increasing the burden of the mother myths. Combine that with the equally powerful cultural assumption of the time that mothers were wholly responsible for the physical and psychological welfare of their offspring (no less an expert than Bruno Bettelheim attributed autism to a mother's emotional coldness!), and you get a glimpse of the levels of denial a new mother had to build up when she felt little or no connection to her daughter or experienced an active disconnection.

Over twenty-five years ago, when I was in my early thirties, I remember talking to the mother of one of my oldest childhood friends—a graduate of one of America's most prestigious colleges who was a stay-at-home housewife and mother from the late 1940s through the early 1970s. When her two children were launched, she began to work in the world of nonprofits, which proved to be a highly satisfying career path. She turned to me and remarked how lucky her daughter and I were to have had so many opportunities and choices. Then, somewhat wistfully and to my utter shock, she added, "I don't think I would have had children if I'd been born when you girls were. I would have been happier working." I always thought she was a terrific mother—I much preferred being at her house than my own when I was growing up—and I was downright jealous of her daughter's relationship to her. After the shock finally wore off, her words had terrific resonance because, at that time in my life, I had decided not to have children. Her words, then and now, helped me realize how having and making an active choice changes everything.

I went on to have my daughter after almost two decades of adulthood thinking about my choice.

"ARE FATHERS ESSENTIAL OR (JUST) IMPORTANT?"

At first glance, this looks like a facetious question—we'd *never* ask it about mothers, after all—but it's actually been the subject of a sometimes heated debate since the mid-1990s. (The question itself is a quotation from a newsletter issued by New York University's prestigious Child Study Center.)

This chapter is called "In the House of the Father" because, in a literal sense, for most of these daughters, it *was* the father's house; his efforts as a breadwinner paid for it and its upkeep. But it's equally valid to ask whether there really is or historically ever was a father's house, since the parenting space a father occupied then (and for many families occupies now) for a daughter was more like a mud room or porch than not. Still, there is another real sense in which the house isn't his nor has it ever been.

Stacked one upon the other, the mother myths cast a shadow over the father and his role in a daughter's life and, in doing so, create another set of cultural assumptions that are his alone. Dr. Linda Nielsen has researched father-daughter relationships for twenty years and begins her book *Embracing Your Father* with a list of common beliefs about fathers that daughters (and almost everyone else in our culture) hold to be true. Among them are: that fathers lack the "instinct" to raise children that mothers have, that they get as much or more satisfaction from their work than from their children, that they have less impact on their daughters' development than mothers do, that they make fewer sacrifices for their daughters than mothers do, and that they are more critical and judgmental than mothers are. All of these assumptions are, of course, reverse reflections of the mother myths.

These cultural tropes—magnified by gender stereotypes of the kind that have us thinking "men are from Mars, women are from Venus"—are an inexorable part of the landscape today, trumpeted by all manner of media, but they are hardly new. From the dawn of psychology, gender differences—rather than gender similarities—have always occupied center stage, even though there is remarkably little scientific evidence to support them. This will come as a surprise to most of us who assume the psychological differences between women and men are vast, but in truth, scientific evidence shows that women and men are more alike psychologically than not. In addition, despite our cultural beliefs, there's little scientific proof that parenting skills are connected to gender, or that by their nature women and men parent differently in ways that are significantly important.

Nonetheless, these ideas actively shape not only how our society views women and men but how individuals—women and men alike—within it see themselves and their roles as mothers and fathers and wives and husbands. These assumptions are pervasive and persuasive social constructs and affect both adult behaviors and expectations of family relationships. Children's expectations are also affected by cultural ideas about the role a father (or mother) "ought" to play; they will be shaped by ideas communicated in books and magazines, movies and television, as well as conversations with peers and other adults.

For example, the long-running television shows of the 1950s and 1960s—*The Adventures of Ozzie and Harriet* (1952–1966), *Father Knows Best* (1955–1963), and *Leave It to Beaver* (1957–1963)—influenced the perceptions of daughters now in their late forties, fifties, and sixties. But, as historian Steven Mintz notes, these shows—which purported to "show American children what middle-class families were supposed to be like"— were, in fact, "part of a concerted effort to combat the deepening disengagement of fathers from family life" and were not "an accurate portrait of postwar fatherhood." Mintz calls *Leave It to Beaver* "a fantasy of a caring father in a modern family," something I wish someone had told me when I watched it and, yes, compared the Cleaver family to my own.

An assortment of cultural assumptions also shapes the family dynamic as a whole. Take the example of Jim, now sixty, a physician from San Diego and the father of Josh, twenty-eight, and Jennifer, twenty-six. He and his wife, Linda, took on traditional roles until their children were in their teens; Linda stayed at home with the kids while Jim worked five days a week. But from the time Jennifer was small, Jim enjoyed a special and close relationship to her; she preferred to have her dad fix her hair in the morning, either brushing it straight with a barrette over her right ear or putting it in braids. Many of the family photographs show Jim with Jennifer either on his lap or nearby, and Josh with his mother, Linda. The two children were very different: while both were smart, Josh tended to coast in school, doing as little as possible, while Jennifer was more serious and industrious.

Even when the children got older, each remained closer to the opposite-sex parent: Josh was fussed over and doted on by his mother, while Jim became the parent in whom Jennifer could confide. Increasingly the two parents clashed over how to deal with Josh, who was undisciplined in school and out. As Jim saw it, Linda undercut his efforts to set boundaries for their son and refused to cooperate by imposing penalties for Josh's behavior; from Linda's vantage point, Jim was encroaching on her maternal domain, and she belittled his views on what should be done about their son. By the time Josh was sixteen or so, he began to follow his mother's lead and disparage his father openly. As Jennifer approached adolescence, Linda's resentment of her husband and daughter's closeness increased, as did the couple's disagreements about Josh's behavior. Here too Linda felt strongly that Jim was impinging on what should have been her territory, preventing her from having the special, confidential bond that mothers and daughters were supposed to enjoy. Tensions in the marriage comingled with Linda's jealousy of the father-daughter relationship, and she became more actively accusatory. The couple divorced when Josh was in college and Jennifer was in her last year of high school.

The cultural assumptions about the roles fathers and mothers play in the family both marginalized Jim's efforts and fueled the family dynamic, a pattern Dr. Linda Nielsen and other researchers assert is far from atypical. It even has its own name: "maternal gatekeeping." A "maternal gatekeeper" is a woman who keeps traditionally female territory—managing the home and raising the children—as her own and actively subverts a husband and father's efforts in that arena. It's thought that between 20 percent and 25 percent of mothers engage in gatekeeping behaviors, although the number may actually be higher.

Maternal gatekeeping, which is closely tied to the mother myths in our culture, explains in part why women's responsibilities for maintaining the home and caring for the children have stayed basically the same for the last ninety years, despite all the dramatic changes wrought by the 1960s and 1970s, including women's political rights, economic privileges, and work patterns. Experts note that many women are often ambivalent about sharing the domestic sphere with their husbands—a place that has always belonged to women alone: "Some women both cherish and resent being the primary caretaker and feel both relieved and displaced by paternal involvement." Gender beliefs about men and parenting may, according to research, result in a wife's "devaluing" her husband's ability to parent, thus discouraging a father from taking a more active role by actively criticizing how he interacts with his children or performs specific tasks.

In some families, maternal gatekeeping may, in fact, keep fathers from forming meaningful relationships with their children. Because of the power of the mother myths, some women will gatekeep because they see paternal involvement as both a threat to their maternal identity and a confirmation of their own inability to mother to society's standards. In addition, from a man's point of view, the social belief that he isn't as nurturing as his wife may prevent him from even trying to nurture his children. Whatever the reasons, as showcased in a 2008 cover story in *The New York Times Magazine,* women do twice as much housework as men—even when both parents work—and wives do almost five times the amount of child care as their husbands, whether they work full-time or not.

Other factors, research shows, are highly predictive of how involved a father will be in his daughter's life. (It's worth noting that, overall, fathers are much more involved with sons than with daughters.) One important factor is the nature and quality of the marital relationship because, as researcher Mary F. Luccie discovered, mothers are "influential agents" in determining how a father relates to his children. Both a positive marital relationship *and* the support of his wife were reliable predictors of

involved fatherhood. Interestingly, a woman's relationship to her father
was also highly predictive of how involved her husband would be with
their children; the more *negative* her relationship with her father had
been, the more likely it was that her husband would become an involved
father. Perhaps, as the researcher suggested, those mothers more strongly
appreciated their husbands' paternal involvement because their relationships with their own fathers were more negative than positive. In a similar
fashion, women who characterized their relationships with their fathers
as "rejecting" were more satisfied than other women with how their husbands parented.

It becomes clear in many daughters' stories that their parents' relationship to each other—whether healthy or not—is as influential as their
individual personalities or behaviors. The marital relationship in any
given household becomes a template for how children in that household—
daughters and sons alike—will behave in their own relationships with
peers and romantic partners, through either participation in the relationship (by taking sides) or simple observation. Without therapy, relationship
patterns thus tend to "remain all in the family," "such that problematic
ways of relating repeat themselves from one generation to the next." How
mothers and fathers resolve their conflicts, what tactics they use, are also
significantly related to how their children will ultimately handle their own
conflicts with peers and intimates, inside the family and out. Sometimes
the marriage itself becomes another character in the family's script.

In Susan's case, her parents' marriage and her mother's vulnerabilities
would shape the narrative of her later childhood, adolescence, and early
adulthood. Susan remembers her early childhood as idyllic, with a loving
and involved mother who cooked and baked and brushed her hair. She
still has a scrapbook her mother made for her then, and some of her happiest moments now are looking at the words her mother wrote and the
pictures she pasted on its pages.

At age sixty-eight, the mother of two daughters and the grandmother
of four, Susan now understands in fullness both how her mother and her
father and their marriage initially shaped her sense of self. Her mother's

childhood had been troubled—there was alcoholism in the family—and her adolescence was extremely traumatic. At eighteen, she discovered the lifeless body of her beloved brother, a suicide; the family was devastated both by his death and then by the loss of the family business that same year during the Depression. Unable to cope, her mother dropped out of college. But her marriage to Susan's father, at the beginning at least, gave her the safety and validation she needed; he was a brilliant businessman and professor and their future looked bright. They had three daughters, of whom Susan was the eldest. But as the years passed, Susan's father spent more and more time working, and progressively withdrew from his wife, who had ceased to be a priority for him. Over time she began to feel the same kind of loss she'd felt as a girl when her favorite brother died. Realizing that her husband was having an affair was the final blow and she began to drink.

So just as Susan approached adolescence, she lost not only the protection her mother provided but also her childhood. "At that point, I was forced to take on my mother's role," Susan tells me, "mothering my younger sisters, cooking the meals. Not knowing what kind of shape my mother would be in, I couldn't bring anyone home from school, and my father stayed at work later and later. I became a star student, using my intelligence as a way of stabilizing what had become a chaotic world. My mother became my problem, someone I had to take care of, make up for, and defend. Of course, then, I didn't know why she drank and I was angry at how weak she was. I didn't then realize how afraid she was of everything and how depressed she was."

Susan's father was a perfectionist, and even though he was distant and unaffectionate, he was an example of how to make your way in the world. He held Susan to high standards: "When I got an A, he'd simply ask, 'Why not an A+?' and he did give me the sense that I could do anything. Even though I wasn't a 'Daddy's girl,' he was an important figure in my life in that sense. But the pattern of their marriage was very destructive, and as a teenager I decided it was better to be a mistress than a wife. I felt that if I were married, I *would* become my mother. It took me years to understand why I chose affairs—I was choosing the opposite of what my mother had chosen."

But Susan hadn't yet found her own path, and the tenacity of family patterns of relating was demonstrated by what came next: "My marriage was a re-creation of my family—brilliant, exacting, demanding, and cold"—and after twelve years and much counseling, Susan knew she had to get herself and her daughters out. "I was the first person I knew to get divorced," she says, and that decision, along with the care of a loving therapist, permitted her to reinvent how she connected to herself and others: "I knew that by becoming conscious of my own unconscious behavior, I could become what I so desperately wished my mother could be—loving but also worldly and successful."

And that is precisely what she is today.

FOR THE DAUGHTER of an unloving mother, the traditional division of labor, the assumption of maternal expertise, and maternal gatekeeping often have very specific ramifications for how her father helps or hinders her growth or, in a broader sense, is at all involved in her development. The role a father plays in a family can vary widely. In some families, the father's mere presence will act as a buffer to the mother-daughter conflict, while in others the father may sometimes actively support his daughter in mother-daughter disputes. Alternatively, the daughter may see her father as her mother's coconspirator, reinforcing her sense of isolation and lovelessness. In some families, the father may actually be a source of the tension between mother and daughter, as they each compete for his love, attention, and validation.

The family Ella grew up in was, she says, pretty typical of a 1950s household, at least from the outside. (She's just turned fifty-five.) Her mother stayed at home until the three children reached the teenage years; her father earned the money and managed it, planned the vacations, and gave her mother an allowance. When Ella was a child, she says, "I was very aware that my mother served my father. She didn't have much say in things, and it seemed to me that everything was done his way. He was the life of the party—the social one—and she didn't have much to say because he dominated every conversation. But they were a team, and as I got older I could see how much they loved each other and supported each other. Their relationship changed for the better when Mom gained more independence, went to work, took over the finances, and the kids left home."

Ella's relationship to her two parents could not have been more different. She felt unloved and uncared for by her hypercritical mother, who was also preoccupied with her two other more needy children, but her father—whom she resembled physically—clearly adored her, and Ella felt sure that she was his favorite child. Unlike her two siblings, she shared her father's love of sports, and they often watched football games and golf together. Ella was the child her dad would take along when he ran errands, and she remembers how, at the grocery store, he would grab her hand and waltz down the aisles, whistling. It was, she admits, both mortifying and wonderfully loving at the same time.

His influence on her reflected both his strengths and his weaknesses: "My dad was a fair man who treated people well. What I didn't like about him was that he always had to have control. It was his way or no way. He wouldn't discuss; he would lecture. Life was black and white, and as long as things went his way, he was happy. I learned the value of listening because he didn't, and I realized very early on that change is the only constant in life because he hated change."

But while Ella's father's love for her sustained her, she also felt very resentful and abandoned because her father didn't protect her from her mother's barrage of criticisms. "My father knew how she treated me," she tells me, "because she criticized him too. He just accepted it as the way she was and expected me to accept it because she was my mother and deserved respect. He said I should just ignore her behavior, but he never made it clear that it was her problem, not mine. Instead, he told me that Mom started every day with a clean slate, which is how he explained the fact that she never remembered any of the horrible things she said to me. In fact, whenever I confronted her with what she'd said, she would accuse me of making it up. I remember thinking, even when I was young, 'Is he nuts? Doesn't he see what she's doing?' But he loved her enough to accept her for who she was. Of course, he was an adult and I was a child, and I felt that my father should have told me somewhere along the way that her behavior wasn't about me but about her. Instead, without that support, it took me a very long time to understand that."

In some families, a father's allegiance and loyalty to a mother may complicate a daughter's journey into wholeness; in another, though, a father's voice may provide an important alternative.

In Jane's family, both parents seemed content within their marriage, and while her architect father was the sole wage earner, she perceived him as an involved parent. While Jane's mother was hypercritical, controlling, and hard to please, her father represented a safer haven. "I've always had a good relationship with my father," she tells me. "He is caring and loving toward me and my brother. He tended to leave the discipline and house-hold issues to my mother, but he was also involved when we were growing up. He'd take my brother and me to parks and play sports with us, and he'd help me with homework. He didn't have any sisters and didn't seem to understand my pretty typical adolescent issues—like why I was so upset not to have a boyfriend for a school dance—but I never took that as a lack of caring on his part. He encouraged me to explore career options, and didn't abide by my mother's much lower expectations for me. But he was still old-fashioned and conservative in some ways."

Most important, in the context of his marriage, Jane's father was free to express his own opinions, even when they differed from her mother's: "I feel that my father was a positive influence on my self-esteem as a child, as an adolescent, and as a young adult. He was certainly proud of my accomplishments. He was a good role model in terms of career, supporting a family, and also spending time with his family." And while her mother called the day Jane got engaged the "worst day" of *her* life, Jane's father's reaction, while critical of her choice, was different in kind. "My father was disapproving because Steven, my fiancé, didn't have a job when we got engaged and didn't appear to have any major career ambition. But my father wasn't hurtful and he didn't say the hurtful things my mother did. And he told my mother to back off on the wedding planning, which she saw as a mother-daughter thing—and which I wanted to do with Steve, our way." While both parents were conservative enough to believe that the husband should be the main provider in the family, it was Jane's father who encouraged her to decide for herself, and it's probably not an accident that Jane is an architect, like her father.

The balance of power in a marriage, cultural assumptions about the role fathers play in the family, and the way boys in American society are socialized all affect how fathers act when the mother-daughter relationship is weak, damaged, or emotionally nonexistent, Dr. Linda Nielsen tells me in an interview. In general, paternal responses to familial dysfunctions, including marital, remain relatively consistent. Fathers tend to withdraw from the family in times of stress, both literally and figuratively—spending more time at work, for example. Coincidentally, mothers become more actively involved. The tendency of fathers is to step back, which is in part a function of the larger cultural script, which tells men that women know more about children and raising them.

In addition, what William Pollack, author of *Real Boys,* has called "the Boy Code"—the myths that shape how males are raised in our culture—affects not only men's perceptions of themselves but their interactions with their families. Pollack identifies four main cultural tenets: First is the vision of men as "stoic, stable, and independent," thus requiring them to hide weakness. Second is the notion that men are "biologically wired" to be aggressive and even violent; this is the "boys will be boys" credo, which sets them off from womankind. Third is the imperative that men are to achieve "status, dominance, and power." Last, but perhaps most important, is the one that "prohibits boys from expressing feelings or urges (mistakenly) seen as 'feminine'—dependence, warmth, empathy."

All of these social constructs pertaining to manhood and masculinity influence how any individual man behaves both inside the family and out. Added together, they may prevent a father from involving himself in his daughter's life or interceding on her behalf or from revealing himself to her. As a result, some daughters may perceive their fathers as shadowy presences in the household, mere visitors to what is essentially their mothers' domain.

Gwen's father, as she tells me, was hardly a presence in the household she grew up in, which was dominated by her outgoing mother, who disparaged both her husband and her daughter: "My mother used to tell me how dumb and 'uneducated' my father was. I always thought that he didn't graduate from high school, but when I went through an old strongbox after both my parents died, I found his college degrees. I was very, very angry. But my father never talked about his youth, so I never knew."

In fact, Gwen doesn't remember ever having a real conversation with her father, nor does she remember her parents talking to each other in any meaningful way: "I never thought my parents were at all happy, and mother would put him down a lot. He didn't respond, but took a lot of naps." The division of labor in the household was traditional—her father ran the family-owned businesses while her mother stayed home, gardened, played bridge, and did volunteer work—but in addition her father was absent from the family in a more profound emotional sense: "He simply didn't take part in any parenting that I remember. My mother was such a strong personality and he just let her have her way and simply didn't step in. I know my parents got married after eleven years of dating, and my mother was forty-two when she had me, which was very old in those days. He was a very good-looking, quiet man. Now, as an adult, I can see that he was never 'into' women in some sense, and I think my mother simply wore him down over time so that he'd marry her. She gave him a nice home, two kids, and all that went with the *Ozzie and Harriet* visuals, just not the same script."

The twice-married Gwen addresses how her relationship to her father affected her: "I never felt that comfortable with men. I liked the attention they gave me, but I think I actually used them and never really 'communed' with them. I just felt flattered that they were attracted to me and appreciated me, and I guess I craved those feelings. I just never had any basis to have a *real* relationship."

In the end, it was the combination of what she didn't get from either her mother or her father that shaped her and her ability to form lasting relationships with men: "I honestly don't think that I ever learned to love from my parents. I learned to survive and be happy on my own and not count on anyone else. Recently I was talking to a girlfriend who's known me since my girlhood, and she told me that when I was younger that she couldn't hug me because I wouldn't let her. It was only after I had my daughter that I learned to hug."

OEDIPUS AND COMPANY:
WHAT DAUGHTERS LEARN FROM FATHERS

Historically, the father in American culture has been viewed largely in his role as breadwinner—succeeding or failing at providing the economic stability his daughter needs—though at various periods up through the present he has also been associated with other roles as well: as "moral overseer," "sex-role model," and "nurturer." Different psychological perspectives, however, highlight different aspects of the way a father shapes a daughter's sense of self.

Both brain science and attachment theory understand the father as presenting another potential model for resonance and attunement, in addition to the one presented by the mother. A securely attached man who becomes a securely attached parent—even with an avoidantly attached wife—can offer an alternative emotional template to his daughter. Alternatively, an insecurely attached father may simply reinforce the model an insecurely attached mother has presented.

Jungian psychologist Linda Schierse Leonard, Ph.D., author of *The Wounded Woman: Healing the Father-Daughter Relationship,* writes that, "As a daughter grows up, her emotional and spiritual growth is deeply affected by her relationship to her father. He is the first masculine figure in her life and a prime shaper of the way she relates to the masculine side of herself and ultimately to men." More specifically, since the father is also "the other"—different from both the mother and daughter herself—"he also shapes her differentness, her uniqueness, and individuality. The way he relates to her femininity will affect the way she grows into womanhood."

In more traditionally structured families—where the father is the breadwinner and the mother is in charge of the home—Dr. Leonard asserts that the father acts as the daughter's guide to the outside world and is largely responsible for communicating attitudes toward work and success. A confident father will instill a sense of confidence in a daughter, while a hesitant or even fearful father will inculcate those attitudes in her. A body of research, in fact, confirms that "fathers may play a special role as intermediaries between the family and the outside world." Dr. Linda Nielsen tells me in an interview that, for younger daughters with working or professional mothers, this aspect of a father's modeling may not be as important as it was once was but that a father nonetheless teaches singular and important skills: "Fathers help daughters develop self-reliance and self-confidence more than mothers do. Because of how men are socialized, they tend not to depend on a network of friends as women do, but develop different ways of problem-solving that are based more on self-reliance than anything else. While it's true that daughters often complain that when they turn to their fathers for comfort, they get advice instead, it's also true that by giving advice fathers teach self-reliance and instill confidence in their daughters that they have the right to be themselves even if they're not immediately met with approval." This paternal role is often a strong theme in the narratives of daughters who had unloving mothers or extremely difficult relationships with their mothers. Many daughters have, in one way or another, followed their fathers' examples, and in some cases have actually surpassed their fathers by realizing unrealized paternal dreams. In some families, though, a daughter's unwillingness to follow her father's example may provide another source of tension.

Elizabeth, fifty, was the eldest of three children. During her child-hood, her father was a successful businessman who ran a small company; her mother volunteered at their church and their children's schools. Both of her parents were very controlling, and by the time Elizabeth was an adolescent the tensions in their marriage were evident. Her mother grew more and more resentful of her husband, who didn't seem to respect her efforts and withheld the approval she so desperately needed from him: "My mother had an idealized notion of family, and she was desperate for affection and approval. She seemed genuinely happy and accepting of her traditional role as the mother, but she was definitely less happy about being the wife of an executive, since she didn't seem to have high self-worth."

While Elizabeth remembers her mother as loving during her child-hood—"She took the job of being a mother seriously. She was thoughtful about her children's activities, schools, and welfare"—during these years she became unpredictable and temperamental. "She began giving with strings attached, and I remember several times she got so angry that she literally dragged me down the hall by my hair. It's clear now, if it wasn't then, that my mother was severely depressed." Her parents separated twice when Elizabeth was in high school and went through an extremely contentious divorce when she was in college.

Her father wasn't really involved in day-to-day parenting but nonethe-less influenced Elizabeth in significant ways: "He was the 'coach' I could confide in if I wanted him to tell me how to fix something. He coached me in other ways too—on business skills, how to communicate successfully, how to work in the world. Of his three children, I was the one he had the highest aspirations for—perhaps because I was the oldest or the highest achiever academically. Neither my sister nor my brother was academically curious the way I was. My father didn't listen to my sister; he didn't seem to respect her the way he did me. In fact, both of my parents never expected very much from either my sister or my brother."

But that respect, Elizabeth says, was shallow and not very substantial: "My father would often embarrass me with these exaggerated displays of affection, like throwing his arms around me or pinching my butt, and all it made me feel was that he was telling me that he was in charge, that he was bigger than I was and could do whatever he wanted. He clearly wanted me to follow in his footsteps and be in business the way he was; I worked for him during the summers in college, and that made him proud. He helped me get my first job out of college, in the financial industry, and I knew immediately this wasn't where I belonged, and my father was terribly disappointed. I think that my decision to be a homemaker and raise my children disappoints him even today. I'm still struggling with my relationship to him because he really doesn't know me and never has. I will say, though, that the skills he taught me—how to communicate, act in the outside world—have helped me in many ways, including the fund-raising I've done for nonprofits."

As the first adult male a daughter knows, a father also models "maleness" and is her first guide to how a man communicates, loves, and relates to women. Seen from a strictly Freudian point of view, daughters move away from the primary attachment to their mothers during the "preoedipal" and "oedipal" stages to establish their own heterosexual identities by connecting to their fathers. In her influential book *The Reproduction of Mothering,* psychoanalyst Nancy Chodorow argued that daughters don't turn away from their mothers or "give up the internal relationship" they have to their mothers but instead oscillate between attachments to their mothers and fathers. Research also confirms that fathers play an important role in helping girls learn to interact with boys during adolescence.

Running counter to popular wisdom, which sees mothers as the primary influence on children's emotional development, recent research suggests that fathers do help to socialize children's emotions. Men play with their children differently than women do, studies show, and it's been suggested that a father's more rowdy, physical style of playing—in contrast to a mother's more modulated play—may be important in teaching a child about emotional displays and self-regulation. In addition, it's been suggested that both a father's management of his emotions and his reactions to his child's emotional displays may have a significant impact on a child's social relationships with peers and friends.

No matter what the mother myths suggest, in both his presence and his absence, a father's role in a daughter's life is an important one.

MARITAL KNOTS: THE PARENTAL DYAD

Even though the cultural myths are pervasive, the balance of power in each household remains unique. When the parental dyad is extremely close, a father may be even more content to play a peripheral role in his daughter's life. Both his love for and loyalty to his spouse and his assumption that the domestic sphere is hers alone may combine to isolate a daughter even more. Both of Lisa's parents were children of the Depression, and her father's worries about money were a constant in her childhood: "My father was the breadwinner and my mother controlled him. She told him what to eat, what to wear, where to go. But he adored and worshipped her, and he could see no wrong in her. There's one family story that once my father stood up in my defense when my mother was yelling at me, but if it really happened, it happened only once."

Her father's lack of involvement in her life made it harder for Lisa to establish an authentic sense of self, because being "known" by a father can make up for not being "known" by a mother: "My mother would become irritated when my father would let his emotions show. I remember him as being detached during my childhood. He never really asked about my life in any sense—not about my feelings or interests. He never knew or remembered who my friends were, and we never really did things together. There were no shared amusements—no hobbies, no movies, no games. We visited relatives together and I attended religious services with him, but all of that was more about *going* together rather than *being* together. I remember growing up feeling like a fifth wheel— my mother and father had each other, my sisters had their husbands, and I tagged along like an extra. At the end of his life, my father tried to write some sort of memoir, and it was all about my mother. The three daughters he had—my two older sisters and me—were relegated to a sentence or two. Literally, he wrote: 'We had Patricia and Jane. Then we had Lisa'—and that was the extent of what he wrote about his children."

In Lisa's family, what remained unsaid shaped her even more than the few words exchanged at the dinner table every evening. Her lack of connection to her emotionally absent, impossible to please, and often controlling mother was compounded by both her father's absolute loyalty to her mother and his own emotional unavailability: "For me, because I so separated myself from my family at such an early age and felt so separated from my parents, it was almost more like stories than experience. My mother would scold my father for getting too emotional. He'd emigrated from Hungary when he was a toddler, and his mother was depressed all of her life and never really adjusted to life in America. My father didn't leave home until he was thirty-three, when he married my mother, but his family was emotional, and impassioned by politics. I think the lack of openness affected me, because I have a really hard time getting in touch with my feelings or expressing my emotions as an adult."

But Lisa locates her father's most important influence in her difficulties connecting to men: "Not having an involved father and one who was, in some ways, stuck in the old world, in a family dominated by women, I think I never learned to relate to men in a real way. I never felt supported or loved by my father. My senior year in college, I was seeing a psychiatrist to address how I felt after my first serious love relationship ended. I came home from spring break, and the only comment my father had was to ask how long this extra expense—seeing the shrink—was going to go on."

A father who adopts the traditional role of pater familias and combines it with active criticism of his daughter will affect her in different ways. Even though Jennifer grew up in the 1970s and 1980s, her household was more like that of the 1950s: "My father was the god of the house. If Daddy wanted to sleep, we all needed to be quiet. If Daddy wanted to watch TV, then we all needed to go outside. If Daddy wanted to eat dinner at 4 P.M., then that was the new dinnertime. The atmosphere in my home was changeable. When my father was home, it was structured and tense. He had to have a routine, and we became part of that."

As Jennifer got older, her father became increasingly distant: "He worked all the time, and when he came home, he was tired. When he did talk to me, he was almost always critical. My father's lack of approval drove me to seek approval elsewhere. It also drove me to seek my own career and independent life, on the one hand, and made me needy for emotional connection with men but cautious about rushing into commitments with them, on the other." But most important, her mother and father were an inseparable dyad.

She tells me, "As an adult, I've developed an intellectual relationship with my mother; we share similar interests in nature and the arts, and she's very well read. My father is and was unavailable, both physically and emotionally. At times, my mother *can* be quite loving. But if I go to her with a disappointment or something that has gone wrong with my life, I can't trust her with information, because she tells my father everything. She cannot keep a confidence."

When the mother-father dyad is extremely close, a daughter (or a son, for that matter) may feel cut off from both parents or shut out, as though there's no emotional room for growth or connection.

Georgia's mother and father both came to parenting with emotional baggage from their childhoods. Growing up with an enmeshed mother— one who had been shaped by the loss of her own mother in infancy, a cruel and unloving stepmother, and a weak father who never stepped in to protect his daughter from his new wife's wrath—Georgia had an intense, often contradictory bond with her father, who could be both loving and volatile by turns. Her mother and father had what she called "a deep and connected bond. They made love a lot and they did everything together. Yet Dad ruled the show. He wasn't a very social man, so they didn't have friends who came to the house, and not very many family members did either." Her father respected and admired his wife for her innate skills as a mother. Georgia says, "The underlying dynamic was undetected by him, and he always made sure that we treated Mom with the utmost respect."

The youngest of three daughters—her sisters are five and two years older than she—Georgia was the "baby" of the family. Her mother stayed home until she turned eleven, filling her workday with cleaning, sewing, and cooking. "My dad came home in the evening, tired, and he didn't want to be bothered. All revolved around his need for rest and calm at home. We were all afraid of him and his temper." At the same time, though, her father was an active participant in both the household and his daughters' lives: "He would build us doll beds and take us fishing. He was a true family man and helped Mom with everything. He was always very involved with her projects, whether it was tiling, making curtains, or doing something at church."

Despite her father's sometimes violent temper—and Georgia's fear of his anger—she adored him nonetheless, and he adored her. "He was scary, yes, but I resonated so much with who he really was. So I worked around his violent outbursts and learned how to spare myself. He could be strict and oppressive, yet I loved his stories, whether they were about the countryside or other things. My father gave me a love of nature and gardening and endowed me with a sense of spirituality, humility, and generosity." Her father helped balance her mother's smothering way of connecting: "During my childhood, I felt isolated and overprotected. I didn't have many friends, and I was shy, not socialized enough. My mother's need to have me pay attention to her, for her to be central in my life, led me not to put myself first. I developed a codependent style of relating to others."

Georgia's father died when she was nineteen, but the two years before his death brought them closer. Her mother has never remarried. But even though Georgia recognizes the gifts her father bestowed on her, the relationship, with all its ups and downs, left her confused by its contradictions, and it also bequeathed her, in her adolescence and early adulthood, a fear of men. "I was afraid," she says, "of their violent potential." Her mother abetted in words what her father taught her by his example in the house: "My mother kept telling me, from my adolescence on, that men only want sex. She worried about my being raped and assumed that all men would push themselves on me. She always saw men as 'hunters' and women as their silent 'prey.' She wanted to control my going out, and as she became more frightened and worried, she became more controlling. And I believed her and felt paralyzed by it. She didn't teach me that I had to be firm with my boundaries, that my body was mine, that I could say no."

COMPETING FOR THE KING OF THE CASTLE: LOOSE CONNECTIONS

In some families where the marital relationship is weak or deteriorating and the father is actively dismissive or rejecting of his spouse, even an essentially loving mother may become competitive with her daughter.

Emily, now forty and the divorced mother of a daughter, nine, and a son, six, recounts how her closeness to her father sparked her mother's competitive feelings and a sense of detachment from her daughter: "At a pretty young age, perhaps at four or five, I began to feel some resentment from my mother. My apparent independence hurt her feelings and made her angry as well. She once said that I barely needed a mother, even as an infant. Of course, how could that possibly be? I think it was her own emotional instability I sensed at a very young age. About the time I began going to school, I also sensed that my mother was jealous or resentful of my relationship to my father. This made me very uncomfortable."

Not altogether surprisingly, Emily's mother's feelings of competition were sparked only by her daughter, not by her younger son: "It felt, always, like a gender thing—another female in the house. My mother had three sisters in her family and there was definitely competition and jealousy among them. I think my mother's feeling of competition or jealousy toward me was a carryover from having sisters and that she looked at me sometimes as a sister, not as a daughter."

Emily's parents' deteriorating marriage was an important part of how her mother related to her: "My mother deeply resented my relationship with my father. He respected me, even when I was a young child, in a way that he never respected my mother. He was incredibly verbally abusive to her (and us kids as well), but there wasn't an ounce of respect or honoring my mother as the mother or as a person. In my household, emotions or emotional sensitivity were seen as a weakness. My mother was emotionally fragile, and he verbally skewered her for her vulnerabilities, which undercut her sense of self terribly. On the other hand, he held me in high regard. I was quick and smart and made of emotional steel—not necessarily a good thing but a survival skill in my family—so that put my status higher in the family. I was independent and not particularly sentimental or emotionally needy—and this earned the respect of my father. I remember my mother saying, from time to time, "Well, your father listens to you more than me!" And, understandably, the whole situation made me very uncomfortable, and it wasn't what I wanted from my parents. I certainly didn't want my father's attentions; I wanted my mother to stand her ground and fight back, and I didn't want my mother to feel bad."

Her mother's jealousy of her fueled not so muted criticism and then spread out to other areas of life in which Emily succeeded and her mother felt insecure: "It bothered my mother that school was easy for me and that I was well liked and comfortable socially. She constantly tried to devalue these qualities by saying that because school was easy, I didn't have to work hard enough and was lazy. Or that because I had so many friends, I was betraying the family. When I got older, she was jealous of my relationship with her parents, my own grandparents. She made comments like 'You must get along with my mother because you are so like her'—not necessarily a compliment at the time because they were not on speaking terms for a brief period and my grandmother was a judgmental matriarch."

Emily is a beautiful woman, and when she turned twelve, her burgeoning looks became another arena where her mother felt threatened: "I'd overheard another mother saying to mine that 'Oh, Emily is so beautiful.' And so, standing in my mother's bathroom, I asked her, 'Is it true that Jackie's mom thinks I'm pretty?' When my mom said yes, I was shocked. And then she added, begrudgingly, 'Lots of people tell me that all the time.' I couldn't believe it. She saw how stunned I was and said, 'Well, I don't want it to go to your head. And it's not important.' I don't think she realized until that moment that she could have told me a nice thing or two—and she did feel mildly bad about it. After all, if your mother doesn't think you're beautiful, who ever will? You can bet that I tell my children that they are beautiful, inside and out."

Emily's parents divorced when she was thirteen and her mother thirty-nine. Reflecting on that relationship now, from an adult perspective, Emily tells me, "I imagine that her jealousy when I was a child was tied into both her childhood—she had a difficult relationship with very harsh parents—and her debilitating marriage. Because she was so deeply unhappy, my youthful exuberance, joy, and perhaps all the opportunities I had ahead of me just bothered her. My mother is quite a different person now, as am I. Because she has spent decades rebuilding her self-esteem, going to therapy, and is in a good marriage now—her second—we have a healed and wonderful relationship. My mother finds me a source of joy, and I feel very supported by her inasmuch as she can give. She is still very emotionally fragile and my expectations are minimal, but overall she can 'show up' as a healthy adult most of the time."

Emily was affected in many ways but has been able to pull the positives out of her experiences with her mother: "As a mother, I'm acutely aware of the responsibility to take care of myself so I can parent my children well from a place of strength and self-love, and the responsibility I have to let my children shine bright. In other words, it's not about me! In the world outside, having experienced both my mother's jealousy and sense of competition, I'm very aware of trying to enjoy the youthful beauty of others, mentoring younger women, and appreciating someone else's success. I don't feel jealous, but I do compare myself to other women, and then often my shrill inner critic shows up to beat myself up, but that voice is getting less frequent and a little softer."

Reflecting on how both her parents and her marriage shaped her relationships with men, Emily tells me: "Because my father was verbally abusive, I thought it was normal to be scared in your own household. I tended to have relationships with men who had very dark sides—the tortured souls and men with dark clouds hanging over them. In my marriage of ten years, it was the 'walking on eggshells' variety, very much like parts of my childhood. Because my father was a philanderer, I very carefully chose a man who would be faithful to me—and he was. I just forgot all of the other things, like that I had to enjoy and like the person I married. I thought I was able to look at my mother clearly and focus on how to 'not be like her.' I would have a career and be financially independent; I would be emotionally strong and stable; I would have community support. Well, that all worked out pretty well, but I forgot the partnership part of things and became independent to a fault."

ROLE MODELS AND RESCUERS

Fathers may also present daughters with alternative visions, different in kind from those presented by their mothers, in the realms of both achievement and emotional development.

In some families, a daughter's need to carve out her own identity separate from her mother's may put her father in the position of being her primary role model. This may happen even in families where the mother is essentially loving and caring of her daughter. Lara, now forty-seven, grew up in Northern California and was the eldest of three daughters. Her father was the scion of a wealthy family, who had grown up in a mansion, surrounded by gates and lush gardens, and had always enjoyed a life of privilege with all that implies. Though not a handsome man, he was charming, thoughtful, and a voracious reader. In contrast, her mother had grown up poor and was the daughter of a cold, withdrawn mother, but she was a stunningly beautiful girl as well as nice and generous. The two fell in love when they happened to work at the same company, he as a partner and she as a secretary.

Their story—and all the stories Lara's mother told her about her life when she was a child—was more like a fairy tale than anything else, with the moral that beauty (and goodness) would always win out. But while Lara's father adored her mother for her beauty—and how having a beautiful wife made him feel—he was dismissive of her intelligence. "I realize now," Lara says, "that my mother's beauty became the way for her to earn some kind of status in my father's world—a counterbalance to the fact that she wasn't born with money, didn't go to private schools or college, hadn't read the 'right' books or known the 'right' people—and to make her claim to being a rightful inhabitant of that world. I loved her stories as a child because she was always the princess being rescued or admired. Even the jars of secret potions on her dressing table and the scores of dresses and shoes in her closet—all the things she depended on to maintain her beauty and the admiration it garnered her—had a kind of mystery to them."

But these stories—and their lessons—took on another aspect as Lara approached adolescence and understood that, unlike her mother, she wasn't beautiful, and that the plot lines of her mother's life—the admiring beaus, the dramatic rescue, the accolades, and the attention paid to her—were not likely to be hers. "I realized," she tells me, "that you have to decide on being *something* to make your way in the world. At school, it seemed you could be either pretty, athletic, or smart, and since I wasn't either of the first two, I concentrated on being smart. My father had always stressed intelligence—he admired intelligent people and looked down on those who weren't—and I cared about impressing him."

The truth was that Lara, who grew up in a Victorian mansion in San Francisco's Pacific Heights, belonged to her father's world in a way that her mother could not. And since she didn't have access to her mother's world—"Being beautiful grants you a kind of natural aristocracy," Lara notes—she moved closer into her father's orbit. Dinner conversations became a father-daughter twosome, effectively shutting her mother out: they were conducted in Italian, a language her mother didn't speak, about topics she knew nothing about or books she hadn't read. "It was unkind, I know, to cut my mother off this way," Lara says, " but I had to make room for myself somehow. I wish it hadn't been through elbowing my mother

out in this way. She never asked to be beautiful, just as I never asked not
to be." Her parents divorced when she started college.

While my own father wasn't precisely a knight in shining armor, he
nonetheless rescued me in important ways. Unlike my mother, he was
worldly, well educated, and well read, with a sharp wit. In the absence of a
male heir (my brother wasn't born until I turned nine), my father did with
me what he might have done with a son, had he had one. He taught me how
to ride a bike, kick a soccer ball, swing a bat, and took me to baseball games,
car races, and the track—none of which my mother was even remotely interested in. We went to the car show at the old Coliseum in Manhattan every
year, just the two of us, since my mother couldn't have cared less about cars.
I learned to read at the age of three, sitting on his lap while he read *The
Wall Street Journal,* and because my mother didn't drive, Daddy and I did
the grocery shopping on Saturdays, ate a hot dog together at the deli, and
stopped at the local stationery store where he bought me a book each week.
Along with my dolls, my proudest possessions were the jacketed copies of
books in my favorite series, the Bobbsey Twins, Nancy Drew, Cherry Ames,
and the Hardy Boys that sat on a bookshelf in my room. On Sundays, he'd
drive me to church school and pick me up after, when, away from my naturally thin mother's watchful eye (she always had the two of us on a diet),
we'd steal off to the bakery to indulge in an otherwise forbidden treat.

We were both readers and talkers, and while my looks and intelligence
sparked my mother's worst impulses, my father was undeniably proud of
both. He was a demanding cheerleader: "Do your best" was his mantra,
and so I did. Most important, during my childhood at least, I knew he
loved me.

Not even the birth of my brother, whom he named after himself,
dislodged me from my special place in my father's world. An infant or a
toddler—even an adorable boy with big blue eyes whom I doted on as my
own living doll—couldn't compete with the company and conversation a
ten- or eleven- year-old-daughter could offer my forty-five-year-old father.
He rescued me in many senses, though not all, since he made it possible
for me to believe, at least from time to time, that my mother might be
wrong, that I might be lovable after all.

But—and in the story of an unloving mother, there is almost always a *but*—there was a limit to our relationship. My father adored my beautiful and willowy mother; she was the antidote to his own insecurities. A man overweight and bald, with thick glasses and crossed eyes, who'd been born wealthy but never qualified as a business success himself, he nonetheless had a beauty queen on his arm and it made him proud. A smile and a kiss from her were enough for him to overlook her temper and her shortcomings, and even though she was careful to hide the way she treated me most of the time—he was at his office every day, after all—there were times when she didn't, and never once did he come to my defense. In the three years or so before he died—as I entered adolescence and actively combated my mother's taunts and cruelty in kind—he often sided with her. This might have been, I suppose, because the home and children were her domain, but I suspect it was really much simpler than that: she was more essential to him than I was, and his love for and need of her outweighed every other consideration. His death, when I was fifteen, forestalled what I now see would have been part of our future: the inevitable conflict between us and clash of loyalties as the battles between my mother and me became more pitched.

That said, he saved me nonetheless. He planted the seed that would, in time, yield a reasonably strong sense of self and confidence. His respect for my intelligence allowed me to see it as an asset, which was largely the foundation for my self-esteem. And his love for me, whatever its limitations, and in turn my love for him left me open—despite all my mother's harm—to the possibility of relationships in my life. Learning how to relate, though, would in the end prove to be harder than I thought. It's hardly an accident that I've been married three times.

In Mary Karr's beautifully written and realized memoir, *The Liar's Club,* her father, despite his drinking and capacity for rage, is the yin to her mother's always volatile, sometimes psychotic yang: "With Mother, I always felt on the edge of something new, something never before seen or read about or bought, something that would change us. When you climbed into a car with her, you never knew where you'd end up. . . . With Daddy and his friends, I always knew what would happen and that left me feeling a dreamy sort of safety." She shares her childhood but not her experience of it with her sister, who is just two years older, and as Karr reminds her readers more than once, her sister's memoir would be a very different book.

Siblings are fellow travelers in one sense, but they often have very different understandings of the journey. How an unloving mother can change the chemistry of the sibling relationship—thus shaping the siblings and their connections to each other—is where we need to turn next.

· Four ·
Siblings and Other Rivalries

D URING EARLY CHILDHOOD THE WORLD OF THE FAMILY IS ALL
each of us knows. Daughters of mean mothers who are only children often dream of having a sibling to share the experience, buffer them
from a mother's hurtfulness, keep them company, and, most important,
provide them with another source of love.

One daughter remembers how her own sibling fantasy helped her
cope during her very difficult childhood with an unloving and often cruel
mother and an emotionally absent father: "I had it all worked out in my
head—I would have an older brother to protect me (two years older), plus
his friends would become handy boyfriends when I was a teenager, and a
younger sister (one year younger) to be my friend. I always had that plan
in my head and thought about it quite a lot . . . thinking it would make
my life much nicer. I really had this powerful fantasy that if I had *that* life,
then I wouldn't have *this* life. I fantasized a lot about a lot of things when
I was a kid—a great coping mechanism. And the brother was cute too—I
don't know why it was important—just to give him more status, I guess.
And the sister was pretty. We would have fun dressing up and doing hair

and stuff like that . . . and she would be the same size I was when we were in high school so we could share clothes. It's such a pedestrian fantasy, I guess, but at the time it was very important to me."

I also longed for a sister, an older one, who would talk things through with me, play dolls with me, run away from home with me if need be, and assure me that what went on with my mother wasn't my fault. But these are the dreams of unloved daughters who are single children. What happens in families with siblings—universally but most particularly when a mother is unloving—turns out to be much more complicated.

If there is a single metaphor that describes the possible range of sibling relationships, perhaps the best one might be the childhood game of pickup sticks—the one in which you hold a bundle of different-colored sticks in your hand over a flat surface and let go, waiting to see how they fall, and then trying to pick each of them up without disturbing the rest. Some of them will end up scattered far apart—in the game, at least, the best of all worlds, though not necessarily among siblings. Others will fall in patterns that have a point or two of intersection—which is where many sibling relationships end up. The rest end up close together but still distinguishable from each other by color. Only a few will land so that they are truly inseparable.

When a mother is unloving or neglectful because she is a depressive or suffering from some other diagnosable condition—and the children in the family are treated in the same way—the bond between siblings may actually be reinforced. This sibling bond, sometimes called a "Hansel and Gretel" pair after the Grimm Brother's fairy tale about two siblings who become each other's caretakers in light of maternal (and paternal) cruelty or abandonment, reflects only one of many possible scenarios for a sibling relationship. While sibling closeness can reflect a feeling of deep connection with parents, it's been noted by Stephen P. Bank and Michael D. Kahn that "some of the most intense sibling ties can result from an *absence* of parental care." While particularly marked when a parent dies—and one sibling becomes a parent to another—it *may* also happen in families where a mother (or a father) is emotionally unavailable or even cruel to more than one child. I've put the emphasis on the word *may* because, as researchers have noted, while sibling closeness *often* occurs in inverse proportion to secure familial attachments—as Stephen P. Bank and Michael D. Kahn asserted in their groundbreaking book, *The Sibling Bond*—it doesn't always.

Siblings with an emotionally absent parent or parents may not bond at all during childhood, as Elizabeth, now fifty, tells me of her relationship to her sister, some twenty months younger: "Our mother didn't treat us differently—she was emotionally unreliable, jealous, critical of both of us—but we never talked about it as children or even adolescents and it didn't make us bond. We just accepted it as the way it was. At the same time, I think we both saw being sisters as being stuck with each other—nothing more or less." The two girls shared a room but little else: "My sister and I were dressed alike for special occasions—the photographs show that—but we were so very different from each other that there wasn't either any common ground or, for that matter, any sibling rivalry. We went to the same schools but had totally different social groups and we were both popular in our own circles. My sister relished her role in the family—the more mercurial wild child, who was messy and crazy—while I fit into my role—the 'good' girl, the responsible one, the achiever—much more begrudgingly." Unlike some other sister pairs, these two women have found common ground as adults.

Patterns of sibling connection can be so complicated and entrenched that even a fundamentally life-changing shared experience—such as the death of a parent—doesn't always reinforce or strengthen the sibling bond immediately or in straightforward ways, most particularly in childhood and adolescence. In fact, the shared experience may paradoxically exacerbate existing sibling dynamics. In her book *Motherless Daughters,* Hope Edelman recounts how she and her sister "grew up on a shared diet of rivalry and rancor as we competed for our brother's adoration and our parents' limited time." When their mother died, Edelman reports that she and her sister found "little comfort in each other. Instead, we intensified the division we knew so well. Familiarity offers false security when change permeates the house, and competition was our established code."

In another family, the loss of their mother also intensified the rivalry between two sisters separated by five years, in part because the rivalry was aided and abetted by the surviving parent, a famously difficult, critical, and often cruel father. Then and now, each girl had a distinct role in the family. One sister, Eve, is a professional writer and the other, Lucy, a professional musician. Eve tells me, "I was the smart one and the scholar and also, after my mother died, the 'trouble' child. My sister was the musician. I can't really say that these roles were arbitrary—I really did excel at school and Lucy was really drawn to music from a young age—but much of this had to do with my father after our mother died. He was only interested in each of us as an extension of himself." The competition between them has never really abated—and reached a minor crisis some years ago when Lucy surprised her sister by writing a novel and thus "invading" what had always been Eve's "domain"—but whatever rivalry there is in adulthood coexists with genuine feelings of love and friendship. Reflecting on being a sister, Eve tells me, "I guess being an older sister has given me a sense of maturity and authority. In many ways Lucy is my best friend, and I always look forward to seeing her. We have the kind of easy conversation that doesn't happen with many other people. But she can still get on my nerves something fierce—far more than she would if she weren't my sister."

When I ask Eve if she thinks she'd be a different person if she didn't have siblings, she answers categorically: "Absolutely, though I honestly can't tell you how. I just know that these relationships have had a lasting impact on who I am, and I'd be someone else—diminished in some ways, maybe enlarged in others—without them." Then she adds: "Having a sister and brother has given me a sense of belonging. Who else, after all, would understand so well what I went through growing up, belonging to this family?"

The common ground of growing up with a mother (or father or both) who is a harsh taskmaster with exacting standards, or competing within a large family for limited amounts of maternal or parental affection and attention, can give very different siblings—separated by personality, interests, or age—a sense of connection they might not otherwise have, particularly if their views of their parent or parents are shared.

That sense of solidarity, though, is hardly universal. In her book *The Sister Knot,* Terri Apter suggests that when sisters have different views "about their childhood, their parents, and their experiences within the family," there is fertile opportunity for conflict between or among them. Why is that? Because, as Apter notes, "Siblings can challenge our memories, not simply as accurate but as 'fair' or 'cruel'; and they may condemn us for the stories we tell. They, like us, are passionately committed to the interpretations that inform our ever-present memories of life-shaping people and events." When there is profound disagreement about who a mother or father was—was she loving or withholding? simply being protective or actively smothering? strict or vindictive?—Apter notes that these different stories may "threaten to dislodge the identity they help construct." As she puts it, "Sisters seldom agree to disagree on such matters."

A sister's alliance or identification with one parent or another—during the normal course of life or in a family crisis or divorce—may make it impossible for two sisters, no matter how close in age they are, to reconcile their visions of the family they share, and may actually contribute to how the siblings are compared to each other and how they see themselves in relation within the family.

The story of Elaine, fifty-two, and her sister, Karen, forty-nine, who were eleven and eight when their parents divorced, is one such example. Elaine was closest to her father but was actually relieved when he moved out; she tells me, "My father was very angry and critical and I'd say that their marriage was just a bad match." Her sister, though, was traumatized by the separation and sided with her mother, who felt victimized in the divorce. Unlike Elaine, Karen actively hated her father for years. This had been an old pattern in the family—Elaine was "her father's child" and her sister was "her mother's"—but it took on special significance once their parents separated. Although Elaine notes that their father is careful to love his two daughters equally, even today she and her sister see and react to the same circumstances completely differently. Their alliances in the family—one with her father, the other with her mother—made it easy for their mother and other family members to expand on those differences. Elaine was perceived as the "smart one, the competent one"—traditionally "masculine" characteristics—while her sister, not altogether surprisingly, was seen as the more "feminine," flirtatious, and prettier sister. The effect on Elaine was, she says, profound: "My sister, more than anyone else, shaped my sense of myself as feminine. And surrendering my sense of my femininity to her was one of the biggest losses of my life, and competing with her goes on even today. For almost forty years, this pattern has repeated itself in my friendships and partnerships with women." The bond between these two sisters is both complex and close and not infrequently continues to be filled with tension.

Sometimes the timing of one daughter's birth may separate her from the family history as her siblings experienced it, especially if an event of particular significance—a change in economic status, illness, death, or divorce—has created a "before and after" in that history and in her mother's behavior. In her book *Jealousy,* Nancy Friday writes that she has avoided confronting the role her sister has played in her life, a life she has always seen as having been shaped by her relationship to her mother and her father's absence. But the very subject of her book—jealousy—leads her inevitably, if unwillingly, to look at the relationship, and this is what she says: "From the beginning, we were a triangle. A mother and two daughters." She continues: "I have always known there was something special between my mother and sister. I used to think it went no further than what I saw—criticism, heated reaction, intense and tearful emotional exchange. I told myself I was well out of it. Why then this lifelong sense of being left out? I now know that 'the something special' my mother and sister shared was my father. A time when my mother was a happy woman. When she had a husband and my sister had a father. I never knew those years. I never knew him." Feeling separated from the family history in a meaningful way may further isolate an unloved daughter from her sisters and brothers.

How family history is understood can become a loaded subject for unloved daughters who, alone among their siblings, are singled out and who, by virtue of the differences in their interpretation of their family, end up feeling disconnected or literally estranged from their siblings, during both their childhood and adulthood. Sometimes a peaceful resolution will lie forever out of reach. Separated in age from her two sisters by eleven and nine years, Jody was the "baby" of the family, though that role didn't bring with it the stereotypical portrait of a coddled and fussed-over child. Instead, her mother wanted little to do with her. As a child she was in awe of her two older sisters, who seemed glamorous and grown-up; she felt connected to both of them but most particularly to the eldest sister, who made an effort to mother her. But at the same time she also knew that her older sisters sometimes saw her as a bother and a burden, and the teasing they engaged in—"Saying stuff like 'Jody, why don't you go play in traffic?' or calling me 'The Shadow' from the Robert Louis Stevenson poem"—had, by her own account, a lasting negative effect on her, adding to her lack of self-esteem in the wake of what she perceived as her mother's rejection. Even today, at the age of sixty, Jody still feels insecure about her capabilities, something she says "definitely relates back to my mother with some fallout from my sisters as well."

Now, as grown women, the sisters' differing views of their mother have isolated Jody once again: "The middle sister is and always has been our mother's apologist and defender. She has a codependent relationship with her, and whenever my oldest sister and I would bitch about our mother, the middle sister would always get annoyed. More recently, the disagreement about who our mother is has created a real rift in the family from which we haven't recovered, with my middle sister taking on the role of 'protecting' our mother. My older sister doesn't see our mother as loving, but at the same time she's too self-involved to be sensitive to our mother's treatment of me. Some of this has to do with her own psychological construct of how the family works; she believes our father was jealous of the attention our mother paid her." It's worth remembering Terri Apter's wise observation that each of us is indeed "passionately committed" to her own version of the family history.

The relationships an unloved daughter has with her siblings seem to suffer the most damage when the mother treats the siblings differentially or with clear favoritism. This dynamic isn't limited to daughters with mean or hypercritical mothers, of course; in the survey she conducted for her book *Mixed Feelings,* Francine Klagsbrun was astonished to discover that 84 percent of her respondents reported favoritism on the part of one parent or both. The taboos against parental favoritism, but most particularly that of a mother, make it unlikely that differential treatment will ever be acknowledged. How this may affect a daughter is both simple and complicated. In their study of sisters in middle childhood, psychologists Brenda K. Bryant and Susan B. Crockenberg found that a child's behavior to her sister related both to the way she was treated by their mother *and* the way her sister was treated. What's worth noting is that when there was a discrepancy, a child will show more negative behavior toward her sister *even when her own needs are well met.* I've added the emphasis in the sentence because it demonstrates that any sibling relationship isn't just dyadic but triadic—with the mother or father being the third point in the triangle. What matters isn't just what psychologist and psychiatrist Frits Boer and his colleagues called "absolute levels of parental behavior" but the "*disparity* in treatment." Differential parental treatment creates a separate reality; the perception of disparity or unfairness outweighs the actual treatment a child experiences.

Daughters of unloving mothers may sometimes find an ally and a source of comfort in a sibling, but, equally, a daughter's realization that her mother is able to love another of her children in ways that she cannot love her may only add to her sense of isolation, of not belonging to the family. The presence of a sibling whom she perceives to be well loved by or to receive better treatment from her mother may actually intensify her feelings of loss and pain. I certainly felt this during my young adulthood when I saw that my mother could be generous and giving of herself with my brother in ways that she was incapable of with me. Rather than feeling jealousy toward my younger brother, I simply felt my pain at my mother's rejection intensified in comparison. Even when a mother isn't necessarily more loving or nurturing to a sibling but is simply less negative and critical, her differential behavior may still feel like a slap in the face.

Leanne's mother always needed to be the center of attention and by all accounts was a woman who—like her mother before her—was concerned with appearance over substance. Leanne, now in her early seventies, recalls her mother as distant and emotionally uninvolved during her childhood; Leanne was usually left in the care of someone else, and what her mother did do for her—driving her to piano lessons and the like— seemed perfunctory. During her adolescence, her mother became highly critical both of Leanne's appearance and of the friends she chose. Her mother's treatment of her second daughter—six years younger—was different, in part because that daughter fulfilled her mother's sense of what made a daughter successful much more closely than did Leanne, who eschewed her mother's "country club life"—playing bridge and canasta and having lunch with her friends. The relationship between the sisters remains distant.

A daughter who bears the brunt of her unloving mother's constant and sometimes cruel criticism may feel emotionally defeated when that same mother lavishes praise and attention on another child in the family. She may find her sense of self limited anew, as Louisa did. As the middle child—with a sister two years older and a brother four years younger— Louisa felt invisible to her mother, on the one hand, and signaled out for criticism by her, on the other: "I felt like an outsider looking in, lonely and confused, as if I didn't exist or belong in the family. I felt as though my own needs didn't matter." Her mother saved her criticisms for Louisa, the child in the middle, and Louisa remained keenly aware that her siblings were taken care of in very different ways. Her sense of disconnection was only enhanced by the way her siblings connected to each other and to her mother: "I was lonely and made even more lonely by the fact that my older sister was devoted to my brother, as was my mother. He was Mom's favorite, and I remember all the special attention she lavished on him." Louisa remembers being compared to her two siblings constantly, leaving her feeling that if a certain talent or domain belonged to her sister or brother, she needn't bother trying unless she could be "perfect." Reflecting on this dynamic, Louisa says, "I think my mother put me down so that my sister could feel better about herself. She felt my siblings needed her in a way that I did not, and she overpraised them and underpraised me."

These experiences left an indelible mark on her, with both negative and positive effects: "There's a part of me that still wonders if I actually deserve the things I have. I don't feel connected to people sometimes, and I rarely think to ask for help. On the positive side, I became very capable of caring for myself, and my childhood experience made me protective of the underdog, a fixer, capable and on guard and ready to fight against the injustices (or even the perceived injustices) inflicted on people. I am definitely the fixer of the family and of the whole world if it would let me! But I often feel more responsible than capable, and even though I know I am capable, I still have a tough time being conscious of that fact. I've struggled with guilt for years—the 'shoulds,' as I call them, as in 'Should I be this?' or ' Should I be that?' "

When I ask her if she ever dreamed of being an only child, Louisa answers quickly: "Yes! My life would be so much easier as an only child. I still get knots in my stomach when I think about my siblings. They're not a source of comfort but a burden." She also tells me that any contact with her siblings is almost always initiated by her—"If I call them, then we stay in touch," she says—but then she adds, without a hint of anger or bitterness: "Honestly, it wouldn't bother me never to speak to my siblings again. I enjoy talking to my brother from time to time, but he's very opinionated and has an air of superiority that offends me. After years of not talking to me, my sister has come back into my life. We talk more than ever before, and although she loves to share insights with me, I still feel the relationship is mostly one-sided. She has some nice things to offer me in the way of advice, but I just accept it without much joy because she remains narcissistic and it drains me. She has no awareness of how her behavior affected the rest of the family."

It's a truism that no two children in any given family experience that family and its nexus of relationships in precisely the same way, despite all of our cherished myths about the closeness and mutuality of family ties. The reasons for this are both simple and complicated and, even though this particular truth seems both culturally subversive and counterintuitive, it's universal. But it's also true that, despite their different experiences and perspectives, siblings influence each other both through their connection to each other and through their differentiation from each other. In addition, the ways in which they are alike *and* different shape how they see themselves and their places in the family, as well as how others, including their parents, perceive and treat them. While most research has focused on the mother-child dyad and secondarily the father-child dyad as the primary influences on the development of the self, it's nonetheless clear that the sibling relationship—in both its presence and its absence—can shape the self and serve as a template for other relationships outside of the family.

Sibling relationships aren't formed in a vacuum, of course; they exist in and are influenced by the larger context of other family relationships and, later in childhood, by peer relationships as well. Sibling relationships are also shaped by what experts call "constellation variables"—the birth order of siblings, the age spacing between them, and last but not least, gender. Not surprisingly, sister-sister, brother-brother, and sister-brother relationships are different in kind and play different roles in the formation of a daughter's self.

Our families—our mothers, our fathers, and our siblings, if we have them—teach us our first lessons, up close and personal, about intimate relationships. What precisely we learn will vary not only from family to family but also within a family from sibling to sibling. Our cultural tropes about family emphasize relatedness and connection, but if we were to examine sibling relationships with a totally open mind, it would probably be helpful to heed the words of journalist Susan Scarf Merrell, who explained why she gave her book about sibling relationships the title *The Accidental Bond:* "in acknowledgment of the phenomenon of chance that forces two vastly different children into relationship with each other and has an amazing, long-reaching impact on both their lives. We are placed in the world with a gorgeous randomness, cheek by jowl with these look-somewhat-alike/talk-somewhat-alike/think-somewhat-alike others, our siblings." Not every sibling, though, will appreciate what Merrell calls that "gorgeous randomness."

How a brother shapes a sister's sense of self is very different from the way a sister does, since a brother—regardless of rivalry—is by definition more "other" than alike, distinct by nature of his gender. Perhaps inevitably, brother-sister relationships are also influenced by the assumptions their mother (and their father, for that matter) hold about gender. As I've mentioned before, a mother may favor a son because she feels his achievements are intrinsically more valuable and important than those of a daughter; she may also see those achievements as being less threatening to or competitive with her own than those of a same-sex child. "My mother saw my brother as her crowning achievement," Helen says. "No matter what I did, it—whatever *it* was—was always compared to what my brother had done most recently. There didn't seem to be any room for me at all, and it was terribly discouraging. It made me feel both unloved and marginalized, and in a kind of self-fulfilling prophecy I started achieving less. I already felt that my mother didn't love me, but my brother's presence made it both clearer and worse."

A daughter's identity may be defined in contrast to a brother's both to her own detriment and to that of the sibling relationship, as demonstrated in journalist Marie Brenner's moving and articulate memoir of her contradictory and contrarian relationship to her brother, *Apples and Oranges*. While her situation was unique, it nonetheless captures what can and often does happen between a brother and sister: "A research study on siblings breaks down the percentages: 52 percent of all brothers and sisters have a close relationship, 12 percent have no relationship, and 21 percent are something called 'borderline.' I am a borderline, defined by and against my brother, locked into some ancient and immutable feud. There is a moat around our conversations. Why? Why did we spend years locked in struggle with each other?" Later in her book she describes how they, this brother and sister, are separated by only three years, "We were moving through uncharted terrain as if we had grown up in separate tribes. In fact, we had. Within the family, there were two clubs: father-son and mother-daughter. Carl and I could never work out the reasons why." Each plays out the role assigned in the family—he the "dominating older brother" and she the "flighty and rebellious younger sister"—each aligned with a different parent.

Research shows that same-sex siblings report greater companionship, intimacy, and affection than opposite-sex siblings do. The shared female-ness of a sister, though, invites a different kind of comparison, and the competition or rivalry between same-sex siblings—particularly when they are spaced less than four years apart—can take on a different kind of intensity, along with meaningful antagonism. That said, sibling relation-ships become less intense as children get older and the amount of time they spend together decreases with their increased connection to peer relationships and the outside world. Most important, sibling relationships are often fluid over the course of time.

If mothers and fathers are bound like Prometheus by the myths that define their roles, then siblings have their own to contend with, the most important of which can be summed up by the adage "Blood is thicker than water." This myth, as Melanie Mauthner has written, can be—like so many other myths about family and relationship—a blessing or a curse, capable of articulating the basis for a close sibling relationship in one family, put-ting terrible pressure on essentially disconnected siblings in yet another, or being the trigger for bitter disappointment and a sense of betrayal in a family where sibling loyalty falls short of the promised ideal. And for all that we enshrine the vision of sibling closeness—those Kodachrome snapshots of smiling children with their arms around each other, with "We Are Family" playing in the background—roughly only half of all sisters (and even fewer brothers) declare their relationship "close," even in essentially loving families.

As researchers note, few valid generalizations can be made about the range of sibling relationships in our culture, but if there *is* one, it is that the dynamic of all sibling relationships is comprised of both a need to establish connection, on the one hand, and a need to differentiate, on the other. The dynamic can be both contradictory and ambivalent, set-ting the need for a sense of belonging to the family—one based in like-ness—against the need to establish a distinct and independent vision of self—one based in differences. Among siblings, the precise nature of the dynamic may tilt in one extreme direction or the other—overwhelmingly toward connection or toward differentiation—or, with siblings who enjoy a close relationship, stay balanced somewhere in the middle. A mother who is unloving to one child and loving to another will change the sibling equation entirely.

The idealization of sibling ties—between and among brothers, sisters, and mixed gender sets—is aided and abetted by literary examples and fairy tales—think Louisa May Alcott's *Little Women* or Laura Ingalls Wilder's *Little House* books—as well as by familial hopefulness and cultural norms. Cultural norms are weighted against only children and heavily invested in the ideal family that includes two siblings or more; as a result, some 80 percent of you reading these pages, for example, will be a sister to at least one person and most probably two. For some unloved daughters, these myths will contribute significantly to their vision of the sibling relationship as yet another area of life filled with disappointment, where their needs to belong and to feel loved, already damaged by the maternal relationship, will find little succor.

THE MYTH THING: ONCE MORE WITH FEELING

It's been suggested that the cultural myths and assumptions about siblings—about the bond itself, the importance of birth order, the ubiquity of sibling rivalry, and the like—as well as those pertaining to being an only child may exert as much influence on the way a daughter thinks about herself as does the actual experience of being a sister, being the oldest or youngest, or, for that matter, being an only child. As psychologist and researcher Toni Falco points out, because being an only child is still "non-normative" in our culture, most only children consider growing up without siblings as a psychological disadvantage, even though there is *no* scientific proof that only children are in fact disadvantaged. She notes that only children who feel this way are likely to attribute whatever problems they experience to their "only" status.

Similarly, as psychologist and psychoanalyst Frits Boer writes, even though there is "very little empirical evidence of a strong effect of birth order on adult personality, the popular belief in its significance is as alive as ever." He goes on to comment wryly: "In fact, birth order could become a serious competitor of the horoscope." Women and men who tell their life stories in the framework of birth order—attributing their identities to being "the youngest" or "the oldest," for example—may not realize that what they are telling isn't a birth order story at all but an individual one, which "is given meaning in family mythology by being attributed to birth order."

Family and sibling myths don't affect just the development of the self during childhood or how that development is understood later in life; they influence how parents—once children themselves—understand their own children as well. An only child will bring her personal and cultural myths to the table as a mother, just as mothers with siblings (and fathers, for that matter) will bring theirs. Without examination, sibling histories along with an individual's understanding of those histories can work their influence on a mother's behavior as well. As Susan Scarf Merrell notes in her book *The Accidental Bond,* each of us has "convictions" about what "position" in a family means, based "on his or her own unique and specific early experiences" so that "A mother who is the older of two daughters may have little sympathy with her younger daughter's eagerness to trail after her big sister. Without realizing it, she has a more empathetic response to the needs of her child who is in her same sibling position. That mother's differential empathy, a remnant of her particular sibling experience but now a factor of luck and chance for her two children, will certainly make its mark on the way in which each of those two young women perceives the world."

But with consciousness and awareness—those essential ingredients often missing from the stories of mean mothers and their daughters—a negative sibling history can become a positive template for the next generation. Louisa worked hard to assure that her daughters had a close connection to each other, exemplifying how, with examination and consciousness, old patterns can be rewritten for a new future. This is what she tells me: "Because my relationship to my siblings was so difficult, it was a priority to raise my two daughters with a strong bond. They are twenty and twenty-three now and best buds. They share their jobs and their clothes, and they are each other's cheerleaders. I have a fabulous picture of my then three-year-old daughter, Amy, holding her baby sister who's only two days old—she asked to hold her the second we walked in from the hospital and she was shocked when I said yes! They fought a bit when they were little—when the youngest became old enough to assert herself and the oldest still wanted to be in charge—and they were always competitive. But Amy was the best big sister and taught Jill all the 'rules' and spent time playing and reading to her, so their bond is tight. Jill was a bit more of a free spirit, so she learned the rules, had a strong sense of self, took what she learned, and broke free by competing with her older sister in every avenue that interested her. My girls never seemed to be afraid to try anything, even if they didn't necessarily succeed, in part because we taught them that failure was just another opportunity to learn. They are each very happy for the other when the other does well."

Other daughters who also had loose or nonexistent ties to their siblings report that working hard to make sure that their children were loved equally and well so that the sibling relationship could flourish was a high priority for them. In this way too, older family patterns can be changed in future generations.

VARIATIONS ON THE SIBLING THEME

As much as only children may dream of a sister or brother to help them deal with an unloving mother, only some daughters—even those with siblings close in age—report experiencing active support or help. Sometimes, though, the mere presence of a sibling who is treated in the same way can help a daughter better navigate the emotional landscape of the maternal relationship, even though the sibling relationship per se doesn't otherwise offer emotional support.

In her book *Altered Loves,* Terri Apter writes about her experience as a baby sister who goes from being adored by her older sister to being treated as a nuisance and embarrassment when they're both in school. But witnessing her sister's battles with their mother during adolescence gave her an edge and a strategy, and endowed her with a sense of superiority: "I took notes, learned lessons, and steered clear of my mother in certain areas, learned about how to keep things private—especially sexual feelings, or feelings of admiration and adoration of others, which my mother was so adept at reducing." The sisters ultimately find a common ground in their unique battles with their mother: "The quarrels we each had, in our very different ways, with our mother took on a smaller, more circumscribed area when we shared our information about her. Our mother's anger, too, which fell on the house like a bank of fog, was thinner, and we had more power within it, because we could turn to each other with our common complaints." What is perhaps even more interesting is that Apter—a researcher and psychologist—admits that her presumption of the "usefulness of a sibling" was so strong that she was positive that the complaints she heard from adolescent girls about their siblings would reveal themselves to be superficial. To her surprise, they weren't.

For one sister-brother pair, shared experience was most certainly a plus. Jane's brother was four years younger than she, and their mother exerted as much control over her son as she did over her daughter. Jane tells me that her mother's treatment of Bob helped clarify that what went on in the house wasn't about her but about her mother's need to control and manage: "It was helpful, even though my brother and I were very different, to have someone there who really understood what I was going through, because he had the same experience." Being a sister, especially an older one, in her particular household was an important influence: "It's interesting because most of my friends when I was growing up were all younger siblings—one of them was actually the youngest of five. I remember one of my friends telling me that I was acting just like an older sister to my brother—I don't remember the occasion, but I guess I must have been acting bossy or something. But being the eldest meant that I was the first to 'break in' my parents with testing boundaries, curfews, issues about money, and the like, and I took on a leadership and teaching role in relation to him, particularly in dealing with our mother and the similar issues that arose for both of us. I think I set an example for him too—I got good grades and always told him about the importance of working hard in school."

Today, Jane and her brother get along well, but she is quick to point out that they are mainly connected by their family history rather than the bonds of friendship. "We are very different in many ways," she says, "with different attitudes about almost everything including politics. But he is an emotional and caring person and very good to my two children." The two siblings have traveled very different paths; Jane has been a successful architect and moved away from the hometown she grew up in, while her brother, now thirty-seven, has suffered from health problems and remained dependent on their parents, both financially and emotionally. He continues to struggle in his relationship to their mother in ways that Jane does not.

The distinction between the sibling relationship and friendship is emphasized by other women as well. As the daughters of an emotionally unreliable mother, Elizabeth and her sister had little connection during childhood but became progressively closer after college and, most particularly, when they each had boys in their thirties, born three weeks apart. Having moved to the East Coast from California, Elizabeth has been physically separated from her sister for over twenty years, and, for just about as long, neither the sisters nor their brother had much contact with their mother: "We'd call her and she'd get angry and hang up on us. We put her aside—and we felt we had to." Recently, as their mother ages, the children have nonetheless come together to help her out.

Even though they weren't close during childhood, in adulthood—as both of the sisters became mothers themselves—their relationship has deepened with mutual admiration, without erasing any of the differences between them: "My sister and I are still as different as we were then. She's into presentation and the way things look in ways that I'm not, and she can still infuriate me when she falls into one of her critical modes. But at the same time, we've invested a lot in our commonness—the things we share, such as family and kids, being female, and even our experiences growing up. My sister's an extraordinary parent, married to a man who is an equally conscious and committed father, and I see her soul and beauty. We love each other now in a deep way, even though I wouldn't choose her as a friend. We do mother each other in small ways since our mother has always been unavailable—by acting as each other's sounding boards and offering each other counsel." Their relationship to their brother—five years younger than Elizabeth—remains distant.

A persistent theme in some women's stories—especially those about sisters—is captured in the way Elizabeth's words about their closeness now coexist with her observation that that she wouldn't "choose her as a friend." The importance of friendships to a woman's life is well documented, and it may well be that sensitivity to the difference between these two bonds—one "accidental" and the other chosen—remains important, even when the relationship between sisters is fundamentally close. I wonder too whether the myth of sibling closeness—that bond of blood that is "thicker than water"—doesn't bequeath many siblings an impossibly high standard of understanding and intimacy. It's no accident that the language both women (and men) use to describe the closest of relationships draws on that idealized sibling bond, whether the speaker has siblings or not: "She is like a sister to me" or "He's like a brother to me."

In another family, being the eldest of three daughters would shape one sister's experience in ways that separated her from her siblings. Susan and her two sisters—one two years and the other six years younger—grew up with the same parents but share neither their experiences of childhood nor their memories of their mother. Even today the three sisters, now all in their sixties, end up giggling when they talk about "their" mother and father, correcting each other to ask, "Are we talking about the same person?" As the oldest, Susan's experience was markedly different from those of her two siblings. "Our mother loved babies," Susan tells me, "and she was great with small children. But she was too self-absorbed and fragile to deal with any kind of conflict, and for her, mothering got hard when we started saying no or when we bickered. She didn't see herself as a model or a coach, and she couldn't really handle anything except the simpler tasks of early childhood caretaking." Susan was four when her mother inexplicably—to her child's eyes at least—withdrew from her daughter emotionally as she became progressively more unhappy in her life and marriage.

Although Susan didn't realize it until much later in her life, her grandmother—her father's mother—was a buffer against her mother's abandonment. She lived next door to the family, and her home was, as Susan tells it, a safe zone for her. "As a child, I felt I lived in a walled-in place, but the darkness didn't come on me until I was in junior high school, when my grandmother died and my mother fell apart." Susan stepped into the vacuum her mother left behind and became—as she still is today—a mother figure to her younger siblings. She cooked, cleaned, did the shopping for the family, and, as she says, "I shielded my sisters, and because they had me, they weren't as dependent on my mother as I was. They had me, but I had no one. My sisters and I were a unit, but from my point of view it wasn't based on emotional closeness but on the bond of responsibility, my responsibility. I took care of them."

During her childhood, Susan felt isolated in ways her sisters did not: "Reading and writing were my friends, and my journal was my very best friend," she tells me. Her sisters' experiences were also different because their mother regained a measure of stability as they got older. Her younger sister, in particular, had warm memories of their mother as the only child still at home, while her middle sister benefited from the care their mother, who was always good with babies, gave her own children. Unlike her sisters—but very much like other daughters of mothers unwilling or unable to give of themselves—Susan continued to struggle with needing her mother's attention and love until she was an adult in her early thirties.

FAMILY SCRIPTS AND ROLES

In their study of families done in the 1950s, James Bossard and Eleanor Bell noted that while in a small family, the "roles" children play in the family are usually "assigned" by parents, in larger families, siblings themselves may assign roles to other siblings on the basis of differences among them. Among the eight recurring roles Bossard and Bell discovered were the responsible one (usually the eldest, who becomes a caretaker to younger siblings); the popular one, who's well liked by the others; the social butterfly; the studious one; the isolate, who pulls out of family life; the irresponsible one; the weak or sick one; and the spoiled one, who is usually the youngest or second youngest.

Comparisons and contrasts between and among siblings, especially same-sex siblings, are inevitable in every family, whether loving or not, and influence both a daughter's perception of herself and the formation of her self. Physical, temperamental, and intellectual differences between and among sisters also work to define their roles in the family. While fractures and extreme differences in siblings' recollections and visions of the family are often connected to a mother being loving to one child and not to another, it's important to realize that family dynamics are rarely either straightforward or ideal when seen from the point of view of any individual child experiencing them. It's important for an unloved daughter to keep that in mind as she looks at her sibling relationships. Two stories of very different families of sisters may be valuable in that regard.

Even in a family blessed with an involved, loving, and totally supportive mother—one willing to afford her children every opportunity and dedicated to making sure she treated them evenhandedly—and an attentive father, perceptions of differential treatment and perhaps the inevitable comparison between closely spaced sisters can shape both the sibling relationship and the girls themselves. Lynne, now fifty-eight, is the mother of two and a successful entrepreneur who also sits on the boards of numerous charities. She is the oldest of four girls who grew up in a prosperous suburb outside of Chicago. Her sister Lydia is one year younger, now fifty-seven; her sister Lily is fifty-four, separated from her by four years; and Catherine, the baby of the family, is now fifty, some nine years younger than Lynne. All the sisters remain very close to their mother; in fact, each of them, Lynne tells me, is closer to her than they are to each other. "My mother is terrific at keeping confidences," Lynne says. "Whatever any one of us tells her would never be shared with any of the other three.

"My parents had high standards," Lynne tells me, "not just for educational pursuits but athletic and social pursuits as well. Our parents were part of the religious community in our town, as were we, and we also had a group of family friends we saw regularly. It was a stable, calm environment—there never was any yelling at our house—and my parents had a good relationship. Our mother made most of the big decisions concerning us, although she always discussed everything with our father. During my childhood and adolescence, I was closest to my sister Lydia—we're only one year apart—and we were both good students and athletes. She and I had separate rooms, even though our younger sisters always shared one. Still, growing up with three sisters, you learn to accommodate; you can't be a prima donna about what you eat, and you recognize that there's just so much energy to go around. We shared a single bathroom and just one phone.

"Because I was the oldest, my father called me 'Number One' and 'Skinny Minnie' because I was really thin. I was a 'Daddy's girl' and used to read *The Wall Street Journal* with him and we'd talk about business. I had a lot of male friends in both high school and college, and I think that maybe having sisters who were friends made me feel as though I didn't need any girlfriends, really. My sister Lydia's nickname was 'Pumpkin'— she needed to lose some weight in those days and thinness was important to my father—and she was a really good student, was serious, and had lots of girlfriends. I didn't feel competitive with Lydia or Lily, probably because I was the oldest and always worked so hard. If my sisters felt competitive with me, they certainly didn't express it overtly, and, to be honest, I'm not sure I would have really understood. I wasn't very sensitive to it."

Even though all four sisters are high achievers and live comfortable lives, Lynne's relationships to them in adulthood are very different, and each has a unique dynamic; their shared childhood and loyalty to their parents are factors in some of these relationships but not in all of them. Her relationship to her youngest sister, born nine years later, is, not surprisingly, the most distant: "Catherine has three children now and is a stay-at-home mother, though she had a very successful career earlier. We're not very close, though I'm not sure whether that has to do with the age gap between us or because of personality issues. She's got a very strong personality and vision of things, and we sometimes disagree about how to handle issues." In adulthood, Lynne is closest to Lily, the sister four years younger than she, even though they too have made different life choices: "Lily doesn't have children and is now in a loving and stable relationship after two unsuccessful marriages, so in that sense we're really quite different. But she's easy to get along with—she's calm and doesn't make waves—and is lots of fun and I enjoy her company." The two sisters see each other often.

In adulthood, it's with Lydia, the sister to whom she is closest in age and with whom she was closest in childhood and adolescence, that Lynne has the most tension-filled relationship, perhaps as a carryover from their childhood, when the girls were compared to each other: "Lydia was always more spiritual and involved in religion than I was, and had a different temperament. I'm very competitive, and while Lydia did well in business, she never liked competition. Time after time she'd be offered a top job and then ultimately she'd decline to take it. I'm much more assertive, and as a result I'm much more in the public eye than she is—I don't mind putting myself out there."

When I ask her about how Lydia might have been affected by the

comparisons between her and her older sister, Lynne becomes more reflec-
tive: "You know, after college Lydia was the only one of us who moved far
away from home and the family to make her own life. She's a purist and
a perfectionist in many ways and has become, over time, profoundly and
deeply religious in ways that I am not. I genuinely admire the role Lydia
plays in her chosen community and the gratitude she displays, but at the
same time, how she lives seems foreign to me. Her life is deliberately sim-
plified, and of course when you have children, as I do, that kind of 'simplicity' just isn't within reach. She's become more critical and intolerant
of other people's choices, I think, when they don't coincide with her own,
and sometimes I feel as though she is both competitive with and critical
of me at once."

Was it the comparison between the girls—the "Skinny Minnie" and
the "Pumpkin" or "Number One" and, by default, the unnamed "Number
Two"—that was the seed for their relationship now? Or was it a function
of their respective personalities? Even in adolescence, Lynne asserted her
needs, which is how she went to private school and her sister didn't. Lynne
doesn't know for certain, perhaps because as the oldest she was always on
the "winning" side of the comparison between them. It was Lydia, after
all, who had to carve out her own space in comparison. It's noteworthy
that their mother, someone who tried so hard to be evenhanded with her
daughters and whom all her grown daughters love and admire, now sometimes wonders out loud whether things might have been different if she'd
known to pay attention to the almost inevitable dynamics between and
among same-sex siblings.

In another family of sisters—one less stable than Lynne's, to be sure—
the dynamic among sisters was very different and yet shared certain similarities. Some of the differences are obvious—there was paternal violence
and a wounded mother in one, not the other, for example. Keep in mind
too that the first story is told by the oldest of the sisters, Lynne, and the
second by the youngest, an importantly different perspective. For Georgia—the youngest of three girls, one five years and the other two years
older—her sense of self is inextricably bound to her sisters: "Being a sister

gave me a direct experience of sharing. Sharing space—the three of us were always in a single bedroom—fun, energies, suffering. It gave me a direct experience of resonance, of not being alone, of being with others who are unique people, not like me but close to me. I could be like them, of the same stock, with so much emotional intimacy and at the same time realize that I was me, a unique being with different tastes, desires, personality, moods, style. I was definitely more outspoken, spunky, and energetic than my oldest sister, Renée, and less confrontational, struggling, and wounded than my middle sister, Charlotte. Our mother's obsession with treating us equally worked well; there was never any competition among us, and there isn't today."

Their influence on her has been pervasive: "They've given me unwavering support and sustained presence. A sense of tribe, of blood resonance. A bond beyond words and beyond struggles. Their impact is visible in my sense of style, my taste in music, in people, things. They've helped in my distress. They have hurt me too and taught me that relationships have their ups and downs but that ultimately we stick with each other in understanding that commitment isn't just a word but a fact of life, a situation that exists beyond our whims. I have two sisters and so I never feel alone. I've been able to find friends who feel like sisters, and I know one when I meet one. As the friendship develops, I recognize the sense of comfort, of transparency in myself, the depth of intimacy. That is an incredibly powerful reference point for who I am."

The household they grew up in, though, wasn't all sweetness and light, and their closeness coexists with their different experiences in the family as well as their disparate perceptions and memories of their mother and father. Their mother was needy and, as Georgia puts it, "emotionally wounded," since her own mother died soon after her birth and she was raised by a cruel and unloving stepmother. As Georgia tells it, their mother's connection to each of her daughters was in part shaped by history and experience by their individual personalities. The eldest daughter, Renée, had been desperately ill as a child and almost died; in her mother's eyes, she was eternally deemed to be "fragile" and was babied out of concern and worry. The middle sister, Charlotte, was Renée's opposite; she was fiery in nature, confrontational, and combative, and she felt overlooked because of the attention showered on the "fragile" Renée. Her personality evoked their father's rage: he hit her while her mother stood by, paralyzed and frightened. As Georgia sees it, "Charlotte was betrayed from every angle."

Georgia, the proclaimed "baby" of the family, felt smothered by her mother's neediness but benefited from her sisters' experiences: "I was freer than they were. They had gone before me and did pave the way for more autonomy. I saw what worked with my parents and what didn't, and learned how to manipulate situations so I could do what I needed to do. But even though my sisters' roles were true at first, they were also projections, which kept us hostages of a proclaimed path." Georgia also tells me that "I understood my relationship to my mother by comparison and contrast. I saw my sisters' relationships to her and defined mine according to what I witnessed. I could use my radar and gauge how to behave. I saw her inability to deal with conflict as well as her capacity to be playful, and seeing her in her powerlessness with Charlotte's victim role scared me and forced me to understand that she wouldn't protect me either if push ever came to shove."

Today, these close sisters often talk about the family they grew up in, acknowledging that each of them had a unique relationship with the two parents they shared. As the first-born, Renée was a "precious gem" to them both. Charlotte felt disconnected from both of her parents; she saw their father as crazy, unsteady, and full of rage and their mother as powerless, a coward, and unprotective. She left home as soon as she could and moved thousands of miles away. In contrast, Georgia saw their mother as clingy and smothering, an emotional blackmailer who threatened to shut down if Georgia challenged her. "She made everything about her, and what a great mother she was, but she was really extremely emotionally fragile and couldn't face any kind of challenge." For her, her father was unreliable; as she puts it, "he could be great and supportive and then flip into his oppressive and violent fits."

Even though the sisters didn't bond over the violence inflicted on Charlotte—"We were each overwhelmed with our own emotions," Georgia says—their shared past is very much a part of their deep connection to each other: "My sisters saw me as a person and truly mentored me in a 'lived in' sort of way, by virtue of their presence in my life. They were very important. They still are. I feel that what we share now is truly a testimony to an emotional intimacy constructed organically of small building blocks of moments shared and challenging, traumatic events survived together, even in silence."

WE LEARN ABOUT LOVE—OR ITS ABSENCE—FROM OUR FIRST TEACHERS, our mothers and fathers. Sometimes, in the absence of love, a sibling may step into the breach because, as Stephen Bank writes, "as warmth-seeking mammals, children will attach themselves to any available object that offers solace, even if that solace is more imaginary than real, and even if the object is hostile or frustrating to them." The lessons an unloved daughter learns from an unloving, hypercritical, or unavailable mother (or father or both) are stored within her, an encoded transcript of gestures, actions, and words that hold the particular truths of her singular experience and her understanding of herself and close relationships. What Bank writes about siblings in dysfunctional families with a "vacuum of parental care" seems applicable as well to a single child; he calls this stored emotional information "a *secret inscription,* a *frozen image,* or *template*" and notes that this information consists of "memories filled with visual and visceral information." Some of it may not even be accessible in words, "because these images were acquired before the children had full command of language and thought." Most important, he tells us that "these templates become operative only under specific conditions that remind us of our old relationships. Like most unconscious processes, secret inscriptions dictate irrational behavior and ignite conflict until they are no longer secret."

We turn next to those lessons learned, those "secret inscriptions" and "templates" bequeathed by an unloving mother to her daughter, to discover how those templates can be uncovered, understood, and ultimately conquered so that the daughter can choose a different emotional life for herself than the one she inherited.

· Five ·

Stilling the Voice of the Mother Within:
The Battle for Self-Worth

HERS IS THE FIRST VOICE EACH OF US HEARS, BEGINNING WITH our existence in utero. From the moment we arrive in this life, her voice informs our sense of who we are and our place in the little world of family we find ourselves in with utter poignancy. For a daughter, her mother is the first mirror in which she catches a glimpse of herself, and her mother's voice—the full articulation of all of her words, gestures, and actions—will limn her sense of self. Her voice may tell us that we are strong, capable, loving, and lovable and that the arena of relationship is a safe place.

For a loved daughter, the discovery of mother is also a discovery of self, pleasurable and safe. In her memoir *An American Childhood,* Annie Dillard captures the process with exquisite lyricism: "A young child knows Mother as a smelled skin, a halo of light, a voice that trembles with feeling. Later the child wakes and discovers this mother—and adds facts to impressions, and historical understanding to facts." For these daughters, internalizing the lessons learned—the mother's voice within—gives them a reliable compass for navigating the journey of life. For other daughters, though, the lessons about the self communicated by their mothers' voices are different in kind.

I tell one of the women I've interviewed about the title of this chapter, and what she e-mails me back has terrific resonance: "Have I done that yet? Will she ever really be out of my head? My mind tells me that by concentrating my efforts on just being me, I will find the confidence in myself that will drown my mother's voice out of my head. My heart tells me I need to forgive her in order to make that happen." Mind you, this is a daughter who, alone among her siblings, is taking care of her aged mother in the wake of myriad health problems and has always, despite their difficulties, lived nearby. What she tells me underscores the complexity of some mother-daughter relationships: "Doing this for my mom is who I am. The difficult part is doing it while fighting with the part of me that is a result of who she tried to make me be by her harsh words and example. This is a war to reclaim my authentic self, and it's no wonder I'm exhausted. She's sad and confused when I arrive and perks up the minute she sees me and it feels wonderful to be so loved. Yet I can't help feeling resentful that she was never there for me and that I felt that I was invisible to her."

In contrast, another daughter who has lived most of her adult life either thousands or hundreds of miles away from her very critical mother has managed, on many levels, to make peace with her mother now that she herself is the mother of a young daughter and son: "Her voice isn't in my head so much as I try to ignore the past and the rockier parts of our relationship. My four-year-old daughter absolutely loves my mother, and the grandmother-granddaughter relationship is very different from the mother-daughter one. It's great not to have her controlling nature get in the way of her relationship to my children, her grandchildren." Even so, she adds, "I wonder if it would be different if we lived closer. My mother still doesn't 'see' me in some real sense, and it's still painful but not hugely so. I try to ignore it because I don't think it would do any good at this point to dwell on it. Part of that is also my personality—I generally avoid conflict—and I am financially and (mostly) emotionally independent. I enjoyed a good relationship with my grandparents, despite my parents' difficulties with them, and want my kids to have the same. And, despite the issues I had and continue to have with my mother, she (and my father) did many other great things for me."

Dr. Marilyn Lyga, a therapist in private practice, whom I ask about strategies she might suggest to a woman working on stilling the maternal voice, emphasizes that "it's important to remember the extent to which a daughter has been loved by someone else. If she's had a loving father or grandmother, for example, the flavor will be very different."

Reflecting on the process of stilling the mother voice, Georgia mentions both therapy and the process of life experience, writing that "By spending so much time listening deeply to the mother within, I have been able to separate from it, see the voice for what it is, see that it is not me. That it's my mother's wound—her fear, her condition, her circumstances—that endowed her voice and made her so controlling and suffocating toward me. Sometimes her voice echoes in my head in strange and unexpected ways, but it doesn't activate any triggers anymore. I can place the voice in the perspective of *her* life. At the end, it is about seeing her truly, letting her be in her life, having compassion for what she endured and what she went through. For me, that's where the healing began—with compassion for her and then for me. But this didn't happen by 'transcending' what I call the 'emotional grind.' I had to put up a fight, be angry, feel lost first."

For some daughters, gaining perspective through therapy or positive life experience can put the internalized maternal voice in a more productive context. This process isn't necessarily easy, Dr. Lyga tells me: "With an engaged but critical mother, a daughter may have trouble recognizing the way she's internalized that voice. Or with an enmeshed and envious mother, it may be hard for a daughter to differentiate that voice from her own."

The stories other unloved daughters tell about their mothers' voices may be filled with anger, pain, and sometimes bewilderment, along with undeniable longing. "I trace my own lack of self-confidence and general unsureness about things back to my mother," Jeanne says. "She was emotionally unreliable—horribly critical of me one day and then dismissive the next. I never knew what to expect—she could be intolerably present and then inexplicably absent—but when I was young, I always thought she was right. Now I know she wasn't, but her voice, particularly when life gets difficult or I feel insecure, is still in my head."

Sometimes, even though our achievements belie our mothers' assessments, their words may still echo in our heads. Gwen writes to me: "The constant reminders that I 'couldn't do anything right' or that I 'wouldn't amount to anything' were my daily diet until I left home for college. I have divorced twice, and I was always looking for someone to love me without paying attention to how I was loved. I made unwise choices. I still can't entirely kick 'the fear of success,' because the prediction of failure is still in my head, even though I have done many things that were well done by any standard. Am I able to still the mother voice within? I would say no. I am continually insecure and tend to recap events and even accomplishments. I go back and think, 'Did I do that correctly?' and 'What will the other person/people think?' It's very annoying, and while a part of me thinks I will never still that voice, I still try. I know I have come a long way." When I ask Gwen how her mother most affected her, she answers simply and bluntly: "I have always and still feel completely *alone*. I compensate—God knows I compensate—but I am always aware of how alone I am."

For other daughters, the maternal voice within can be the source of turmoil and pain and of terrible self-doubt or self-criticism. The voice of an emotionally absent mother may convey the message that we are not worth bothering with or listening to, while that of a hypercritical or mean one may say that we are lazy, stupid, or fat, or that nothing we do is ever good enough. Some inadequately loved daughters feel inauthentic and worry about being "found out"—having their true selves revealed—as I did when I was young. Others simply continue to feel unworthy of love, of attention, of connection. These legacies may get in the way of an unloved daughter's finding the support and sense of connection she needs in female friendship.

In their book on female friendship, *Between Women,* Luise Eichenbaum and Susie Orbach underscore the obvious but often ignored fact that all female friendships have their roots in our first relationship with a woman, our mothers: "For each friend involved, woman-to-woman relationships duplicate aspects of the mother-daughter relationship and simultaneously extend the promise to repair some of the hurt and difficulties of the original relationship." Not surprisingly, some daughters who had unloving mothers or emotionally untrustworthy ones have difficulty forming close female friendships or choosing healthy supportive ones; they may also put too much pressure on a friendship to give them what that first relationship, that of the mother and daughter, lacked. When I was young, trusting other girls and, later, women was nearly impossible for me and, perhaps because I expected to be betrayed, being betrayed wasn't an uncommon experience for me. Patterns of behavior and expectations learned from the maternal relationship may end up self-fulfilling in ways that may be hard for a daughter to see and so may be even harder to fix.

Sometimes the legacy of an unloving mother manifests itself in other ways. Sarah, fifty-two, tells me: "I learned not to ask my mother for anything because she never gave anything freely. There were always strings attached. Holidays associated with family and closeness and even my own birthday have always been hard for me and still are. I approach them with low expectations and am always ready to be disappointed because I always was with my mother. I have trouble asking for help from people, especially women, because of my mother's inability to give. I hid things from my mother that were important to me so she couldn't take them away, and there's a part of me that still has trouble revealing myself, exposing my feelings and my needs."

Growing up with a mother who was controlling and smothering by turns and who most of all made Sarah feel as though she didn't exist, Sarah had few girlfriends as a young woman, and even now she has trouble dealing with women in a position of authority or whom she's trying to impress. "I have ghost images of my mother," she admits, "most usually when I want a woman to like me, hire me, include me in her circle. Nothing I did ever pleased my mother, and it made me feel as though nothing I did was ever good enough." Sarah's relationship to her father was different—he supported both her academic and artistic efforts—and how she connects to men is very different from how she relates to women: "I took a martial arts class and I was surprised, years later, when my former teacher—my sensei—told me that, of all the women in the class, I was the most fearless. It was, I'm sure, because of my comfort level with men."

Reflecting on the girlfriends she's chosen over time, one woman e-mails that: "If I have all these narcissistic friends who aren't necessarily in the friendship because they like me but because they like what I can do for them, then I'm always in the position of being judged unworthy or unuseful. When I pick these kinds of women, it comes from this place of my not having any value and my feeling that I always have to give 100 percent to get 2 percent, or 10 percent, if I'm really lucky." Another woman whose mother was both distant and dismissive tells me that she was never able to connect with her female peer group at any age because she didn't have "a model of female closeness." When I ask about the role girlfriends play in her life, another woman e-mails me: "I never felt sure that anyone really liked me. Why should anyone like me? That little voice that says I'm not good enough still reminds me I shouldn't think too much of myself." In her book *Tripping the Prom Queen,* Susan Shapiro Barash reports that many daughters learn about female envy, rivalry, and competition from their mothers' modeled behavior.

An emotionally unreliable mother or one who is actively abusive— either emotionally or physically—may affect a daughter in a broader way, even when she's been able to still the voice of the mother within and long after she's become a loving and emotionally available mother herself. Here is what Alissa tells me: "The way in which my relationship with my mother affected me the most deeply is fairly straightforward but also so funda- mental that to this day it affects basically every part of my life all the time. I was *never, ever* safe around my mother, and so now, even after all these years, I still *never* feel safe. My mother's crazy, unpredictable behavior stripped away the normal sense of denial that allows humans to go on through the day and not worry about car crashes and pesticides on their foods and other dangers. I am always on alert in a primal, life or death way. It's exhausting."

What makes a mother's voice so potent, so capable of shape-shifting a daughter's perception of herself, even long after she is out of her mother's house and her reach, years and years later? Some of the power of the maternal voice derives from a child's original, absolute, and unequivocal need for her mother—for her love, her protection, her care, and her validation—which is part of the child's first inkling of being. With an unloving or mean mother, that need produces a growing sense of powerlessness in the daughter as her mother abuses the power she has over her child. The mother's voice—the bigger and louder of the two—informs her child's universe, with all the authority motherhood and a child's neediness grant.

Growing up, one of my greatest sources of distress wasn't what my mother said or did; it was instead her absolute refusal, then or ever, to acknowledge any of her words or acts and her active denial of them. I couldn't have been more than six or seven when I realized that the two versions—hers and mine—of what went on at our house were utterly incompatible. She insisted that her treatment of me was deserved—I was difficult, unruly, in need of punishment—but I knew that what I did or said, or didn't say and didn't do, had no effect on her actions or words. One of us was wrong, or maybe even crazy, and that thought left me breathless. I was scared of someone thinking I was crazy; who would love me then? She was the Mommy, after all—could she be wrong? It had to be me, didn't it?

That thought alone can rob the self of the keel it needs to right itself. As Linda tells me: "My soul, my instincts, told me that what happened *did* happen, but as a young child I would still second-guess myself because she was my mom. This was a dangerous dynamic because it made me doubt my authentic self. As I got older, I would get angry, but she would come at me with either denial or, if I pressed her, she would say I was 'too sensitive.' I hated her when she said that. Like being sensitive was a negative? Or even more hurtfully, she'd say, 'Why would I say that to you?' Like *I* was lying. I never answered her. Eventually I learned it was about her, not me. I sometimes thought she said things in anger and then 'forgot'. . . as though it was too painful for her to admit, so she buried it. But that didn't make it any easier." Even now, Linda admits: "I need more therapy in this area because it still hurts. It's distressing and maddening to me that I still give her so much power, that she's still capable of hurting me. The issue remains unresolved. I feel unloved and worthless when I think of how she treated me, and I think of how I still feel 'less than' when I hear her words. I always felt I had enough ego to survive but, as I went through menopause, these issues resurfaced and I feel vulnerable once again."

This pattern—a mother's active refusal to validate a daughter's perception of her experience—is, as Deborah Tannen writes, most heartbreaking and destructive when there is real physical and emotional abuse or, as Tannen puts it, "domestic terrorism." But Tannen also makes it clear that every daughter needs her mother to recognize her experience as real: "As bad as the experience of being abused as a child is, what is most damaging—and most tenacious—is having her own perceptions cast in doubt. . . . But even for women who, like me, were never physically assaulted, the desire to have a mother see things from our point of view, to acknowledge the world we lived in as we experienced it, is poignant and real." Mother need and the self are intertwined on myriad levels.

Vivian Gornick's now classic memoir of her relationship to her widowed mother, the aptly named *Fierce Attachments,* is perhaps the most articulate rendering of how a daughter's need for her mother's acknowledgment survives even in a relationship that threatens to smother her in its intensity. Gornick's crafted and bare prose transmits the fierceness of their mutual attachment: "My mother's way of 'dealing' with the bad times is to accuse me loudly and publicly of the truth. Whenever she sees me she says, 'You hate me. I know you hate me.'" The dynamic between them has the staccato rhythm of a version of ping-pong, played to the death: "Then she'll turn to me and plead, 'What did I do to you, you should hate me so?' I never answer. I know she's burning and I'm glad to let her burn. Why not? I am burning too."

But elsewhere, in what appears to be a mutual game of tit for tat, Gornick's need for her mother's acknowledgment becomes the soft under-belly primed for her mother's wounding. It takes place on a day filled with promise, when Gornick is on her way to meet her mother, filled with joy. She writes, "I'm flying. Flying! I want to give her some of this shiningness bursting in me, siphon into her my immense happiness at being alive. Just because she is my oldest intimate and at this moment I love everybody, even her." What happens instead is this: Her mother begins by ignoring Gornick's offer to tell her about her day, and begins haranguing her about whether she has enough money to pay her rent. Then she asks if Gor-nick will be paid for a review she wrote and ends by criticizing what her daughter is wearing. Gornick is utterly deflated, commenting with tart irony that her mother has a "gift" for saying the right thing at the right time. Her mother neither hears her irony nor does she realize how her words affect her daughter. Gornick continues: "She doesn't know I take her anxiety personally, feel annihilated by her depression. How can she know this? She doesn't even know I'm there. Were I to tell her that it's death to me, her not knowing that I'm there, she would stare at me out of her eyes crowding up with puzzled desolation, this young girl of seventy-seven, and she would cry angrily, 'You don't understand. You have never understood!' "

The importance of a mother's attunement to her daughter begins in infancy but, as Deborah Tannen and others make clear, continues through-out her life, albeit in different forms and to different degrees. Judith Viorst, in her book *Necessary Losses,* reminds us that when a mother is sensi-tively attuned, her responses tell us: " 'You are what you are. You are what you are feeling.' Allowing us to believe in our own reality. Persuading us that it is safe to expose our early fragile, beginning-to-grow true self." An attuned mother does this without thinking—responding in that instance when her baby looks up for a moment needing reassurance, permission, or validation, when she reaches for a toy or, later, is about to crawl or take her first step—and that maternal gesture of attunement is enough, Viorst reminds us, to allow us to "trust our own wish: 'Yes, I want this. I do.' "

In contrast, Viorst writes, when our mother responds by "misreading our needs, or replacing them with her own, we can't trust the truth of what we feel or do. Her lack of attunement may make us feel that we have been repudiated, assaulted. And we may then defend our true self by forming a false self." Some unloved daughters will develop false selves to present to their mothers and the world at large—compliant images reflecting what their mothers expect and need—while others will continue to struggle with their lack of connection to the women they've been born to. Either way, the engagement with her mother or the disengagement from her, will shape a daughter's sense of self.

Writer Dani Shapiro has plumbed her familial relationships in both memoirs and novels, but one of the most stirring descriptions of her daughterly self is contained in the beautifully titled essay "Not a Pretty Story," in which Shapiro explores her connection to and disconnection from her mother in the light of her decision to bear a child at the age of thirty-six and the devastating and rare disease her son suffers and ulti- mately recovers from. Her words will strike a specific but still familiar chord: "I had always wondered if she was really my mother—not just in that hateful childhood-fantasy way, but as a real ongoing question." Not even her mother's C-section scar—proof of their connection—is enough to completely convince her, given that Shapiro can only see the differences between them. She is fair and small-boned, while her mother is tall and dark. But more important, Shapiro tells us, "On a *soul* level it seemed impossible that this woman was my mother. All my life, I had had trouble looking her in the eye. Her presence brought me no comfort."

Shapiro cuts off her relationship to her mother when her son becomes deathly ill and she realizes she has a choice between saving her son and herself or allowing herself to be sucked into the vortex of the maternal relationship. Her child is saved, and reluctantly Shapiro lets her mother back into her life, only to see that the grandiosity and insensitivity of her mother's behavior had set up a pattern in which the more Shapiro with- drew, the more her mother "attacked."

And yet, as Shapiro writes, despite all that appears clear from the outside—her mother's need to dominate, to badger her daughter, to hold the center stage—the view from a daughter's perch is, perhaps inevitably, different. Shapiro confronts her feelings, her guilt and her anxieties, with painful tenderness: "Understand this: I never stopped caring about her. I hesitate to use the word 'love' but it's true. In a way, I did love her. She was my mother. She was inside me, a constant voice in my head. Sometimes, I thought her thoughts and was unable to distinguish them from my own."

That is the conundrum an unloved daughter faces. It comes down to a deceptively simple statement that carries with it the full weight of both our too-human need to be loved and accepted and our cultural conviction: "She was my mother."

IN EVERY RELATIONSHIP between a mother and a daughter, loving or not, it is the mother's voice that first defines the boundary of the self we call "I." As daughters, and as girls, and later women, we find our own voices in comparison and contrast to hers.

This process happens in ways that are both literal and symbolic. I remember trying on my mother's lipstick and clothing, both for dress-up and to try on for size what it was like being her. In retrospect, I think it was her power over me that I wanted to assimilate: I wanted to be big and loud like her, so I could shout back in her voice, not mine, and make *her* cry alone in her room. Even then I knew that I didn't want to be her, because I didn't admire her.

The game was very different when my own daughter played at being "Peggy Anne"—my given name, which no one has called me since my early childhood. Along with putting on my jewelry, makeup, clothes, and heels, it entailed a bit of acting in which I could see myself as she saw me. Her lowered voice would take on the inflections of mine and she'd wrinkle her forehead the way I do when she'd talk. Sometimes, as "Peggy Anne," she'd simply be "glamorous" with my shiny lipstick and eye shadow, my earrings dangling from her ears, strutting with her feet jammed into the fronts of my high heels. Other times, she'd "read" her doll a story, bake pretend cookies, or bandage an imaginary "boo-boo," but I might also hear her voice mimicking another tone with which she was familiar. The voice was firm and not exactly sweet, which is doubtless how she heard me and why she addressed her doll by her own given name, the formal name I use only when I'm irritated: "*No,* Alexandra, that's enough. Mommy is on the phone. Just wait until I'm finished."

Recently, I asked her whether she ever hears my voice in her head and she grew somewhat quiet and said, "Of course. But not all the time." I admit I didn't quite have the courage to ask her what that voice was saying. I fervently hope it's telling her that she's a simply splendid young woman and that it reassures her when she's in need. That's not what the mother voice in my head tells me, now or ever, of course. That voice is more muted now, all these years later—it's been twenty years since I heard her speak—but I would hardly call it mute. I haven't dreamed about my mother in ages, but in the last weeks, while I've been outlining this chapter and listening to other women's stories, it's not surprising that I have. My dream testifies to the power of the maternal voice.

In my dream, my mother and I are arguing; I am still small and she looms over me. We are shouting at each other, but I realize vaguely that we are in my home in Vermont, not the apartment where I grew up in New York. Our voices get louder and louder, and finally I scream "I hate you" at her. In the dream, she bursts into tears and I feel satisfied because I have finally made her cry. It's this moment that yanks me into wakefulness at 3 A.M. to find myself in bed next to my sleeping husband. I know immediately why the dream is important, because the reality is that I never saw my mother shed one tear over me—not once, not ever, not even when I made good on my promise never to speak to her again. And even after all these years, her tearlessness delivers a rebuke more stinging in some sense than anything she ever said or did to me. It tells me precisely how unimportant I was to her.

The absence of mother love leaves a void that may be filled with sometimes desperate and misguided attempts to mother the self. In her book

Motherless Daughters, Hope Edelman rightly connects the experience of daughters who've lost their mothers and those who never had their love: "This emptiness turns the unmothered into emotional hoarders. Accustomed to receiving less than they want or need, they try to take in as much as they can, as quickly as possible, as if excess today guarantees a stockpile for tomorrow. . . . Back-to-back relationships, overeating, overspending, alcoholism, drug abuse, shoplifting, overachieving—all are her attempts to fill that empty space, to mother herself, to suppress feelings of grief and loneliness, and to get the nurturing she feels she lost or never had."

In her memoir *Loose Girl,* writer Kerry Cohen recounts how, after her father left the family, her mother's neediness sucked the air out of life, leaving no emotional breathing room for her two daughters. Her mother literally abandoned her and her sister to fulfill her dream of becoming a doctor, leaving them in the custody of their father, a man who was lost himself and emotionally absent in every important sense. Cohen's "need to feel loved and less alone" led her to try to fill that need with boys, men, and sex. Cohen confirms Hope Edelman's observation by adding to the list of vain efforts to fill the inner space left by the absence of love, saying that her story "is the story of any girl who finds herself with pain and then makes a choice to do something about it. Some girls turn to anorexia. Others to alcohol, drugs, cutting, sports, ambition. I chose promiscuity." Not surprisingly, filling the emptiness in this way leads Cohen only to more emptiness in the end.

Not every daughter will take this path, but some will, sometimes with behaviors that aren't as public as drinking or sleeping around but that are still efforts to address their pain. One woman tells me that, by middle school, she had begun seeking out pressure points on her body, pushing so hard that her fingernails would sometimes pierce her skin. As she got older, she turned to cutting herself. She adds that it never felt destructive to her; it simply helped her feel less overwhelmed. She isn't alone. As the authors of *Bodily Harm* write, "self-injury represents a frantic attempt by someone with low coping skills to 'mother herself.' Operating without a paradigm of parental care, she feels alone and terrified, with no hope that a soothing presence will come 'make it all better.' Bodily care has been transformed into bodily harm; the razor blade becomes the wounding caregiver, a cold but available substitute for the embrace, kiss, or loving touch she truly desires." Remembering the pain of my own childhood, it isn't lost on me that when a daughter can't trust the mother to whom she's been entrusted, cutting may be a way of putting the pain in the control of someone you *can* trust: yourself.

An unloved daughter's relationship to food—the ultimate emblem of nurturance and, especially, maternal attention—may also be shaped by her connection to her mother. In her groundbreaking book, *The Hungry Self,* Kim Chernin asserted that disordered eating and female identity, most especially in the context of the mother-daughter relationship, were closely tied. One daughter explained to me how this worked in her family: "My mother expressed her love and attention through food. She was always cooking and baking, pressing food on other members of the family, without eating herself. But at the same time she always pushed me not to eat—my weight was always an issue for her—and so it was an extraordinarily mixed message. When I was anorexic, I felt in control of my life. Of course, when I came home and I saw my mother again, the first thing she said was 'We'll have to fatten you up.'" This daughter is sure her mother was also anorexic; certainly food and eating were potent symbolic activities in the household when she was growing up: "When I was anorexic, I think my mother saw my not eating as a rejection of her, because she gained acceptance through people eating her food." Of course, by not eating, this daughter had control of the dynamic—something she didn't have when she ate and was criticized for it.

Being in control emerges as a significant theme when daughters talk about potentially self-destructive behaviors developed in response to the hurtful or rejecting mother. In her book *When Food Is Love,* writer Geneen Roth—the daughter of a physically abusive mother and an emotionally absent father—explores the connection between disordered eating and armoring the self. She writes: "As children we have no resources, no power to make choices about our situations. We need our families for food, shelter, and love or else we will die. If we feel as though the pain around us is too intense and we cannot leave or change it, we will shut it off. We will—and do—switch our pain to something less threatening: a compulsion." But, as Roth explains, those compulsions, which begin as acts of self-protection, ultimately stand in the way of the things a daughter really needs. They stand in the way of self-revelation, self-worth, and love. She puts it plainly and simply: "It is not possible to be obsessed with food or anything else and be truly intimate with ourselves or another human being; there is simply not enough room." For some daughters, these behaviors will stand in the way of healing themselves.

In her book *Mothering Ourselves,* psychotherapist Evelyn S. Bassoff describes how daughters with nurturing and protective mothers are able "to absorb her healing spirit so it naturally becomes part of themselves—an internalized, or inner, mother on whom we can later call to quell the emotional distress that life entails." In contrast, unloved daughters do not have an inner mother to call on, and substitutes may become the only answer, as Dr. Bassoff notes: "For some, alcohol—which warms, fills, and anesthetizes the inner emptiness or aching—becomes the soothing mother. . . . For others, food represents the nourishing mother. And for others still, the sexual partner is compensation for the absent soothing mother."

A daughter's deep-seated need for her emotionally absent mother or even her mean one paradoxically coexists with the pain and suffering that same mother has inflicted on her. Nowhere is this paradox better illustrated than in Kathryn Harrison's disturbing and sparely written memoir *The Mother Knot*. Harrison's mother was only eighteen when she gave birth to her, not long after a hastily arranged marriage to her father; within a year her mother had divorced him, and her father was effectively banished from Harrison's life. Her mother's decision to have her—rather than seek an abortion—was an effort to break free of her own mother, a jealous woman who, Harrison says, thwarted her only daughter's every effort at independence. Harrison was to be the "surrogate" for her mother—a "hostage" left to her mother's mother, the grandmother who raised Harrison after the age of six. The memoir opens with Harrison, now the mother of three herself, once again struggling with anorexia and depression, years after her mother's death, and it becomes clear that Harrison is not yet free of her. Harrison returns to therapy, and perhaps the most extraordinary moment in the memoir takes place when the analyst looks up and says simply, "Your mother was a sadist." The terrible push-pull of the situation—the way the need for mother love stands in equipoise with pain and suffering—plays itself out as Harrison returns in the next session to defend her mother.

She challenges her analyst's assessment, saying, among other things, "Anyway, doesn't sadism imply conscious cruelty? A conscious intent to inflict cruelty? Whatever she did, my mother didn't . . . she didn't set out to damage me. Whatever happened, happened in the moment—it wasn't premeditated." Finally, Harrison comes to see what she has done, how she has "embraced" her mother and "Remade her. Inside myself. Refused to let her go." Finally, the therapist asks Harrison why she can't let go of her mother—her enemy and adversary, after all. Her answer resonates, illuminating the central paradox of the unloving mother and the unloved daughter and letting us glimpse, through one woman's specific experience, how the lack of mother love and the eternal quest for it can actually become the bedrock for a daughter's identity: "Who would I be without my mother? All my life I've understood myself as her child, as the child who strove to make her love me. Without her, there'd be all this . . . this room left over inside." It is at this moment that Harrison comes to see the choice before her: to let go of her mother and her quest for that mother's love so that she can hold to the love she does have in her life, that of her husband and three children.

Harrison's example is extreme—as are the circumstances of her childhood and young adulthood—but the way in which mother need and mother loss or deprivation can become a central part of a daughter's identity isn't. Because the experiences of early and later childhood are internalized—in what Dr. Stephen Bank has called "a secret inscription" or "template" for relationships—breaking away from the mother line will be easier said than done for many daughters.

But it *can* be done. Not always, of course, and not always completely—but it can be done nonetheless.

COMFORT ZONES AND PERSISTENT PATTERNS: GOING BACK TO THE WELL

In no area of life more than that of relationship do we live what we know and do the unexamined "secret inscriptions" of our childhoods play a more important role. The daughter of a loving and attuned mother will learn about love, trust, and reliability not in the abstract as ideas but as experience lived and emotional knowledge extrapolated from experience. She will learn that a raised voice doesn't signal a loss of love or safety, for example; she will have a reasonable expectation that her mother will listen to her with attention on most occasions; she won't be afraid when her mother drops her off at school or some other unfamiliar place, because she already knows her mother will be coming back. She will learn the importance of touch, of physical proximity, and the sheer joy of being known.

The daughter of an unloving mother absorbs other lessons, and what she learns instead has all the staying power of its positive counterparts. It's the process of unlearning—of finding a way to get to a different place after she has moved out of her original family into the larger world—that presents the greatest challenge to the unmothered daughter. Paradoxically, the impulse to recreate the emotional circumstances of our childhoods is very strong, so it's not unusual—even if it seems highly counterintuitive—for a daughter in flight from her mother's meanness or unloving nature to find her mother's counterparts in friends and lovers alike.

It's ironic, of course, that these familiar "comfort zones" offer no real emotional comfort but feel "comfortable" nonetheless. Various perspectives on the psychology of human relationships yield different insights into the phenomenon of the comfort zone. What Freud called a "repetition compulsion," Judith Viorst explains in simpler terms: "It impels us to do

again and again what we have done before, to attempt to restore an earlier
state of being. It impels us to transfer the past—our ancient longings, our
defenses against those longings—onto the present. Thus whom we love
and how we love are revivals—unconscious revivals—of early experience,
even when revival brings us pain."

Seen through the prism of Internal Family Systems Therapy, which
understands personality not as unitary but as made up of multiple parts,
what I am calling a "comfort zone" owes its existence to the needs of a part
or parts of the self. Richard C. Schwartz, Ph.D., argues that, while we tend
to think of the "self" as monolithic and coherent, each of us contains within
us a multiplicity of parts of the self, which may act in harmony or dishar-
mony. He writes: "If a child is told, verbally or nonverbally, that he is or
she is of little value, young parts of the child organize their beliefs around
that premise. They become desperate for redemption in the eyes of the
person who gave these messages. Thereafter these parts carry the burden
of worthlessness, which makes them believe that no one can love them—a
belief they will maintain no matter what feedback is received from others."
As Dr. Schwartz explains it, this feels like a "theft" of self-esteem, and
the child, in order to survive, tries desperately to get that self-esteem from
the very person who took it away. Ironically, the person responsible for
the "theft" becomes the "redeemer." In this way, seeking the comfort zone
becomes an operative pattern in the adult's life: "These burdened young
parts exert a powerful influence over the person's intimate relationships
as they constantly seek redemption—the lifting of what feels like a curse
of unlovability. They will return to the person who stole their self-esteem
in this quest, or they will find someone who resembles that person." This
is, of course, another form of what I have called "going back to the well."
In addition, Schwartz asserts, other parts of the child's self are "likely to
take on the qualities of the person who stole his or her self-esteem and
sense of safety." These become "inner critics" or "moralizers"—taking on
the role of the original outside authority. For some daughters, this may be
the part of herself that tells her she's worthless or unlovable, despite all
she has achieved.

More recent explorations of how early attachments shape adult lives explain the dynamics in important ways that can deepen our understanding. As discussed in the first chapter of this book, Mary Ainsworth used the Strange Situation to categorize infants' attachment to their mothers or caregivers as secure (when a mother is consistent and attuned), avoidant (when a mother is unattuned, rejecting, and often intrusive), or anxious-ambivalent (when a mother is inconsistent in her responsiveness and attunement). Later research by Mary Main found that how a child was attached was highly predictive of how that child would parent when she or he was an adult. Securely attached children would, as adults, raise securely attached children, while insecurely attached children, whether avoidant or anxious/ambivalent, would, without intervention, grow up to be parents who would, in turn, raise insecurely attached children.

Research in the last two decades of the twentieth century expanded to look at the way early attachments predicted adult romantic involvement and other close relationships, as well as other measures of psychological coping in life, such as the handling of stress, conflict resolution, and the like. It turns out that how securely or insecurely attached we are as infants and children is also highly predictive of how we see ourselves *and* others. Not surprisingly, these "mental models"—the basic views of the self and the other, along with the established expectations each of us has for the self and the other—will permeate all relationships, if left unexamined or not replaced with earned security. For some unloved daughters, these expectations will put them on a path that is both repetitive of their childhood experiences and, on another level, confirms all their worst feelings of unworthiness. This is not to say that a daughter is necessarily destined to repeat her earliest experiences; she isn't. But science does illuminate why for some unloved daughters—myself among them—the model of attachment and the unfilled needs of our early experiences will spill over into our first efforts to find love and connection in adult life.

How does this work? Psychologists Cindy Hazan and Phillip Shaver first proposed a connection between early attachments in childhood and romantic relationships in adulthood, using the three classifications drawn from Bowlby and Ainsworth, i.e., secure, avoidant, and anxious/ambivalent. They hypothesized that the experience of love by a securely attached person would be characterized by "trust, friendship, and positive emotions." In contrast, they expected that for avoidant adults—who as children experienced rejection, unresponsiveness, or intrusion from their mothers—love would be "marked by fear of closeness and lack of trust." For adults whose earliest attachments were anxious/ambivalent—the situation where the child is never sure which Mommy is going to show up, the loving or the unloving one—they expected an experience of "love as a preoccupying, almost painfully exciting struggle to merge with another person." What they found was that "avoidant" lovers were "characterized by fear of intimacy, emotional highs and lows, and jealousy." Anxious/ambivalent lovers, on the other hand, reacted to their partners as they had to their mothers, who were sometimes there and sometimes not; not surprisingly, their love involved "obsession, desire for reciprocation, emotional highs and lows, extreme sexual attraction, and jealousy."

In later research, which partly draws on Hazan and Shaver's work, psychologist Kim Bartholomew proposed that there were, in fact, four rather than three prototypes of adult behaviors in close relationships. She characterized secure adults as having both a positive self-model and a positive model of others. Their sense of self-worth is internalized, and they have flexible coping mechanisms since they are comfortable with others, warm, and affectionate. Both the friendships and romantic relationships of securely attached people are "characterized by intimacy, mutual respect, and closeness." Bartholomew went on to expand the categories of insecurely attached adults to three, making important distinctions among them. I have found these distinctions useful not only for understanding what constitutes any individual woman's comfort zone—including my own—but also for understanding why these patterns of relating are so hard to change and how they connect to the coping strategies of infancy and childhood. That said, it's important to remember that not every individual will fit neatly into each category; in fact, in one study conducted by Kim Bartholomew and Leonard Horowitz, their subjects reported a mix of tendencies "both across time and within and across relationships."

In Bartholomew's model, the first "insecurely attached" group is called "preoccupied" and corresponds to the anxious/ambivalent attachment in childhood. While the preoccupied daughter has a negative view of herself, she looks to others for validation and acceptance since she has a positive view of them. She wants relationships and friendships, often with intensity and desperation, even though that desire coexists with feelings of insecurity and worthlessness. These daughters are both needy and demanding in relationships—Bartholomew notes that their relationships are "punctuated by emotional extremes, including anger, passion, jealousy, and possessiveness"—and they tend to be clingy and dependent. Not surprisingly, because preoccupied women need the validation a relationship provides them, they are likely to be involved in one romantic relationship or another, often bouncing from one to the next, and tend to have difficulty breaking off a relationship, no matter how problematic.

Bartholomew's innovation was to look at "avoidant" individuals and to split them into two different categories: "dismissing" and "fearful." It's the latter designation—"fearful"—that was new, and Bartholomew distinguished between these individuals because, while they share a negative model of others, their self model is distinctly different. While fearfully avoidant individuals actually want social contact and intimacy, they "experience pervasive interpersonal distrust and fear," most notably a fear of rejection. These are rejected children who, Bartholomew notes, "could tend to conclude that others are uncaring and available and, perhaps, in addition, that they themselves are unlovable." These are daughters who, because of their negative view of self, tend to come across as "insecure, hesitant, vulnerable, and self-conscious." They both want and fear intimacy at once, and worry openly about never finding an emotional connection. In relationships, they tend to be both passive and highly dependent; they avoid conflict and have difficulty communicating.

On the other hand, the "dismissing" avoidant appears, on the surface at least, to have a positive model of self along with a negative view of others. Bartholomew explains how this is also an adaptive behavior derived from early childhood experience: "A way of maintaining a positive self-image in the face of rejection by attachment figures is to distance oneself and develop a model of the self as fully adequate and hence invulnerable to the negative feelings which might activate the attachment system. . . . Over time, the strategies used to defend against the awareness of attachment needs become so ingrained as to operate automatically and largely outside of awareness." As a result, these "dismissing" avoidants steer clear of close relationships, may assert vehemently that relationships aren't important, and, not surprisingly, may put their emphasis on other aspects of life such as work or hobbies or other achievements. Bartholomew notes that the dismissing individual may come across "as cool (or cold and arrogant, in the extreme), matter-of-fact, rational, unemotional, and aloof." Bartholomew further notes that the friendships of dismissing individuals usually aren't based on closeness or disclosure but on the much more impersonal plane of shared activities and interests.

The romantic relationships of dismissing daughters or sons aren't altogether different from their friendships. These women and men remain outside of the emotional connection in a very real sense, staying less involved than their partners and steering clear of emotional exchanges, both positive and negative. Hence, they tend to avoid conflict. While they appear to be "in" a relationship—even a long-term and stable one—there are also obvious ways in which they are disengaged from it. Bartholomew notes that it's "the approach to and quality of these relationships, rather than their presence or absence, which is critical." She also points out that, while dismissing individuals appear to feel positive about themselves, on an unconscious level they feel negative, and thus "their adoption of a detached stance toward others is a way of defending a fragile sense of self from potential hurt by others."

The research on adult romantic relationships and their connection to early experiences in childhood can help us understand why these patterns of attachment may continue to assert themselves in a daughter's life. Sometimes the patterns are relatively transparent, though they may exist in more complicated variations and not always easily recognizable ways. Science suggests that these patterns of relating may persist for many reasons. For example, people may act in ways that evoke specific behaviors from others, and then go on to interpret those behaviors in ways that fit or validate their own internal models. Alternatively, we may select partners—unconsciously—who are likely to confirm both our internal models and our expectations of how relationships or people "are." Or we may act so as to elicit responses from our partners that, again, confirm internal models. Real-life examples of how the comfort zone may work in a daughter's life reveal a range of possibilities.

One daughter e-mails me with all the stunning clarity of twenty-twenty hindsight, reflecting on her twenty-six-year marriage, which ended in divorce: "I still have issues with feeling capable and doing things right. Unfortunately, I married my mother and was never able to feel competent in my husband's eyes either. I also never really felt loved by him in the same way I didn't feel loved by my mother."

My own history of intimate relationships included patterns that will be familiar to some unmothered daughters. I fell in love for the first time at the age of fourteen with a boy three years older. Passionate, tumultuous, and completely inappropriate—we were both still children, but neither we nor our parents understood that—the enormity of his needs matched my own. I needed him to love me or, better put, to show me that I was love-worthy, and that, of course, was precisely what he couldn't do. He needed me for his own still developing sense of self and manhood, which involved conquest, sex, and love to fill his own emptiness. Our relationship—which stretched out over some years and continued to haunt me (and him, as it happened) for years after—had all the hallmarks of two young people desperately trying to run away from what their families didn't give them and hoping to find and warm themselves in the heat of love and romance. In truth, neither of us realized that we'd chosen, with unwitting but unerring accuracy, the one person who wouldn't and couldn't give either of us what we so desperately wanted. On the surface, he was handsome, funny, smart, charming; inside, he was obsessive, self-absorbed, and incapable of seeing me whole. Feminized, all of those descriptions probably fit me equally. While he looked like an escape from my mother, the way he connected to me reiterated all the patterns of my relationship to her.

So it continued throughout my late teens and twenties as I moved, pretty much seamlessly, from one relationship to another—the pattern associated with the "preoccupied" category of attachment, perhaps. While all the men in my life were different from each other in highly visible ways—how they looked and thought, what they did for a living and for fun, even how old they were—they shared one common denominator: they made me feel needy, unloved, unlistened to, unseen. The more they withheld, the more I cajoled or begged for their attention and the more unhappy I became. I rejected the men who actually were able to offer me something else—real intimacy and caring—out of hand, although when I did, it was usually for other reasons, such as lack of ambition or drive. Most frustrating of all, while I understood the loop I was in intellectually, I had absolutely no way of functioning in a different way emotionally.

That demonstrates in fullness the power my internalized mother still had over me, even though in the physical world I was an emancipated, independent, and relatively successful adult over whom my mother had no control. In the end, it would take an experience with a man in which the comfort zone of emotional neglect and abuse threatened to become physically realized to make me understand that this was a path I had to abandon to save my life, both literally and emotionally. I know now that I am not the only daughter who has gotten that wake-up call.

THE INTERNAL MOTHER: REMOTHERING THE SELF

In her book *Women Who Run with the Wolves,* Jungian psychoanalyst Clarissa Pinkola Estés writes that all daughters have an internal mother, a "legacy" from their "actual" mothers and other influences. This internal mother is an aspect of her psyche "that acts and responds in a manner identical to a woman's experience in childhood with her own mother. Further, this internal mother is made from not only the experience of the personal mother but also other mothering figures in our lives as well as the images held out as the good mother and the bad mother in the culture at the time of our childhoods." Her observation underscores how cultural perceptions—the myths of motherhood surrounding us—also become internalized and shape how we absorb, think about, and ultimately judge actual experiences with our own mothers and other "mothering" figures—relatives, friends, teachers, therapists, and the like. In her analysis of the possible range of "internal" mothers, Pinkola Estés is quick to point out that, while each of us inherits an internal mother, it can be revised, strengthened, and even dismantled if necessary.

Pinkola Estés's analysis of the archetypal internal mother adds another layer of understanding, albeit from a very different point of view, because it connects a daughter's experience with her actual mother to the effect the internal mother has on her psyche and well-being. Keep in mind too that every mother of a daughter has her own internal mother in her identity as a daughter. These observations can help us understand the generational links and shed light on why our mothers treated us as they did.

The first archetype is the "ambivalent" mother—one who sees only her daughter's "otherness" and the ways she is different from herself and perhaps also others, because of her own expectations. Internalized, this ambivalent mother can leave a daughter who may "find herself giving in too easily; she may find herself afraid to take a stand, to demand respect, to seek her right to do it, learn it, live it in her own way." The second, the "collapsed" mother may be a woman who has lost sight of herself, or may be a narcissist who "feels entitled to be a child herself." Internalized, the "collapsed" mother becomes a voice that doesn't support a sense of self-worth, or keeps a daughter in "exile." The third archetype is what Pinkola Estés calls the "child-mother" or "unmothered mother," which she also identifies as the most "common kind of fragile mother." This mother is the one we've met most often in these pages, even though we've looked at her in different, perhaps more unforgiving, ways. Unmothered herself, she is unable to become what Pinkola Estés calls the "radiant" mother both she—and the culture—expect. This "child-mother" doesn't have the support to teach her mothering skills in our culture and she's unable to support or guide her children; in addition, as Pinkola Estés says, "Without realizing it, the child-mother tortures her offspring with various forms of destructive attention and in some cases lack of useful attention."

Finally, Pinkola Estés addresses those daughters who have experienced "truly destructive mothering." Of those she counsels: "Of course that tune cannot be erased but it can be eased. It cannot be sweetened up but it can be rebuilt, strongly and properly, now."

What Pinkola Estés suggests is that "the remedy is gaining mothering for one's young internal mother." Relationships between women, she writes, can accomplish this—"through bloodlines, through friendships, through relationship of mentors and students, analyst and analysand."

With those words of encouragement in mind, we'll turn to the stories daughters have told me.

WHEN SUSAN MARRIED at the age of twenty-one, it seemed as though she had escaped from the dynamics of her own family, one in which problems and feelings were never discussed and never resolved. As the eldest daughter, Susan had become the caretaker in the family as her parents' marriage deteriorated and her mother became depressed and later hospitalized. Susan was effectively left motherless at a young age, burdened with the care of her two younger sisters, with no one there for her save a brilliant but emotionally distant father. Looking ahead, marriage and adulthood seemed filled with possibility. "I was looking for a healthy spouse, and he was a child psychologist, and I thought, 'What's healthier than that?' I also thought he would make a good husband and father. My parents never argued anything through, and I really thought that with him, my life would be different. We would talk, communicate. He was adoring, gave me presents, and it was all very enticing. I thought he would give me what I wanted most—all the things I never had growing up. "

All these years later, Susan now realizes that no one—not a husband or a friend or anyone else—can actually give us back what we lacked as children. At the beginning of the marriage, the discussions she and her husband had were "exciting" and constructive; they resolved issues and kept on the same page. But over time their arguments became more and more angry and destructive. "At the time, I couldn't see that I had chosen someone with a violent temper," Susan says. "I had been so hungry for the communication that I hadn't had in my childhood that I didn't see all the anger mixed in with what I thought was openness." Susan and her husband went on to have two daughters. Over time, her role in the marriage took on aspects that were very familiar: "I felt the same isolation I'd felt growing up. Once again I became the fixer, the 'good little girl' who took care of everyone, feeling at the same time that no one was taking care of me." After twelve years of marriage—and a huge leap of faith in herself and concluded she deserved better—Susan left the marriage and set about reinventing herself and raising her two small daughters.

At sixty-eight, she reflects on those early years, reminding me that if a situation feels "familiar," it is likely that "it is because we experienced it in our family. Notice that the word *familiar* contains the word *family* within it." When we talk about her marriage and how it proved to be familiar in unexpected ways, she is remarkably clear: "I was looking on the outside to get what I needed on the inside. And, of course, that is the wrong place to look." When I ask her how she stilled the voice of the mother within— and in her case the voice was her need for an available mother—she tells me about her therapist, who was loving, affirming, and, most important, acknowledging of her thoughts and feelings. There was a breakthrough moment when her therapist said simply and plainly that Susan was an "abused" child. Susan protested, pointing out that she had never been hit or hurt, and her therapist explained it wisely and plainly, saying that the kind of abuse she experienced was actually harder to deal with because there were no bruises as evidence. Those words freed Susan to trust her own experience and begin to acknowledge her inner self who needed to be mothered. She tells me, "I have finally learned to give myself what my mother wasn't able to give me, what I needed then. I am compassionate and understanding of myself when that part screams out to me. I look at the younger part of me in the mirror and tell her what she always needed her mother to say. I'm able to express the emotion and feel the support I need." Over time, Susan has filled that childhood void, and her world now reflects that fullness back to her. She has been in a communicative and supportive relationship for many years.

The daughter of a hypercritical mother, Linda has long been married to a man who is accepting of her—even though they have very different styles of relating. John, she tells me, is a man who doesn't easily share his feelings and tends not to react emotionally—the legacy of his own difficult childhood during which he learned that keeping silent was safer than being reactive. At times this has been frustrating for Linda, whose childhood left her needy for overt and expressed responsiveness, but it has also given her the room she didn't have during her childhood to be herself: "He accepts me for who I am, and I suppose we could have a better relationship if I could let my guard down and accept the love he has for me. I sometimes jump through hoops to get a response from him, and it's been hard for me to understand that his way of expressing his love for me is different from my own. He shows me that he loves me by doing, not by confronting or demanding, as I sometimes have." Linda's sensitivity to not being heard or seen—her own childhood legacy—sometimes gets in the way of seeing how John supports her in fundamental ways. If the emotional side of life belongs to Linda in their marriage, it is John who provides the supportive structure that allows her to be herself—in fullness, with both her strengths and weaknesses in view. Over time, she tells me, their relationship has become a partnership in many important senses: "We respect each other, something we each felt was lacking in our parents' marriages, and we've been able to look at our differences as pluses. I have what he lacks and vice versa. And I am learning to be more like him—patient, kind, and accepting."

An important romantic relationship can also be the mirror in which the unmothered or undermothered daughter first sees herself truly, even though the effects of childhood experience may still linger. Georgia, reflecting on how "some wounds really do heal and fade away with time and new experiences," puts it this way: "For years I kept bringing men into my life who were communicating the message that I was okay as a girlfriend but not as someone to whom anyone would commit, to start a life or a family. Through these relationships I kept sending myself the message that I really wasn't worth it. Then I met the man who became my husband, and for the first time I felt that someone 'got' me and that I was understood. I saw that I had finally brought a sign into my life that I was deserving of the best. Yet even in this really good marriage, I see how I can revert at times to an inner place of not daring to be me, feeling small again. Then I consciously go back to events and instances and try to show up differently, to provide a place of healing for the child inside who doesn't want to make herself feel small any longer. Now it's up to me to notice it, to provide myself with healing."

LOOKING FOR THE WAY OUT:
LEARNING TO MOTHER THE SELF

Almost forty years ago, at the age of twenty-one, I find myself back in New York, going to graduate school at Columbia and lying on the couch in my first therapist's office. I tell him that I'm here to try to reclaim myself from my mother's grasp. Since I know no one who has a mother like mine, I'm also here to find out if it's my fault. I suspect that I may be somehow unworthy.

He is famous, the author of several acclaimed books, though, at a glance, he looks more friendly than imposing. He is round and shorter than I, with blue eyes that twinkle, and he always wears a tie and a jacket, sometimes a tweed one with suede patches at the elbow. I know nothing about him, not even how old he is, although I know the apartment he lives in lies just beyond the door behind his desk and I have read his book about dreams and symbols. The furniture is solid, all dark wood and leather, and the walls of his office are lined with books, making it feel more like lying in a library than anything else. That makes me feel safer than I otherwise might, even with all the boxes of Kleenex on every surface within my reach.

He sits behind my head, silent, and, at the beginning the process makes me feel strangely disembodied. My words, my stories about my mother, tumble out of my mouth without evoking any comment; only when I pause do I hear the faint scratching of his pen on the notepad he has in his lap. Beyond my feet, framed by a large picture window, I can see the Hudson River, and I imagine my memories floating like so many balloons over the water, sailing high over the crags of the Palisades, then scattering over little New Jersey towns I've never visited.

This goes on for what seems like weeks and weeks. Pain and anger flow out over my edges into the quiet, vying for his attention. He speaks only when I fall silent, and then only to prompt me with a question or two: "Is that your earliest memory of your mother?" or "How did that make you feel?" I tell him I feel lonely and alone—motherless, fatherless, anchorless. Every time he calls me by name, I react with surprise, both because he says so little and because the me lying on the couch, the one who's letting the words out of the place they've been so tightly held for so long, doesn't feel like me. Leaving his office—going back to my own little apartment and the present of my life, which still includes my mother even though I don't live with her—I feel lighter, but not better. A large part of me is still defensive, and deeply worried that I'm to blame.

Then, on an autumn day so bright that the Hudson looks like molten gold, he speaks and, to my amazement, his words rush out into the air, over my shoulders, and into the void inside of me: "Hasn't it ever occurred to you, Peg, that your mother is unspeakably cruel and punitive—perhaps even crazy? Think about it for a minute: What could a three- or four-year-old child possibly do to deserve that treatment? What are you saying or doing now that justifies the terrible things she continues to say to you, the ways in which she makes you feel awful about yourself?" Without meaning to, my middle rises and my knees jackknife, leaving me upright on the couch, gasping for air, my tears streaming.

He has thrown me a lifeline. It's probably just as well that, in the revelation and relief of the moment, I do not yet know how steep the walls of the pit are, and how fragile the rope.

SOME DAUGHTERS, like Susan, have learned over time to mother themselves, to fill in the hole or void the lack of attentive mother love left in them as young children and girls. Others discover a way of rewriting the narratives of their lives through therapy or close relationships—establishing the "earned" security that permits them to go forward more whole, more healed than before. Elizabeth writes to me: "After a lot of therapy and self-examination, I realize that I am not who my mother thinks I am. I have worked and strived to take care of my own needs, cultivate my relationships, and tell people when I need help. I am not expecting myself to be perfect." Still others begin to mother themselves with the help of other mother figures. Some daughters, like myself, only really begin to self-mother when they become mothers themselves, by boldly writing a new maternal narrative for the future and thus giving the maternal story of the past an entirely new context. Alissa, who never felt safe in her childhood, tells me that, while the child within her still doesn't fully trust other adults, that same child within—the one who loves babies and children and is a caretaker—is an ally in mothering, and she has learned to use that inner child to help her chart the waters of motherhood.

Some daughters embark on this journey by cutting their mothers out of their lives—literally separating themselves from the physical maternal voice—but many do not. Each story of healing is unique, though the broad outlines of daughters' stories often share much in common.

What does it mean, ultimately, to "self-mother"? I ask therapist Françoise Bourzat whether she thinks my title for this chapter is accurate, whether it's really a question of "stilling the voice of the mother within" or something more complicated than that. Her answer illuminates the journey of the unloved or unmothered daughter from another point of view, that of the therapist: "When a child doesn't receive love from her mother as a young child, the mirroring of her very existence is absent. Safety is missing, and there's a sense of withdrawal that has to do with being alive. A mother's love is what we are wired to need in times of hunger, loneliness, in physical and emotional crisis. It's in our mammal genes to be related to and comforted by the presence of the being who brought us into this world. If that is missing, the hardest part of healing has to do with feeling worthy of existence. Looking for love outside becomes a quest that never ends, unless the focus gets turned inward. Even though we must receive a mother's love to know what love is, we all have it within ourselves to experience the feelings of love and connectedness as part of the human tribe. What is most difficult for the unloved daughter is to get to love herself, to feel beautiful, lovable, and good enough for herself. It is a long and step-by-step healing that builds upon itself slowly so the strength is self-generated."

Bourzat tells me that the ability to self-mother comes out of connecting to that maternal voice in a new and different way: "The daughter has to spend time with that voice, to learn to listen to it, truly hear it. She has to acknowledge that it triggers anger, frustration, even rage in her, because giving her ugly emotions a place allows her the opportunity to be 'in relation' to the voice. She will find herself getting fed up with the voice, wanting to push it away and begin reclaiming a sense of self. Once a daughter has listened to it long enough, she begins to see herself in relation to it, which will bring out the hurt child in her as well as her rightful expectations and birthright." In this new relationship, the daughter no longer "identifies" with the maternal voice but is separated from it, and in therapy the relationship now has three aspects: the maternal voice, the daughter as child, and the daughter as adult. This relationship yields a dialogue in which the internal voice says "its nasty things," the child listens and feels, and the adult daughter defends and re-parents the child. The adult daughter can truly listen to the voice, separating out what might be of value—warnings and concerns—from what isn't, such as jealousy and overprotectiveness. In the process, the internalized voice is out, dealt with, "de-dramatized," and its mythic power dissolved. As Bourzat puts it, "Being with the voice—listening to it—is key to unraveling the power it holds over a daughter's psyche." It doesn't matter whether we call it "stilling" or "making peace" with the maternal voice within. It's getting there that matters.

COMING TO A NEW UNDERSTANDING: EARNED ATTACHMENT

An unloved daughter's past experience can't be expunged or erased, of course, but it is nonetheless true—miraculous, even—that our own supremely flexible human brains can actually be "rewired" through new understanding. Advances in brain science tell us that the old expression is literally true: we *can* change our minds. By making sense of our childhood experiences—going from what Daniel Siegel and Mary Hartzell call an "incoherent" or insecure functioning of the mind to a more "coherent" or secure functioning—the patterns of connection in our own brains can actually be altered on the level of neuron activity and synaptic connections. The old habits of mind—the filters through which we react to situations and emotional encounters and respond to the emotional cues and gestures of others—can actually be changed, freeing us to make different choices than the ones bequeathed to us by our childhoods. By making sense of our experiences as child-daughters, we can bring those "secret inscriptions" and unconscious repetitions out into the open and choose a different path.

When those "secret inscriptions" stay secret, what Selma Fraiberg called the "ghosts in the nursery" move right in and take over. Most unloved daughters can only guess at what their mothers were thinking or feeling, uncensored, at the time we were born. But in her unflinching and well-written memoir, *The Three of Us,* Julia Blackburn describes how her mother treated her as a sister, a confidante, and ultimately a sexual rival. We learn that this relationship has its beginning literally at Julia's birth, because when Julia is about to have her own child, her mother gives her the diary she kept when Julia was born. It is, to be sure, nothing short of extraordinary—excruciating and painful in all of its detail: " . . . as soon as my mother looked at the little creature lying beside her, something from her own troubled past kicked into action. She hadn't given birth to a new life, but instead had given birth to herself. . . . And when it was time to feed the baby, any feelings of love and protectiveness were swept to one side by what she called a *wave of ambivalence* and she was overcome by resentment at the demands that were being made of her." Her mother dreams of taking the wrong child home from the hospital, of drowning the baby in the bathtub and going out to a party. Her mother actually sees her infant as an antagonist—responsible for her inability to paint—and as a critic, one who sees through "her pretense of love." Julia doesn't read the journal when her mother gives it to her, but when she does, this is what she writes: "I wonder if she sat down and studied the contents of this strange and sad account of what motherhood meant to her before passing the notebook on to me. I think not, but perhaps what I really mean is—I hope not."

In the next chapter, we'll look at how unmothered daughters work to become the mothers they didn't have, and the challenges each of them faces as unique individuals—even with the nursery windows flung wide open, with the sunlight illuminating the corners of the past, dispelling the ghosts at hand.

· Six ·

Turning the Wheel:
Mothering the Next Generation

NOT EVERY UNLOVED DAUGHTER WILL GO ON TO BECOME A mother herself. That choice is, of course, deeply personal for every woman, but for a daughter who has had a damaged history with her mother, it may be framed differently than it is for her well-loved counterpart. Sarah, who grew up as an only child with a controlling, withholding, and unloving mother, says her decision evolved over time: "I didn't begin with an interest in children. I didn't play with dolls as a child and I never babysat when I was older. It was clear to me, even at a very young age, that being my mother didn't make my mother happy, and so the idea of being someone else's mother myself didn't seem even remotely desirable. And given my childhood, I did know that, on some level at least, I lacked the skills to raise another human being well. I was afraid of hurting and being hurt. But that wasn't the whole story or even the main story as I told it. For a long time the economics of how I lived my life as an artist gave me permission not to have a child. How could I have a baby without health insurance, after all? And then there was the 'how' of how I lived my life. How could I travel if I had a child? My choice was complicated, and I don't think it came down to one thing or reason but, in the end, for me to be myself, to do what I wanted to do, I needed to be without children." Nonetheless, now fifty-two, Sarah has worked with and nurtured other women's children throughout her working life. She has taught, mentored, and counseled older girls and young women for decades.

For some daughters, becoming a mother constitutes a leap of faith, one that can be both exhilarating and unnerving at once, because the faith involved is belief in the self—often the very aspect of her identity most affected by her relationship to her own mother. For some, taking that leap requires time and deliberation, making sure that the old wounds are sufficiently healed and the new patterns of seeing and connecting established so that the past will not be repeated. For others, deliberation followed by an active choice helps to establish emotional clarity. Several daughters I interviewed aborted first pregnancies, even though they were already with the men who would father their children later in time, because of hesitation and doubt about whether they would mother as their mothers had. Some decided in their twenties that they wouldn't have children, only to reverse themselves in their thirties, even in their late thirties, as I did, often with the active encouragement of their husbands. Then again, some daughters always knew that they wanted children; the only question was when. For some daughters, becoming a mother entails nothing less than an act of self-invention.

Elizabeth, fifty, now the mother of an adolescent girl and boy, confides, "I was skeptical about the 'joys of motherhood.' I remember discussing not having children with my husband, and his answer struck a deep chord. He said, 'I can't imagine *not* having children and our world without them.' Now I would say that parenting has been the most rewarding, most challenging, and fulfilling 'job' I have ever had." Not surprisingly, the support of a husband or partner is mentioned by most women as crucial to their choice, even if that relationship ultimately foundered or failed. One woman, the daughter of a distant and critical mother and mother of two daughters herself, confided: "I actively considered having my tubes tied in my twenties, but my husband opposed the idea. At that time I probably would have gone through with it. But then, when I was in my early thirties, I wanted kids and had my first several years later. For whatever reason, mothering came naturally to me. I didn't read books about parenting. Even when my daughters were young, I treated them like people. Someone said to me that she never heard me complain about my girls, and I think that's true. At one point during our very extended couples' counseling, I realized that my kids proved to me that I could love fully. That didn't happen in my marriage, and that was very validating." But she adds: "There were definitely—and continue to be—experiences that I wasn't prepared for, didn't know how to counsel, or even things I did that frustrated or made my daughters angry. And often I felt like I was too close to them and the boundaries got difficult and blurred—moving back and forth between parent and friend."

Once a daughter chooses to become a mother, being pregnant may involve another confrontation—symbolically or sometimes literally—with the mother she had. Alissa, the daughter of an abusive mother who died when she was eighteen, is now the mother of three daughters, all in their twenties. This is the moment of confrontation she remembers, a symbolic one: "I was five months pregnant, and one day I just absolutely freaked. There I was pregnant with a *baby* that was going to need me to love it and love it well, and what if I wasn't me after all and I turned out to be my mother? I couldn't live with the thought of that. I sought out one of my grad school professors, a woman I really loved, who was both a mother and grandmother. I was twenty-two, and I ended up telling her about my fears and a little bit about my childhood, and then I just broke down in tears. It was a huge release. Anyway, she just sat there with me in her VW van and listened and, at the very end, said, 'Well, one thing you don't have to worry about is this: you aren't your mother.' And a bell went off in my head: I *wasn't* my mother. She helped me so much, and then went on to set me up with counseling. I met every week with a kind woman in her fifties, and she mainly told me stories about how being a mother was hard at times and wonderful at others and how she hoped I would have both girls and boys because they were so very different. I don't think I talked much because I couldn't—it was too scary. But she was so comforting, and her warm, kind, caring self helped me a lot."

The confrontation between an unloved or hurt daughter and her mother—whether she is physically in her life or not—may intensify as the daughter experiences motherhood herself. When her daughter was born, Alissa had another revelation, one that both separated her from and connected her to her mother at once: "With Jenny, all there was was love. I used to snuggle with her the first days and months of her life and just be blown away that it was possible to love someone so much. I happily gave up ideas of working until work found me later. I was so devoted to Jenny— I didn't know until then that I was such a devoted person. I had always been a free spirit, but having someone to love changed everything for me, someone who needed me in ways so much more absolute than the way my husband needed me. Jenny needed me, and I loved caring for her, being tender, being funny and attentive. I loved that she loved me back. It was bliss. I didn't know I could be so happy. A few months later, I decided that maybe I was somehow wrong about my mother; if I loved Jenny so much, my mother *must* have loved me. And, in that moment, that thought really rattled me."

Over two decades later, I ask her whether she believes all mothers love their children, and what she tells me packs an extraordinary emotional wallop: "I believe children love their mothers unconditionally; they are hardwired to love like that. And I also believe that mothers are supposed to learn about love from their children, and when they do love, the love exchange is beautiful. A healthy mother is wired to respond to the love an infant offers, but if she is broken, she can't always do it, and things get very screwed up. A child will continue to love her mother unconditionally even if she also hates her for the hurt she's caused. It's terribly dissonant to love and hate someone so fiercely. The child has the right to those feelings of hate, but she loves her mother nonetheless, and she'll find it hard to let go of the past because the love she *should have had* would have made all the difference. This kind of love is so intrinsic to life, so much a part of it, that when it's distorted, it's very hard to untangle."

Every unloved daughter faces this moment of confrontation differently. In my own case, the decision to have a child—at the age of thirty-eight reversing the course I had chosen for myself in adulthood—involved both a symbolic and a literal confrontation. Having chosen to bear a child, I also chose to cut my mother off completely. It was radical and drastic but, at some level, realistic. I had grown sufficiently to know, finally, that having a baby wouldn't turn me into my mother and to feel that I could trust myself to be loving and attentive, first to an infant and later on to a growing child. I wanted my child to a have a safe, loving, and protective environment, and I thought that I, along with her father, could provide it. But I also knew that I needed to trust myself and my own instincts, something I had always found hard to do when my mother attacked. At the same time, I understood with great clarity that I couldn't trust my mother not to continue the old patterns of hurt—not simply with me but with my child, most particularly if she were a girl. It was a decision that came with loss—most certainly the loss of a grandmother for my child—but, despite an enormous amount of familial pressure, I didn't capitulate. I wanted a fresh start more than anything—an opportunity to undo what generation after generation of mothers in my family had done to their daughters.

Listening to daughters' stories, the word *conscious* is the first word that comes to mind. It strikes me that by having been the daughters of decidedly imperfect mothers, these women seem less haunted by the myths of perfection that pervade our culture as a whole and more focused on meeting their children's needs in ways that their own needs weren't. This is not to say that they don't admit to or regret sometimes making mistakes, ignoring boundaries with their daughters, or trying to "do it all" or "too much"; they do. But there is a sense that their own experiences have, in the most helpful way, put the idea of perfect mothering to rest, along with all the egocentric energy associated with the perfect mother moving seamlessly through every arc of her and her daughter's lives. Perhaps having been hurt or disappointed in childhood, and having gone through the process of making sense of their experiences and the roles their mothers

and fathers played, endow them with a different, more heightened awareness of the role they will play in their daughters' lives. The work they've
done to move out of their mothers' sphere of infuence may allow them
to act with greater consciousness. Perhaps their acknowledgment of their
mothers' imperfections gives them a more realistic vision of their own.

In her sometimes angry, sometimes overbearing book, *The Mask of
Motherhood*, Susan Maushart, herself the mother of three, explores and
exposes how cultural pressures and expectations enforce a code of silence
on mothers. Unable to acknowledge the difficulties, ambivalence, and
confusion that can accompany the transition into motherhood, women are
sometimes forced to put on what she calls "the mask" of motherhood—pre-
tending that all is fine and right when it isn't—making them feel as though
they are "faking" motherhood. It's not simply that we don't acknowledge
the difficulty of mothering, the hard work, or even, sometimes, the sheer
tedium. "Perhaps more than anything," she writes, "we fail to anticipate
the depth and breadth of the mothering experience, its sheer transforma-
tive power in a woman's life." She goes on to say, "No one mentions the
psychic crisis of bearing a first child, the excitation of long-buried feelings
about one's own mother, the sense of confused power and powerlessness,
of being taken over on the one hand and of touching new physical and psychic potentialities on the other." It seems possible that the daughter of an
unloving mother may have a slight edge on her loved counterpart precisely
because of the emotional and psychological self-examination that brought
her to decide to become a mother herself.

Melinda, now in her fifties and the daughter of a withholding and
critical mother, tells me: "Personally, I always loved and wanted children.
I knew I was meant to be a mother from my earliest memories. And I knew
I would be a good one because I loved babies. What I hadn't thought
through was how good a mother I'd be when they got older. And, yes, I
am an even better mother because of my mom. I consciously did not want
to make her mistakes. I never violated my daughters' trust, never read
their diaries, and always trusted them." Reflecting on her growth through
motherhood, as well as her strengths and weaknesses, Melinda says, "I

am most pure with small children; I can give them all my attention and respond with no thought of myself. When my daughters got older, there were times when I wanted to be in control, because that was what was valued in the family I grew up in, but when my daughters became empowered and I saw the look of confidence in their eyes, it was intoxicating. I wanted more of it for all of us. It was a thrill to see them own their power. I didn't feel I got that from my own mother."

At the same time, though, she admits that reinventing herself through mothering was an imperfect process: "Looking back, I can see that I overdid it as a stay-at-home mother. I threw myself into doing what I did best, organizing, bringing people together. I won an award for volunteer of the year at the grade school and actually made six hundred cupcakes one year! So there were many ways I grew as a person, but I failed at balancing it all. I didn't stay well connected to myself or my husband; I just went into 'Mom mode.' It affected me personally more than the marriage, because we had the kids and parenting classes in common so that we really didn't have to notice that intimacy was disappearing."

Now that her daughters have entered young adulthood and moved out of the house, Melinda has a different perspective and understanding of how she needs to reclaim her self: "I see now that my real personality needed to concentrate on fewer things. It's such a contradiction—being a talker and having the need to be quiet. I see now that I didn't have to be in charge of everything, and it's taking a long time to unlearn, but I'm a better person for the experience and, like all good lessons, I couldn't have learned it without the experiences. And now that the girls are grown, intimacy is making a comeback!"

Although she struggled with her mother, Melinda consciously chose to live near her. I ask her why, knowing that it might have been easier to place physical distance between them. She answers as a mother, not a daughter: "My dad's folks were such wonderful grandparents that I couldn't imagine depriving my girls of that experience, even if it cost me. And I knew, as hurtful as mom could be, that the relationship between a grandmother and grandchild is different and better than that of a mother

and a daughter. And, most important, the girls would have me to protect
and support them."

Melinda's reflections on her relationship to her mother include a sense
of real loss: "She could have taken pride in being my mom. What a gift
that would have been to me! We could have had fun just being friends,
and it wouldn't have had to feel like a competition. We could have done
more things together and enjoyed the time we spent together, instead
of always feeling on edge. We could have shared books, recipes, information, without either of us feeling judged or criticized or 'less than.'"
Finally, though, she says something that captures the two-way aspect of
the mother-daughter mirror: "I'm not sure whether my mother saw me
for who I was. It was too hard for her to admit my gifts and talents. And
perhaps she felt too small herself to allow me to be bigger than she was.
That is the difference. I expect my daughters to be better than I am, and I
celebrate the ways in which they are."

I realize too how *conscious* the decision to become a mother was for
most of these women, particularly set against the backdrop of maternal
relationships that were unsupportive at best and destructive at worse.
Some of this is generational, since these women—now in their forties, fifties, and sixties—by and large saw motherhood as a choice to make, not
a socially decreed norm or cultural script, made easier by access to more
reliable and easier-to-use birth control as well as opportunities for career
and work that didn't exist for their mothers in the same way. Lisa, forty-
one, admits that "I really can't imagine what it was like for my mother in
terms of cultural assumptions. She was the oldest of six and therefore was
always in the mother role. She grew up in a small town in the Midwest
where her parents never pushed her in the direction of a career. She married right out of her parents' house. Did she really see no other options
for herself, and then did she not realize that there were other options for
me? Is that why she was unable to provide me with support or guidance
in terms of helping me figure out who I was and who I wanted to be?"
There's no question that many daughters' experiences with their mothers
and sometimes fathers underscore the element of choice. Their need to

make sense of their experiences, coupled with a growing societal acceptance of therapy, also gave them a very different outlook on parenting
than their mothers had. When I ask therapist Françoise Bourzat whether
unloved daughters struggle with motherhood, her answer enlightens but
doesn't surprise me: "When unloved daughters embark on a journey of
therapy, they are actually *very* good mothers: aware, careful, awake to the
pitfalls of 'repeat performances' or overcompensation. They treat their
children with the respect and affection they wish they had had and actually heal themselves in the process too."

Motherhood may be an act of self-invention as a daughter becomes a
mother and begins to stretch the outlines of the mother she would like to
be. This is what Gwen tells me, at the age of sixty-two, with the perspective of almost three decades. Her daughter is now in her thirties and the
mother of four girls herself: "I never pictured myself as a mother. I never
babysat and didn't know the first thing about children. Honestly, I was so
unhappy generally that I didn't think I would ever even get married—sort
of the 'Who would ever want me?' syndrome. I had a terrible self-image.
But when I got pregnant, I never worried about making my mother's mistakes, because we were so different. I could never be that mean to a child,
and in the end I went in completely the opposite direction. I felt very confident and knew, as I know now, that it was the best thing I had ever done.
My mother set a negative example which taught me a great deal. I knew
that I needed to love, demonstrate that love, encourage, and connect to my
child—all the more so because I was never hugged, asked what I felt or
thought, or had good heartfelt counseling. I also knew that I always had to
give my daughter a reason for my decisions and not simply be authoritarian. I desperately wanted her to learn that life was all out there and that
she could do absolutely anything she wanted. She was allowed to make
mistakes, fail at something, and know that this was just one thing she
didn't excel in and that it wasn't a reflection of who she was. My childhood
was the opposite. In my mom's eyes, I couldn't do anything right."

In contrast to her mother's experience with her, Gwen says, "Being a
mother to my daughter was a joy. I found myself, my confidence, in being

her mother. I made better choices. I learned from being her mother, and, in many ways, she has taught me. Now that she is an adult and a mother herself, I get love and encouragement from her as well. Sometimes I even feel mothered by her." Finally, she confides, "We get along wonderfully, and she looks up to me as her mother, as she should. I think she is the person I could have been if I hadn't had my mother. If I had been loved and encouraged, I could have gone very far."

Time and age may give a daughter distance and the ability, if not to empathize with her mother, to see all that transpired from another vantage point. I ask Gwen what she thinks her mother missed: "My mother missed all the wonderful things with me that I now have with my daughter and will have with her girls. I honestly don't think my mother had it in her to love, so in the end she lived her life with what she had inside her. I think she was simply an unhappy person all her life, and I was the easiest one for her to take things out on. Being young, I couldn't fight back, and my father's way of reacting to her was silence. In a way, I felt like I was being beaten, not physically but mentally. I have moved on, and I don't think much about her now. When I do think about her, I don't 'hate,' but I feel sorry for her that she didn't have a better time. She missed a lot, to my way of thinking. She felt that she was a good mother to my brother, so in the end she did mother—she just didn't mother me."

Gwen never broke with her mother; her sense of filial duty was too strong. In this, she is hardly alone.

BEYOND THE MYTHS OF PERFECTION

For every woman, whether her own mother was loving or not, becoming a mother is a genuine sea change. Pregnancy transforms us physically and mentally, but also creates a distinct "before and after" that is really unlike any other in life, mirrored both in the outside world and a woman's interior one. The ensuing birth of a child with its new priorities shifts every representation of the self we have, in each and every role we play in life, and may engender as many conflicts in us as it does reconciliations, even if we are fully prepared to love the new baby in our arms. In that sense, becoming a mother is always an act of self-invention for every woman. There's not much societal support for the turbulence these changes may bring to our lives, not to mention our psyches—unless you chose to see a baby shower as a real form of support.

No matter who our mothers were—or how they loved or behaved— each of us comes to this moment with our own specific nexus of feelings and confusions. Myths about mothering as "instinctive" make it difficult to acknowledge whatever anxiety or ambivalence a woman may feel at this cusp moment in her life, or the sometimes profound feelings of dislocation even a desired pregnancy can bring with it. Our pastel-tinted vision of motherhood often gets in a new mother's way, as Beth explains, almost seventeen years after her daughter was born: "I think over time I began to see myself as more competent, more dependable as a mother. Initially the effect was just the opposite—when it began to sink in that this little, demanding, needy person was so very dependent on me, I panicked. I felt desperately inadequate, and I was terrified that I was going to mess up the job. It took quite a few years before I realized that what I thought was an act I was putting on—that I was grown-up, competent, and dependable— was actually more true than not."

Each of us dreams the baby she carries. The portrait a pregnant woman paints of her soon-to-be child is culled from a mixture of past experience and future expectation. Leslie tells me that she thought her daughter would be "a lot like me, but I hoped she'd be braver. In fact, before my daughter was born, my husband and I talked about what we'd most like her to be. I said 'brave' and John said 'happy.' I think that maybe we most wish our children to be what we weren't but wish we'd been." Mary Ellen had a dream during her first pregnancy that was so vivid and crystal clear that "it's wiped out any other image I might have had. In my dream, even though we didn't know the gender of the baby, I was carrying a two-year-old girl, all smiles and sweetness. I was feeling utter happiness with the easy, charming child. She said, with a broad smile and a face that's now replaced by my own daughter's face, 'I love you, Mommy. My name is Cassie.' I didn't name my own daughter Cassie, but the dream image stuck with me, and Mary Kate has embodied it—by being always the optimist, peacemaker, perspective provider, sweetly funny girl. I dreamed for her to be independent because independence is big in my list of important characteristics. I might have too much of it myself, but I wanted her to be happy but also strong enough to know her own mind and make her own way in the world." Not every woman will dream so specifically, of course, as Karen reminds me: "I didn't do a lot of imagining while my daughter was in utero. I was so, so pleased to be pregnant after so many years that I felt she was a miracle. I did imagine her being like both of us, and she is in ways. But she was also born with certain personal characteristics and talents neither of us has."

What's amazing about the process, as research has shown, is that those representations are part of the internal mental process of becoming a mother, moving us from our original identity as a daughter to our new identity as a mother. This isn't a linear process but one that, like the experience of motherhood, over time encompasses cycles of both close connection and separation. During pregnancy, a woman's representation of self is "reorganized around the child," as Diana Diamond and Kimberly Kotov note, entailing "a review of relationships with one's parents, as well as an upsurge of reflections, concerns, and doubts about the self as a mother, the spouse, and past attachment relationships." This is both a conscious and unconscious process, rooted both in past relationships, particularly with the woman's mother, and her "own current evolving relationship with her child." Needless to say, other outside factors, such as the support systems available to the mother-to-be, the experience of pregnancy, and later the birth itself, affect the ways in which the representation of self re-forms itself, as do the appearance and temperament of the baby herself.

As the representation of self undergoes change, so does the mental representation of the baby, although not in an entirely parallel fashion. Not surprisingly, the representation of the child takes on increasing specificity beginning in the fourth month of gestation—when the baby begins to move in her mother's body and when ultrasound images and other technologies bring the image of the child more clearly into the present. Research confirms that between the fourth and seventh month "there is a rapid growth in the richness, quality, and specificity" in representations of the baby-to-be, but this elaboration stops at month seven. In fact, there's evidence that the representations actually lose their specificity between the seventh and ninth months. Dr. Daniel Stern offers an explanation of why this happens the way it does, in his book *The Motherhood Constellation,* writing that "mothers intuitively protect their baby-to-be and themselves from a potential discordance between the real baby and a too specifically represented baby. After all, birth is the meeting place for the baby in her arms and the one in her mind." Writing from a clinical point of view, Ruth F. Lax, Ph.D., has detailed the problems that can ensue from a too fully realized "fantasy" child in a mother's life when her "real life" child is too markedly different from the one she had imagined.

With the birth of her first baby, a woman's identity is fundamentally altered, along with what Dr. Stern calls her "fixed representational world." While part of this shift in identity has to do with her change in status—her primary, lifelong identity as a daughter, which "occupies a kind of historical center of gravity" shifts to being "the mother-of-her-daughter"—it also involves both a conscious and unconscious repositioning, psychologically and emotionally. One aspect of this change—which I think is of special interest to the daughters of unloving mothers—is what Dr. Stern thinks happens on a psychological level along with this shift: "The new mother must give up, in large part, whatever long-held fantasies she has safeguarded about repairing, correcting, or redoing her childhood or being able to return there when she needs to. Now, all the faults, disappointments, and omissions that occurred in her girlhood become fixed forever as past history. She can perhaps repair the past, but never again as a girl."

I don't think I realized that fully when I first held my daughter in my arms—I was too focused on the door that had just opened in my life—but there is no question, in retrospect, that another door closed at the same time. This is not to say that my past history—my childhood, girlhood, and adult relationship with my mother—was suddenly erased; it wasn't. But the birth of my daughter permitted me to put the narrative of the past in a new perspective and out of my present; my own history didn't disappear, but it did lose its power over me. Understanding my history also permitted me to shape my own role as a mother, paying special attention to the things I needed and never got and making sure that I understood what my daughter needed. Putting my history into the past may well have been easier for me since I decided, at the same time, to cut my mother out of my life. It doubtless helped too that I was just one month shy of turning thirty-nine when Alexandra was born.

Not every daughter will feel this way, as I learn from another woman, who tells me that while her relationship with her mother never "shifted into the past tense," the birth of her daughter did change the sense of self her childhood had bequeathed her: "I began by feeling so inadequate that the idea of having a baby—when I honestly thought I could do nothing right—was such a huge idea, such an enormous responsibility that I never went there. If I couldn't take care of myself, how could I take care of a baby? But then I got pregnant by accident, while on birth control, and I had my daughter. Being responsible was very new to me, but I seemed to be doing a good job of it. Over the years, that sense built, and there was proof that I 'worked' as a mother. Having my daughter was a huge shift for me, in my self."

Dr. Stern suggests that with the emergence of what he calls "the motherhood constellation," every new mother will, consciously or unconsciously, reevaluate her own mother. During what he calls the "postpartum crucible of change," both new or more "elaborated and understood" views of her own mother emerge for the new mother. This reevaluation includes "her mother as a mother to her when she was a child, as a wife, as a woman, and as the grandmother to the new child." He reminds us—relying on attachment theory to do so—that in every case, it's not the literal history of what happened during our childhoods that matters; it's how we have come to make sense of it. As a result, he writes, "A woman can learn from a negative model ('I will never act as she did') as well as from a positive one. . . . The aspect of the mother's representation of her own mother that is most predictive of her future maternal behavior is not necessarily what happened in the past—whether she had a good or bad mothering experience—but rather the way she thinks and talks about her mother now." As he puts it, "Narrative coherence has won out over historical truth as the stronger predictor." He goes on to say: "This finding is counterintuitive. Yet it opens the door for a woman to overcome a bad past or escape the fate of repeating it by way of the psychological work she has accomplished in understanding, putting into perspective, and rendering coherent her past, especially her experience of being mothered."

In other words, while an unloved daughter may find herself learning to mother on her own—without the positive example a loved daughter has—a negative maternal model, understood and made coherent, may be just as valuable to the business of mothering. This is a truth every unloved daughter needs to have needlepointed onto a pillow in her bedroom. Elizabeth, now the mother of a teenage son and daughter, reflects: "When I think about it, my mother gave so sparingly of herself, in deeds and emotion, after my early years of childhood. She was a closed person and I knew little about her. I didn't know what made her happy or sad—she is and was opaque to me as a person. We never had an honest conversation. And there was no lightness—we never laughed together. In some ways, I am like my mother—a serious person who has trouble being 'light.' Being casual—the way so many people are—is hard for me. But I knew when I had children that I had to be generous with them, with myself, with my time, my energy, and focus, and I was. I put my energy into being there for them, talking to them, listening to them, making sure that we had conversations." Elizabeth was able to draw on both the negative and positive examples her mother set—she tells me that her childhood home was always comfortable and welcoming—and find her own path in giving her children what her mother couldn't give her.

Recognizing one's own mother's limitations is the first step on the path to mothering differently. That said, it isn't always easy, as Elizabeth admits: "You know, some aspects of mothering can be difficult. Some-times you don't feel like it. It's sometimes hard to discipline yourself to speak honestly and be responsive, but it's so important to create a routine of life that's reliable and orderly." She says that her proudest achievement as a mother is "being intuitive about what each of my children—and they are very different people—needs in the moment. Each stage of life has its own difficulties. I remember sitting with them, reading the same book over and over, and thinking that was hard. But, of course, doing it right has gotten harder, as they've gotten older, in other ways. It certainly was easier and less complicated when they were under the age of five."

When I ask Elizabeth how being a mother has changed her, she tells me that "I've never been a patient person, and I became more patient because of my children. My mother wasn't patient, but she was a perfec-tionist, and I was one too. I've become less of a perfectionist, because now I get that life is messy, and even though I fight it, I accept it." Her mention of perfectionism prompts me to ask her if she thinks it's pos-sible to be a "perfect" mother and whether that's something any of us should even strive for. Her answer is right on: "Only if the definition of *perfect* includes within it lots of imperfections. I think being a perfect mother has to do with intuition and understanding both your children and yourself."

Susan, the mother of two daughters and now a grandmother, tells me that the negative model her own mother provided actually gave her insight into mothering that she might not otherwise have had: "I didn't just turn to looking at what my mother didn't give me but also asked, 'What did I want instead?' Being able to answer the questions pulled me out of the old patterns of my childhood." Focusing on the "instead"—the positive exam-ple—Susan believes is most important, permitting a woman to move past the old habits of mind and action. In her role as a counselor, Susan rightly points to the importance of seeking out positive examples of mothering—it could be the mother of a friend or a grandmother—as being vital to women who "can't imagine mothering in any way other than the way they were mothered. You need to load those positive examples into your brain so that you have those to draw on, so that your brain doesn't just go back to your own experiences."

Because I had never imagined becoming a mother myself, I'd never forced myself to look at precisely what my mother had done that was so wrong. Yes, I had a catalog of hurts—large and small—and the knowledge that, in an essential way, my mother did not love me, but that point of view belonged to the little girl child inside of me, still reacting to the past, not to a woman on the brink of motherhood herself. Cutting off my mother "forever" when my pregnancy was confirmed—the first time in my life I had ever taken that draconian step with full intention—completely changed the dialogue my inner self had with her and my past. I needed to know precisely what she had and hadn't given me, so that I could make sure that the past didn't flow heedlessly into the future I would have with my own daughter. Ten lunar months of pregnancy gave me ample time to think.

At the end, what I discovered had all the simplicity and mystery of a Zen koan. What she'd done and hadn't done distilled to a single truth: It had always been about her, not me. She remained hermetically sealed, emotionally untouched by the experience of bearing and raising me, unable to see me in any real way and, equally, unable to see herself as my mother. I don't think being my mother gave her real pleasure or joy, even though I think she was able to experience both with my brother to the extent that she could. When she was pleased with me—as a beautifully turned-out little girl with blond curls or, later, as a star student she could brag about to friends—she was pleased because I enhanced her social standing. At those moments—and they stood out from the day-to-day experience of life with her—she saw me no more clearly than she did on other days. I think my mother became a mother because it was socially expected of her, and it was at the level of social expectation that mothering me held the most meaning.

In the end, my experience with my mother gave me a rare, if hard-earned, gift: a profound understanding that whatever else motherhood might be, it *wasn't* about me. It's an understatement to say that if I had not had the mother I had, there's no way I would have become the mother I did. My experience with my mother bequeathed me a reliable enough compass, a sure knowledge of what I wouldn't do *to* my daughter and what I needed to do *for* her. From the moment she was born, I tried to see my daughter whole—not as a reflection or an extension of me or my hopes and dreams but as herself. If I've succeeded as a mother—and I fervently hope that I have, since it's the most important role I've ever played—it's simply because I gave my daughter an environment in which she could be herself. Raising her has been more like gardening than anything, an experience not unlike that of coming to understand the plant in all of its stages and figuring out what it needs to thrive and ultimately to flower. Not surprisingly, while I've been able to mother this way in large part, it hasn't been perfect. How could it be, after all, when I'm not?

Nowadays, getting out of the way—making sure it's *not* about me—is easier in some ways and harder in others. I asked my daughter, as I was writing this, in what ways I had sometimes failed and what she needed from me now, as she approached twenty-one. Her answer had all the clarity of truth: "I need you to simply keep accepting me as who I am, and to support my actions as I come into my own light. I sometimes feel that you expect me to react to situations in the same way you do, and that I sometimes fall short." Her point is well taken; as a mother and a person with strong opinions, it's not always easy to get *me* out of the way.

The unloved daughters I've spoken to who chose to have children all felt enlarged by the experience of mothering and, whether they continued to communicate with their own mothers or not, felt they had managed not to repeat the past. This doesn't mean, of course, that they see themselves or their ability to mother as "perfect," or that they don't have any regrets or doubts about how well they mothered their daughters and sons. One woman confided that, because her childhood had left her so needy, she sometimes worries that she hasn't respected her daughters' boundaries enough, sometimes confusing the role of mother with friend and confiding in them too much. Eleanor, fifty-nine, the daughter of a distant and critical mother and now the mother of a son and daughter in their thirties, says, "I didn't know how to mother; I just knew how not to be my own mother. I think I overcompensated and probably did too much for my children. I do feel that I am a good mother, and I say this because of what my children tell me. The irony is that, when I look back, I feel I haven't been the best mother I could have been."

But who among us has been?

It's worth reminding ourselves that even a well-loved daughter will go through the processes of envisioning herself as a mother and of reevaluating her own mother with the birth of a child. In the best of all possible worlds, these processes will continue as her child or children progress from infancy to adulthood. Christine, fifty-eight, has an especially close relationship with her mother, to whom she speaks every day. Her mother, she tells me, is always her biggest supporter, and when she gives me some examples, I am astonished that anyone could be so blessed as to be born with such a terrific cheerleader in her life. Her experiences with her mother and father were extraordinarily positive, and she always knew she wanted children. Her father had always communicated well with his four daughters, and she looked for that quality in a husband herself.

But, Christine tells me, her mother was so good at helping and managing her choices growing up that, in her twenties, Christine went into therapy to learn "to make choices on my own." Her own experience of needing to create a more independent self has influenced how she mothers her son, fifteen, and her daughter, fourteen: "I approached parenting the way a person approaches learning a foreign language, and, at some level, I felt that mothering was a skill I had to master, even though I was confident I would be a good mother. I went to classes, read books, got help when my children needed something I didn't know how to give them. I've really focused on letting them be—giving them the room to make their own choices and mistakes, even letting them quit on something they started but didn't want to finish. I've tried hard to let them be as independent and self-reliant as they can be in age-appropriate ways, because I wasn't."

Christine's story underscores what we all know intellectually: that "loving" isn't a synonym for "perfect." If we could get out from under the weight of the mother myths, we might be able to cut ourselves a bit more slack and come to a better understanding and acceptance not only of the limitations each of us has as a person, woman, and mother, but also the conflicts and ambivalence different stages of motherhood may engender in us. For some women, reading *Goodnight Moon* to a two-year-old for what feels like the fiftieth time may mark the nadir of the motherhood experience, while for others the moment of truth may take place in a kitchen with a screaming adolescent or with a twenty-four-year-old who appears to have chosen a life path that appears to make no sense. No matter when it happens, each of us ought to be free to acknowledge that moment without feeling guilty or unloving. Put more directly, if we could all allow ourselves to admit our ambivalences every now and then—and if we saw ambivalence as both natural and perhaps inevitable at times—we would all find it easier to mother our daughters.

Susan tells me a story that may have special resonance for a daughter with a difficult childhood but that should be of value to every daughter nonetheless. It is a story she included in her own book, *Our Children Are Watching,* and it's notable for both its complete honesty and its self-forgiveness. Her daughter is getting married, and Susan and she are out shopping for a mother-of-the-bride dress together, looking at rack after rack of fancy, lace-trimmed garments. "It was nothing I wanted," Susan says. "I was doing what she wanted and, in that moment, the past welled up inside of me and all I could feel and think was how much I didn't want to buy this dress. Without thinking, I fled the store and immediately realized that I was wrestling with that younger version of me—the one who hadn't had a wedding like the one my daughter was about to have, the one who didn't get the love and attention I gave my daughter so freely—and I had to take that younger self by the shoulders and wrestle her back into the store. That was the part of me that didn't want to give my daughter the things I didn't get. The part of me that still felt the pain of my childhood and which expressed itself in the most physical, visceral way."

If there is a lesson in Susan's story, it is that each of us must learn to self-mother ourselves with empathy and understanding throughout each stage of parenting and when the work of mothering gets tough, as it inevitably will. In their amazing book, *Parenting from the Inside Out,* Daniel Siegel, M.D., and Mary Hartzell, M.Ed., write, "Being a parent gives us the opportunity to re-parent ourselves by making sense of our own early experiences. Our children are not the only ones who will benefit from this making-sense process; we ourselves will come to live a more vital and enriched life because we have integrated our past experiences into a coherent ongoing life story." Each of us—whether a loved daughter or not—has experienced hurts, slights, and disappointments that, even if half-forgotten or mostly unseen, remain remembered and a part of us nonetheless. Sometimes they are rooted in the deep past but, equally, they may be part of the lived present, and there may be moments when our own unresolved feelings may endanger the equilibrium of our relationships with our daughters. From the point of view of brain science, whether we address those feelings from what Siegel and Hartzell call the "high road"—the powers of reflection embedded in the prefrontal cortex of the brain—or the "low road"—automatic responses embedded in the past applied to the situation at hand—will make all the difference.

The mother myths marginalize the difficulty each of us has living coherently, keeping our life narratives focused and in touch. They undermine the simple fact that the stress points in each woman's life—no matter what her history—will be different and individual. A woman unsure of her own worthiness and who needs her children to love her more than anything else may be more comfortable mothering small children and find herself floundering with older children who talk back or need boundaries set for them; she may find it painful or even impossible to set those boundaries if the cost is watching her daughter pull back in anger, even momentarily. For another woman, a daughter's adolescence, which coincides with her own entry into midlife, may create a crisis that awakens feelings of ambivalence no other stage of mothering has tapped into. Another mother may find herself confronting new challenges when her daughter or children grow past the age where "hands-on" parenting is really necessary, as Elizabeth wrote me, reflecting that the years when her children were young "were the sweetest time in our marriage to be sure. It's been tougher these past few years since the kids no longer really want to hang out with us. I find that we are more challenged in our marriage and have a tough time acknowledging that we are both very sad that this time has passed."

The journey of self-invention that mothering entails is perhaps more obvious for an inadequately loved daughter than a loved one, since mothering is a learned behavior. Nonetheless, becoming a mother will always entail real adjustment and some measure of self-invention, regardless of what the mother myths tell us, and understanding how unloved daughters cope with the challenges of mothering will be of use to every daughter.

THE ROLE OF PARTNERSHIP

Mothering doesn't take place in a vacuum, of course; it's shaped by our primary relationships, our definition of self, our social and economic circumstances, and our support systems. The choices available to women in terms of how they manage mothering and work have changed enormously, and along with those choices has come a different vision of the partnership between wife and husband, mother and father. For some daughters with either an inadequate or absent model of mothering, partnership may play a special role. Elizabeth puts it simply and directly: "If my mother's example taught me anything, it is that you can't parent well without a partner or support. She was without both. My husband has been everything my father was not. He worked hard in the very early years parenting two young children, even though he was traveling half of the time and we were living far away from the support systems of family and friends. He was very reliable and consistent in his support on all levels. Whether it was changing a diaper or reading a story, his answer was always yes. I could tell that he got great pleasure out of being with the children and developing his own relationship with them. I surely would have been a different mother without his being so involved." She adds that the time her husband put in when their children were young has reaped very evident rewards.

Jane tells me: "My husband was there for the time when I was finally able to break free of much of my mother's hold on me. He was an integral part of that process—he was there for me and I didn't have to do it alone." When I ask her if she would be a different mother without him as her partner, she states categorically, "I can't even imagine being a mother without him. We have different strengths, and he helps me be more well-rounded as a mother because his actions remind me of things that aren't normally at the top of my priorities or that I may inadvertently ignore but that need to be addressed. I'm more of the taskmaster—cleaning up, getting homework done, scheduling activities—but he won't let them get away with the little things like not listening to us or attempting to manipulate us. My natural tendency is to let it slide to avoid conflict, but I know he's right and that it's important even when children are young."

The right partner can actively help a woman overcome the legacy of the household she grew up in, not just by providing understanding but by modeling different parenting behavior. Melinda tells me how her husband helped her learn to let go of the controlling behavior that was part of her upbringing: "I know I would have repeated some of the same mistakes if Jim hadn't helped me to lighten up, see the humor in situations, and learn to play with our girls. He helped me to let go and be less serious, and I wouldn't have been as much fun as a mother without him."

The right partner can also help a daughter acknowledge her own strengths and weaknesses and ease the cultural pressure on a woman to be all things to everyone. Women making different choices than their mothers did—working rather than staying home, for example, or vice versa—may look to a partner for special support. Claire, the daughter of a loving mother and now the mother of two adolescent girls, works full-time while her husband, a musician, is in charge of their daughters. This is what she tells me: "David is very supportive of me as a mother, but our roles are conflated at times, as far as traditional definitions go. When I'm feeling low and absent, he reassures me that I am the glue, that they talk or ask about me all the time. If my being a professional is part of my being a mother—and it is—then his easygoing nature in being the at-home dad has made me able to be well balanced and laissez faire. Sometimes I am overwhelmed at how he does not do 'it'—home/kids/house—right and I could do it *so much* better. Then I realize I'd be so unhappy at home full-time and would certainly take out my frustration on the kids. I am moody and judgmental and he is neither, and the latter is much better in a full-time parent."

Some women may find that motherhood enlarges them in unexpected ways that flow into other parts of their lives, including their marriages: "Motherhood has shaped me by giving me patience, humility, and resilience. It has given me a sense of myself as having qualities I didn't know existed in me: confidence, intuition, protectiveness. It has bonded me with all kinds of women I wouldn't have met otherwise, feeling united by the fact of having children and facing the same issues, preoccupations, and joys. As a wife, motherhood gave me a renewed sense of femininity and grace, a sense of nurturing that could extend past my child into caring for my husband in a way that was nourishing without turning him into 'my other child.'"

For other women, the amount of support and understanding a partner is able to offer the enterprise that is motherhood will ebb and flow over time. Linda lost a child before conceiving her daughter, and while her husband had been incredibly supportive after their mutual loss, the birth of their daughter felt like a different story: "He was working in an office at the time, so he left in the morning and came home at night, and in between I had to deal with this howling bundle on my own. And he just didn't get it. Here I was, with the thing I wanted more than anything else in the world, and now I was miserable. How was that possible? I don't have a whole lot of regrets, but I do regret not leaving her with him for a week so he'd have had some perspective. On the other hand, once we got over that very bad patch, he was certainly very supportive of me, and he continues to acknowledge, on a regular basis, what a wonderful mother

I am." Other women, though, still see mothering as a relatively solitary activity, most particularly when a husband is largely invested in work or when husbands and wives disagree about how to discipline or set limits for their child or children. Yet they too talk about the importance of partnership nonetheless.

For some daughters, like myself, the sea change of motherhood will be so absolute as to change the very premise on which the partnership between wife and husband was founded. Whether we call it "the motherhood constellation" or something else, my entire mind-set about myself and life changed once Alexandra was born and she became the main focus of my attention. I had promised my husband that nothing would change after we'd had the baby; my feminist self was adamant that motherhood wouldn't become central to my identity as it had with former girlfriends who, I thought then, had become so consumed by motherhood that our relationships didn't so much end as fade away as we had less and less in common. I was absolutely sure that I would continue to define myself as I always had. I would just add "mother" to my other list of accomplishments.

Of course, nothing could have been further from the truth, and if the words *sea change* suggest transformation wrought by soft lapping waves, in my case the transformation was more the result of a tsunami than anything else. I now realize that underestimating or marginalizing the changes in the self brought on by motherhood is part and parcel of the mother myths, allowing an easy reconciliation, on paper at least, of the needs of the self and the needs of the child. It is ironic as well that much of my confidence about becoming a mother was rooted in no small part in that very relationship with my then-husband—the "earned" secure attachment—which would founder in the end. Perhaps, in my case, the shift from being a daughter—*my* mother's daughter—to being the mother of a daughter required an emotional and psychological housecleaning so thorough that very little of who I'd been before remained.

This isn't a particularly pretty story, but it's a true one. In retrospect, it's clear to me that the changes in me were so enormous, the shift in

my focus so monumental, that my then eight-year relationship and marriage had little chance of thriving, as did some of my close relationships
to women without children. We separated when our daughter was eight.
Marriages, we've already seen, are not necessarily strengthened by the
addition of a child or, for that matter, by the changes that accompany the
emergence of the motherhood constellation in a woman.

Growth in a new direction sometimes comes at great cost.

RIPPLES ON THE POND: REFLECTIONS
ON THE MOTHER-DAUGHTER RELATIONSHIP

If our mothers provide the first mirror in which we catch a glimpse of
ourselves, then we too become the mirrors in which the next generation
of daughters first see their own outlines. If I have learned anything during
the course of writing this book—reading, researching, listening—it's that
the depth of a mother's influence on a daughter cannot be overstated. A
mother leaves her imprint on a daughter both inside and out—in both the
well-traveled and untraveled pathways of her brain, in how she chooses
her clothes or decorates her rooms, in how she connects to friends and
strangers, in her feelings about new experiences and familiar comforts.
Her influence is felt in ways that are obvious or subtle, literal or mysterious—or a combination of both. It's probably just as well that I didn't
understand this in the detailed way I do now when I had my daughter
some twenty-one years ago, because to be honest it would have scared the
hell out of me.

But—thank goodness for that little qualifier—while this truth makes
it seem that mothering well remains hopelessly out of reach, I don't think
it is. By looking at this darker side of motherhood—at mothers who, by
their daughters' lights at least, failed to meet many, if not most, of their
daughters' most important needs—it's possible to look at mothering in a
more pared-down way. As a culture, we've gotten to a place—and I think

this is most particularly true of women—where we've actively bought into the idea that we have to be all things to everyone, 24/7, and that everything we try, we ought to be able to do well, if not brilliantly, all the time. This cultural stance incorporates the mother myths without a hesitation or even a blink, conveniently permitting us to forget that, in life generally, we just need to be able to do a few things and do them well or even well enough. Mothering can, I think, be seen along the same lines. If we can accept that we can't be perfect mothers to our daughters 24/7, in every way, every day, then we ought to be able to take responsibility for being the best mothers we can be most of the time, particularly in the areas that are most important to our daughters' growth and well-being. Learning from the stories of unloved daughters, we need to be honest with ourselves about the awesome power a mother wields over a daughter, most particularly in childhood but perhaps always, and make sure we always use it respectfully.

If there is a single common attribute to be ascribed to the unloving mothers we've met in these pages it's their lack of awareness, their inability to be conscious of the effect and the import of their words and gestures on their daughters' development, and, for most of them, their incapacity or refusal to take responsibility for their actions. In her book *The Common Thread,* which is both an exploration and a celebration of the mother-daughter bond, psychologist and writer Martha Manning writes about the necessity for an empathic connection between mother and daughter and, later in life, between daughter and mother. The obstacles she cites as "barriers to empathy" shed a different light on why some mothers are unable to mother their daughters in the most important ways. I've chosen the ones I think have the most resonance to the subject at hand, although she includes several others.

Her initial observation is more sociological than psychological: that the way in which women are socialized to deny negative feelings such as anger, resentment, or jealousy can result in a mother's dismissal or diminishment of a daughter's emotions. She writes that "one of the greatest—and most common—emotional cruelties we can commit against our daughters is to deny them their intuition, to teach them to distrust their own wisdom, and to defer to adults' perceptions." We've seen how this can work in a daughter's life in these pages. She also highlights the neglect of a daughter's privacy and integrity, ignoring her right to be herself and to have her own thoughts and feelings. At the simplest level, this can be an invasive act such as reading a daughter's diary—as my own mother did—but it can also manifest itself in more important betrayals.

Even more useful is the barrier to empathy Manning calls "Disruptions in Service." These have to do with the cultural assumptions about the mother-daughter relationship, exempting it from the rules that govern all other relationships, even though, as Manning remarks, "An essential aspect of every close relationship involves a realization that 'close' does not mean absolutely perfect, totally generous, or selfless." These disruptions occur when a mother isn't able to understand what her daughter is feeling or, alternatively, when what a daughter is feeling hits too close to home, reviving the mother's own buried feelings. A variation on the theme is when a mother can't see past herself to see her daughter whole.

Other barriers to empathy have to do with the mother: her past, her present, and her self. What Manning calls "emotional poverty" taps into the mother's past for, as she writes, "Motherhood tests every inch of sanity, patience, and strength a woman has. A woman who lacks emotional resilience, who has little to give anyone, is going to have a very tough time with children." Similarly, a mother who is "so burdened by her own problems," past or present, is unlikely to be able to "sustain empathic connection" with her daughter even if she loves her. Maternal dissatisfaction with her own life, Manning writes, can have the same effect, leading mothers to "emphasize their daughters' failures and trivialize their successes." Manning identifies these mothers as more likely to be diagnosed with personality disorders; some of whom may see their children "as little more than narcissistic extensions of themselves." Manning does note one possible variation, which we also have explored in these pages: "Sometimes one girl is the designated scapegoat, while other siblings are treated fairly well. And a woman looking back on being scapegoated as a child may never get a satisfactory answer to the question, 'Why me?'" Manning identifies another kind of narcissistic behavior in which the mother defines a very narrow "range of acceptable behavior" to her daughter; that is, the "daughter must be very pretty, very popular, and very smart." Any variation from these standards—which reflect the mother's achievement—proves unacceptable.

Throughout this book, I've emphasized the daughter's point of view, stressing her need to "be known" by her mother throughout all the stages of her life. Answering that need to be known requires attunement, consciousness, and, yes, empathy on a mother's part. At the same time, as we move from being a daughter to a being a mother and then perhaps to watching our daughters become mothers themselves, it's important to recognize the extraordinary empathic agility all of these tasks require of any woman. If we can dig our way out from under the weight of the mother myths, we can perhaps see the task of mothering more purely and simply, and focus on staying attuned, aware, and, yes, empathic to the best of our abilities, most of the time. And we can help our daughters do the same.

AN ADDED BENEFIT: A TOAST TO RESILIENCE

Looking at the stories of unloved daughters has another benefit, permitting us all to recognize the extraordinary resilience not only of the human spirit but of the human brain, in its ability to grow and expand, to learn new ways of connecting emotionally and of understanding the past. While none of us can rewrite the past, each of us has the power to script the future of our relationships and to disempower the hold the past has over us. Marilyn Lyga, Ph.D., a therapist in private practice, tells me that she's had patients—both daughters and sons—who decided when they were children as young as eight or nine that they would parent differently than their parents when they were grown. But, as she says, "this isn't a one-time decision. It begins with becoming aware that there's another path, and, once you see that, the struggle is remaining conscious. Remaining in your own voice, as opposed to someone else's, may be a challenge."

If we as mothers model both consciousness and awareness for our daughters—making sure that we remain the authors of our own life narratives—we will have given them the tools to deal with whatever else we have failed to give them when they needed it.

Beyond the Mother Myths: A Coda

A S IT HAPPENS, MY DAUGHTER IS HOME FROM COLLEGE JUST AS I am finishing this book. My daughter didn't know my mother, her grandmother, of course, and what she does know, she knows only through the filter of my experience. She knows too that the ways in which I have mothered her have much to do with turning whatever my mother did inside out and upside down; generally, the compass bequeathed to me in my childhood tells me to run fast in the opposite direction. Alexandra asks me what seems like a simple question on the surface: "If you could speak to your mother one more time, what would you say to her now?"

Her question takes me aback, particularly because I don't have a ready answer at hand. The burning question from my childhood—"Why don't you love me?"—was once enveloped by both bewilderment and pain, but it isn't any longer. I know now that the answer to that question is both simple and complicated, but no matter what answer would be forthcoming, it doesn't and didn't have anything to do with me, the child I was or the woman I am now. Nowadays, more than anything, it seems both unlucky and unfair that in the lottery of life I drew the mother who was my mother.

Whatever question I would ask her would be posed by someone who's been a mother herself for over two decades, and who's not beyond calling motherhood "the endless and thankless profession," even within my daughter's earshot. I challenge any mother to deny that sometimes, at certain moments, it feels exactly like that.

The question would be framed by a mother who has come to realize that, no matter how hard I try or how much I love her, being my daughter isn't always easy. Just because being my mother's daughter was downright impossible and painful most of the time doesn't grant either my daughter or me a pass in the arena of inevitable moments of conflict and friction, in those areas of life where my borders and hers coexist in a somewhat uneasy peace. Our job definitions—mine as her mother and hers as my daughter—continue to shift and evolve as she comes into her own more and more. She still has the task of carving out the territory ahead of her— the life she'll call her own, her work, her relationships. In time, she'll answer the question of whether she wants to be a mother herself, and her answer will be shaped as much by her experience with me as mine was by my own mother.

If I could speak to my mother one more time, I'd say this: "You didn't mean to, but you made me stronger and more aware than I might otherwise have been."

I am not turning into my mother's apologist by writing those words; I would certainly trade in my childhood experiences with her in a heartbeat. But I—and you, for that matter—are more than the sum of the parts our mothers, loving or not, bequeathed us. The process of confrontation—of feeling the pain of not being loved or known—and of becoming conscious of how we were mothered offers an unloved daughter possibilities of growth another experience might not have yielded. Coming to terms with how we were mothered, setting aside the bundle of mother myths once and for all, is an important exercise for every daughter. As one woman wrote me, "Making mistakes and apologizing for them have yielded some of the deepest moments in my relationship to my children. Realizing that I carry my childhood wounds and blind spots makes me human, compels me to feel compassionate toward myself, and ultimately makes me more a part of the human race."

Amen to that.

Acknowledgments

P ARADOXICALLY, WHILE SITTING AT A COMPUTER AND WRITING A page or a chapter is a lonely activity, writing a book takes collaboration, and *Mean Mothers* is no exception. First and foremost, I want to thank the women who shared their stories and experiences, patiently answered intrusive questions, and helped me grasp the subject with greater understanding and insight. The ability to share made the goal of the book that much clearer. I can't and won't name you, but you know who you are. An especial thank-you to Susan Ford Collins, wise woman supreme. Thanks too to my friends and friends-of-friends who sent my e-mail asking for interviews barreling across the United States via the Internet. Daughters of loving mothers helped too, illuminating aspects of their own experiences, and I am particularly grateful to those whose stories demonstrated that maternal care is never perfect and that negatives can coexist with positives in a loving mother-daughter relationship. Thank you to Linda Nielsen, Ph.D., Françoise Bourzat, and Marilyn Lyga, Ph.D., for their interviews and professional expertise. A special thank-you to Rachel Harris, Ph.D., for her graceful introduction. The endnotes tell all, but this book could not have been written without the important work of researchers, scientists, and writers who provided the foundation for anecdote and story.

My editor, Mary Ellen O'Neill, was, as she has been before, a superb help, making this book as good a book as I could write. Her assistant, Matt Patin, was always at the ready; thank you. Karen Gantz Zahler was a fine agent, and proof positive that the Riverdale Country School for Girls could turn out strong girls back in the day, who could team up as stronger, if older, women some three or four decades later. Jane Lahr, an old friend (though I am her new one), offered love, her story, encouragement, and the occasional city and country respite, for which I will always be grateful. Friends and other loved ones offered advice and support and helped me keep writing through a winter or two in Vermont: in alphabetical order, many thanks to Rita Eisenstein, Loren Eskenazi, Leslie Garisto, Susan Greer, Ray Healey, Lori Stein, my Tante Greetje Van Moppes, and Barbara Van Raalte. Merci to John Jiler and Peter Israel for confirming that not every memory, most particularly mine, is selective. Many thanks to my husband, Craig Weatherly, for living with the piles of papers, books, and articles and the ghosts of family relationships and for sitting in a library with me, patiently photocopying, and carrying my books once again, four decades later. And last but always first, kisses to my daughter, Alexandra Emily Israel, for giving me the opportunity to mother differently than my own mother did.

Notes

One: The Myth of Mother Love

Page

4   The parent of a child: Deborah Tannen, *You're Wearing That? Understanding Mothers and Daughters in Conversation* (New York: Ballantine Books, 2006), 188.

5   "Mother's love is bliss": Erich Fromm, *The Art of Loving: An Enquiry into the Nature of Love* (New York: Harper Colophon, 1962), 39.

6   Our insistence on maternal instinct: Sarah Blaffer Hrdy, *Mother Nature: Maternal Instincts and How They Shape the Human Species* (New York: Ballantine Books, 1999), 299–308.

7   A major study: Ranae J. Evenson and Robin W. Simon, "Clarifying the Relationship between Parenthood and Depression," *Journal of Health and Social Behavior* 46 (December 2005): 341–58.

8   Popular books on parenting: See Susan J. Douglas and Meredith W. Michaels, *The Mommy Myth: The Idealization of Motherhood and How It has Undermined All Women* (New York: Free Press, 2004).

9   Roszika Parker has suggested: Roszika Parker, *Mother Love/ Mother Hate: The Power of Maternal Ambivalence* (New York: Basic Books, 1995), 7.

9   "My children cause me": Adrienne Rich, *Of Woman Born: Motherhood as Experience and Institution* (New York: W. W. Norton, 1986), 21.

9   "Every mother knows": Anne Roiphe, *Fruitful: A Real Mother in the Modern World* (Boston: Houghton Mifflin, 1999), 82.

9   as Laurence Steinberg has written: Laurence Steinberg with Wendy Steinberg, *Crossing Paths: How Your Child's Adolescence Triggers Your Own Crisis* (New York: Simon & Schuster, 1994), 67.

10   Even researchers are taken aback: Carol Ryff, Pamela Schmutte, and Young Hyang Lee, "How Children Turn Out: Implications for Parental Self-Evaluation," in *The Parental Experience in Midlife*, ed. Carol D. Ryff and Marsha Mailick Seltzer, 407 (Chicago: University of Chicago Press, 1996).

10.   Nancy Friday . . . astutely observed: Nancy Friday, *My Mother/ My Self* (New York: Delacorte Press, 1977), 10.

10   In a similar vein, Harriet Lerner: Harriet Lerner, *The Mother Dance* (New York: HarperCollins, 1998), 249.

11   "love gives and it takes away": Deborah Tannen, *You're Wearing That?*, 174.

11   Experts of the time: Shari L. Thurer, *The Myths of Motherhood: How Culture Reinvents the Good Mother* (Boston: Houghton Mifflin, 1994), 256.

12   Psychoanalyst René Spitz: Ibid., 274.

12   The model of the good mother as the sacrificial mother: See Carin Rubenstein, *The Sacrificial Mother: Escaping the Trap of Self-Denial* (New York: Hyperion Books, 1998).

15   Therapists, it should be said: Marianne Walters, Betty Carter, Peggy Papp, and Olga Silverstein, *The Invisible Web: Gender Patterns in Family Relationships* (New York: Guilford Press, 1988), 66–67.

15   "The danger lies": Kathryn Black, *Mothering without a Map: The Search for the Good Mother Within* (New York: Penguin Books, 2004), 152.

18   "The quarrels we each had": Terri Apter, *The Sister Knot: Why*

We Fight, Why We're Jealous, and Why We'll Love Each Other No Matter What (New York: W. W. Norton, 2007), 94.

19   Research confirms: Stephen P. Bank and Michael D. Kahn, *The Sibling Bond* (New York: Basic Books, 1997), 19.

19   "Ghosts in the nursery": S. Fraiberg, E. Adelson, and V. Shapiro, "Ghosts in the Nursery: A Psychoanalytic Approach to the Problem of Impaired Mother-Infant Relationships," *Journal of the American Academy of Child Psychiatry* 14 (1975): 387–88.

19   Mary Ainsworth was able: Mary Ainsworth, *Patterns of Attachment: A Psychological Study of the Strange Situation* (Hillsdale, NJ: Laurence Erlbaum Associates, 1978).

20   seen through the lens of brain development: Daniel J. Siegel and Mary Hartzell, *Parenting from the Inside Out: How a Deeper Self-Understanding Can Help You Raise Children Who Thrive* (New York: Penguin Group / Jeremy P. Tarcher, 2004), 104.

21   "In this situation, the child": Ibid., 106.

21   Mary Main: Ibid., 141–151. Also, Siegel, *The Developing Mind*, 77–83.

23   "Mothers and daughters": Christina Robb, *This Changes Everything: The Relational Revolution in Psychology* (New York: Picador, 2007), 262.

25   "Love and the lack of it": Thomas Lewis, Fari Amini, and Richard Lannon, *A General Theory of Love* (New York: Vintage, 2000), 89.

25   "love means protection, caretaking": Ibid., 116.

26   As Irene Stiver observed: Robb, *This Changes Everything,* 372.

29   If, as Hope Edelman has so eloquently: Hope Edelman, *Motherless Daughters* (New York: Delta, 1994), 238–39.

35   "It is hard to write about my own mother": Rich, *Of Woman Born,* 221.

Two: My Mother and Her Mother Before Her

Page

36   "For each woman": Barbara Zax and Stephan Poulter, *Mending*

the Broken Bough: Restoring the Promise of the Mother-Daughter Relationship (New York: Berkley Books, 1998), 3.

41   Both patterns of relationship . . . as exemplified in a case: Marianne Walters and others, *The Invisible Web: Gender Patterns in Family Relationships* (New York: Guilford Press, 1988), 66–75.

42   "life-shaping process": Thomas Lewis, Fari Amini, and Richard Lannon, *A General Theory of Love* (New York: Vintage, 2000), 155.

42   Much of what a baby learns: Ibid., 155–56.

43   How necessary this limbic resonance is: Ibid., 157.

43   each of them "featherweight": Ibid., 160.

43   "How is it that some children": Edward Z. Tronick, "Emotions and Emotional Communication in Infants," *American Psychologist* 44, no. 2 (February 1, 1989), 112–19.

43   Tronick describes this scenario: Ibid., 112.

44   Extrapolating from this: Ibid., 113.

45   researchers had nondepressed mothers: Jeffrey F. Cohn and Edward Z. Tronick, "Three-Month-Old Infants' Reaction to Simulated Maternal Depression," *Child Development* 54 (1983): 185–95.

45   when a mother is fully attuned: Jeffrey F. Cohn and Edward Z. Tronick, "Mother-Infant Face-to-Face Interaction: Influence Is Bidirectional and Unrelated to Periodic Cycles in Either Partner's Behavior," *Developmental Psychology* 24, no. 3 (1988): 386–92.

45   on a visual cliff: James F. Sorce and others, "Maternal Emotional Signaling: Its Effects on the Visual Cliff Behavior of 1-Year-Olds," *Developmental Psychology* 21, no. 1 (1985): 195–200.

46   "actively seek out affective information": Tronick, "Emotions and Emotional Communication," 114.

46   The Adult Attachment Interview: Daniel J. Siegel, *The Developing Mind: How Relationships and the Brain Interact to Shape Who We Are* (New York: Guilford Press, 1999), 77–83.

47   What's truly astonishing: Siegel and Hartzell, *Parenting from the Inside Out,* 141.

47   "The parents' narratives": Siegel, *Developing Mind,* 81.

47   Relational psychology: Carol Gilligan, *In a Different Voice: Psychological Theory and Women's Development* (Cambridge, MA: Harvard University Press, 1993).

48   "I have written it many times": Anne Roiphe, *Fruitful* (Boston: Houghton Mifflin, 1996), 5–6.

48   "earned secure attachment": Siegel, *Developing Mind,* 91–92. Also Siegel and Hartzell, *Parenting from the Inside Out,* 143–47.

48   While adults with earned secure attachments: Siegel, *Developing Mind,* 91.

54   "Daughters worked deliberately": Terri Apter, *Altered Loves: Mothers and Daughters During Adolescence* (New York: St. Martin's Press, 1990), 19.

54   "mutual desire to understand": Janet Surrey, "The Mother-Daughter Relationships: Themes in Psychotherapy," in *Daughtering and Mothering: Female Subjectivity Reanalyzed,* ed. Janneke Van Mens-Verhulst, Karlein Schreurs, and Liesbeth Woertman, 120 (London: Routlege, 1993).

55   "mutual authenticity": Ibid.

55   "A consistent theme": Louis Cozolino, *The Neuroscience of Human Relationships: Attachment and the Developing Social Brain* (New York: W. W. Norton, 2006), 331.

55   In her study of midlife daughters: Karen L. Fingerman, *Mothers and Their Adult Daughters: Mixed Emotions, Enduring Bonds* (Amherst, NY: Prometheus Books, 2003).

55   Fingerman's sample: Ibid., 23–29.

56   Mothers and daughters not only saw: Ibid., 89–91.

56   Fingerman notes that this runs counter: Ibid., 91.

56   Fingerman offers several explanations: Ibid., 91–92.

56   "Probably there is nothing": Adrienne Rich, *Of Woman Born: Motherhood as Experience and Institution* (New York: W. W. Norton, 1986), 225–26.

58   "By attributing certain characteristics": Stephen P. Bank and Michael D. Kahn, *The Sibling Bond* (New York: Basic Books, 1997), 22.

58   the Gallup Poll: "Americans Continue to Express Slight Preference for Boys," July 15, 2007, http://www.gallup.com/

poll/28045/Americans-Continue-Express-Slight-Preference-Boys.aspx.

59   Mothers tend to match their sons': Erin B. McClure, "A Meta-Analytic Review of Sex differences in Facial Expression Processing and Their Development in Infants, Children, and Adolescents," *Psychological Bulletin* 126, no. 3 (2000): 431.

59   Some researchers have suggested: M. Katherine Weinberg and others, "Gender Differences in Emotional Expressivity and Self-Regulation during Early Infancy," *Developmental Psychology* 35 (1999): 175–88.

59   parents talk more to girls: Robyn Fivush, "Exploring Sex Differences in the Emotional Content of Mother-Child Conversations about the Past," *Sex Roles* 20, nos. 11/12 (1989): 689.

59   "spoke more to their daughters": Ibid., 675–91.

60   "Mother can see her son as 'other'": Luise Eichenbaum and Susie Orbach, *Between Women: Love, Envy, and Competition in Women's Friendships* (New York: Penguin Books, 1987), 59.

60   "identify more with their girl babies": Jane Flax, "The Conflict between Nurturance and Autonomy in Mother-Daughter Relationships and Within Feminism," *Feminist Studies* 4, no. 2 (June 1978): 174.

64   cite two separate studies: Judy Dunn and Robert Plomin, *Separate Lives: Why Children Are So Different* (New York: Basic Books, 1990), 74–75.

64   findings both surprised and enlightened: Ibid., 78.

65   "witnessing *differential* treatment": Ibid., 79.

67   "Children's perceptions of events": Ibid., 162.

67   searing memoir of her mother: Susanna Sonnenberg, *Her Last Death: A Memoir* (New York: Scribner, 2008).

68   "We don't want to fight . . . ": Ibid., 3.

68   "She doesn't see what I see": Ibid., 12.

69   By 1819, the Grimm Brothers: Marina Warner, *From the Beast to the Blonde: On Fairy Tales and Their Tellers* (New York: Farrar, Straus & Giroux, 1994), 211.

69   "I'd have to swallow": Charlotte Phillips, "When the Green-

Eyed Monster Is Mum," November 24, 2007.

69 on the paper's website: "Feedback," December 1, 2007, http://www.women.timesonline.co.uk/tol/life_and_style/women/body_and_soul/article2929870.

70 "Once, long ago": Phyllis Chesler, *Woman's Inhumanity to Woman* (New York: Plume, 2003), 284.

70 "We are not envious": Peter Salovey and Alexander Rothman, "Envy and Jealousy," in *The Psychology of Jealousy and Envy,* ed. Peter Salovey, 262 (New York: Guilford Press, 1991), 94.

72 while the majority of mothers: Laurence Steinberg with Wendy Steinberg, *Crossing Paths: How Your Child's Adolescence Triggers Your Own Crisis* (New York: Simon & Schuster, 1994), 61.

73 "goodness of fit": Stella Chess and Alexander Thomas, *Know Your Child: An Authoritative Guide to Today's Parents* (New York: Basic Books, 1987), Chapter 3.

74 "the brain is primed to grow": Cozolino, *Neuroscience of Human Relationships,* 331.

Three: In the House of the Father

Page

76 "children's presence and marital quality": Jay Belsky, "Children and Marriage," in *The Psychology of Marriage: Basic Issues and Applications,* ed. Frank D. Fincham and Thomas N. Bradbury, 172 (New York: Guilford Press, 1990).

76 for couples with a single child: Philip Morgan, Diane Lye, and Gretchen Condran, "Sons, Daughters, and the Risk of Marital Disruption," *American Journal of Sociology* 94, no. 1 (1988): 110–29. Also Aphra Katzev, Rebecca Warner, and Alan Acock, "Girls or Boys? Relationship of Child Gender to Marital Instability," *Journal of Marriage and the Family* 56 (1994): 89–100.

76 "the divorce culture": Barbara Dafoe Whitehead, *The Divorce Culture: Rethinking Our Commitments to Marriage and Family* (New York: Vintage, 1998).

76 This more relaxed societal tolerance: Ibid., 6.

77 no less an expert than Bruno Bettelheim: Bruno Bettelheim, *The*

Empty Fortress: Infantile Autism and the Birth of the Self (New York: Free Press, 1972).

78   The question itself: "All about Fathers," *Child Study Center Letter* 4, no. 2 (November/December 1999), NYU Child Study Center, http://www.aboutourkids.org.

78   a list of common beliefs: Linda Nielsen, *Embracing Your Father: How to Build the Relationship You've Always Wanted with Your Dad* (New York: McGraw-Hill, 2004), 1.

79   scientific evidence shows: Janet Shibley Hyde, "The Gender Similarities Hypothesis," *American Psychologist* 60, no. 6 (September 2005): 581–92.

79   "show American children": Stephen Mintz, *Huck's Raft: A History of American Childhood* (Cambridge, MA: Harvard University Press / Belknap Press, 2004), 298–99.

81   "maternal gatekeeping": Sarah M. Allen and Alan J. Hawkins, "Maternal Gatekeeping: Mothers' Beliefs and Behaviors That Inhabit Father Involvement in Family Work," *Journal of Marriage and the Family* 6, no. 1 (February 1999): 199–212.

81   "Some women both cherish and resent": Joseph H. Pleck and Brian P. Masciadrelli, "Paternal Involvement by U.S. Residential Fathers: Levels, Sources, and Consequences," in *The Role of the Father in Child Development,* ed. Michael E. Lamb, 249 (Hoboken, NJ: John Wiley & Sons, 2004).

81   as showcased in a 2008 cover story: Lisa Belkin, "When Mom and Dad Share It All," *The New York Times Magazine,* June 15, 2008: 44 *ff.*

81   nature and quality of the marital relationship: Pleck and Masciadrelli, "Paternal Involvement," 249. Also E. Mark Cummins, Marcie C. Goeke-Morey, and Jessica Raymond, "Fathers in Family Context: Effects of Marital Quality and Marital Conflict," in Lamb, *Role of the Father,* 196–221.

81   "influential agents": Mary F. De Luccie, "Mothers: Influential Agents in Father-Child Relations," *Genetic, Social, and General Psychology Monographs* 122, no. 3 (August 1996).

82   a woman's relationship to her father: De Luccie, "Mothers," 295–96, 302.

82   the marital relationship . . . becomes a template: Mary Roberts
      Gray and Laurence Steinberg, "Adolescent Romance and the
      Parent-Child Relationship," in *The Development of Romantic
      Relationships in Adolescence,* ed. Wyndol Furman, B. Bradford
      Brown, and Candice Fiering, 245–46 (Cambridge: Cambridge
      University Press, 1999).

82   How mothers and fathers resolve: Parke and others, "Fathering
      and Children's Peer Relationships," in *The Role of the Father
      in Child Development,* ed. Michael E. Lamb, 317 (Hoboken,
      NJ: John Wiley & Sons, 2004). See also Gray and Steinberg,
      "Adolescent Romance," 255–57.

87   The balance of power: Dr. Linda Nielsen in discussion with the
      author, June 2008.

87   "the Boy Code": William Pollack, *Real Boys: Rescuing Our Sons
      from the Myths of Boyhood* (New York: Henry Holt, 1998), 23–25.

89   "moral overseer": William Marsiglio, "Contemporary
      Scholarship on Fatherhood: Culture, Identity, and Conduct,"
      Journal of Family Issues 14, no. 4 (December 1993): 486.

89   "As a daughter grows up": Linda Schierse Leonard, *The
      Wounded Woman: Healing the Father-Daughter Relationship*
      (Boston: Shambhala, 1998), 11.

90   "fathers may play a special role": Michael E. Lamb and Charlie
      Lewis, "The Development and Significance of Father-Child
      Relationships in Two-Parent Families," in Lamb, *Role of the
      Father,* 287–88.

90   "Fathers help daughters": Dr. Linda Nielsen in discussion with
      the author, June 2008.

92   "give up the internal relationship": Nancy J. Chodorow, *The
      Reproduction of Mothering: Psychoanalysis and the Sociology of
      Gender* (Berkeley: University of California Press, 1998), 127.

92   Research confirms that fathers: Parke and others, "Fathering and
      Children's Peer Relationships," 310.

92   recent research suggests: Brenda L. Volling and others, "Parents'
      Emotional Availability and Infant Emotional Competence:
      Infant Attachment and Emerging Self-Regulation," *Journal of
      Family Psychology* 16, no. 4 (2002): 448.

92   a father's more rowdy: Lamb and Lewis, "Development and Significance," 276–77.

92   a father's management: Parke and others, "Fathering and Children's Peer Relationships," 315–16.

103   "With Mother, I always felt": Mary Karr, *The Liar's Club: A Memoir* (New York: Penguin Books, 2005), 58–59.

Four: Siblings and Other Rivalries

Page

106   a "Hansel and Gretel" pair: Stephen P. Bank and Michael D. Kahn, *The Sibling Bond* (New York: Basic Books, 1997), 113*ff.*

106   "some of the most intense": Bank and Kahn, *Sibling Bond,* 19, 123.

107   "grew up on a shared diet": Hope Edelman, *Motherless Daughters* (New York: Delta, 1994), 134.

109   "about their childhood": Terri Apter, *The Sister Knot: Why We Fight, Why We're Jealous, and Why We'll Love Each Other No Matter What* (New York: W. W. Norton, 2007), 225.

109   "Siblings can challenge": Ibid., 224.

109   "threaten to dislodge": Ibid., 225–26.

110   "From the beginning": Nancy Friday, *Jealousy* (New York: M. M. Evans, 1997), 444.

112   astonished to discover that 84 percent: Francine Klagsbrun, *Mixed Feelings: Love, Hate, Rivalry, and Reconciliation Among Brothers and Sisters* (New York: Bantam Books, 1992), 157.

112   What's worth noting is that: Brenda K. Bryant and Susan B. Crockenberg, "Correlates and Dimensions of Prosocial Behavior: A Study of Female Siblings with their Mothers," *Child Development* 51, no. 2 (June 1980): 538.

112   isn't just dyadic but triadic: Brenda K. Bryant, "Sibling Caretaking: Providing Emotional Support During Middle Childhood," in *Children's Sibling Relationships,* ed. Frits Boer and Judy Dunn, 56–58 (Hillsdale, NJ: Laurence Erlbaum Associates, 1992).

112 "absolute levels of parental behavior": Frits Boer, Arnold Goedhart, and Philip D. A. Treffers, "Siblings and Their Parents," in Boer and Dunn, *Children's Sibling Relationships,* 41–54.

112 Differential parental treatment: Judy Dunn, *Young Children's Close Relationships: Beyond Attachment* (Newbury Park, CA: Sage Publications, 1993), 85.

115 sibling relationship—in both its absence and its presence: Rosalind Edwards and others, *Sibling Identity and Relationship* (New York: Routledge, 2006), 39.

115 "constellation variables": Duane Buhrmeister, "The Developmental Courses of Sibling and Peer Relationships," in Boer and Dunn, *Children's Sibling Relationships,* 20.

115 "in acknowledgment of the phenomenon": Susan Scarf Merrell, *The Accidental Bond: The Power of Sibling Relationships* (New York: Times Books, 1995), 8.

117 "A research study on siblings": Marie Brenner, *Apples and Oranges: My Brother and Me, Lost and Found* (New York: Farrar, Straus & Giroux / Sarah Crichton Books, 2008), 42–43.

117 "We were moving through": Ibid., 207.

117 same-sex siblings report: Buhrmeister, "Developmental Courses," 31.

117 sibling relationships become less intense: Ibid., 37.

117 sibling relationships are often fluid: Victor G. Cicirelli, *Sibling Relationships Across the Life Span* (New York: Plenum Press, 1995).

117 as Melanie Mauthner has written: Melanie L. Mauthner, *Sistering: Power and Change in Female Relationships* (London: Macmillan / Palgrave, 2005), 48–55.

118 being an only child is still "non-normative": Toni Falco, "Social Norms and the One-Child Family: Clinical and Policy Implications," in *Children's Sibling Relationships,* 78–79.

119 "very little empirical evidence": Frits Boer, "Epilogue," in *Children's Sibling Relationships,* 54.

119 "convictions" about what "position": Merrill, *Accidental Bond,* 14.

121 "I took notes, learned lessons": Apter, *Altered Loves,* 181.

125   the "roles" children play: James Boassard and Eleanor Bell,
       *The Large Family System: An Original Study in the Sociology of
       Family Behavior* (Westport, CT: Greenwood Press, 1975) cited in
       Francine Klagsbrun, Mixed Feelings, 74.

131   "as warmth-seeking mammals": Stephen Bank, "Remembering
       and Reinterpreting Sibling Bonds," in *Children's Sibling
       Relationships,* 146.

131   "a secret inscription, a frozen image": Ibid., 147.

Five: Stilling the Voice of the Mother Within

Page

133   "A young child knows Mother": Annie Dillard, *An American
       Childhood* (New York: Harper & Row, 1987), 35.

135   "it's important to remember": Dr. Marilyn Lyga in discussion
       with the author, December 2008.

137   "For each friend involved": Luise Eichenbaum and Susie
       Orbach, *Between Women: Love, Envy, and Competition in
       Women's Friendships* (New York: Penguin Books, 1987), 75.

138   learn about female envy: Susan Shapiro Barash, *Tripping the
       Prom Queen: The Truth About Women and Rivalry* (New York:
       St. Martin's Press, 2006), 49.

140   "domestic terrorism": Deborah Tannen, *You're Wearing That?
       Understanding Mothers and Daughters in Conversation* (New
       York: Ballantine Books, 2006), 185.

140   "As bad as the experience": Ibid., 188.

140   "My mother's way of 'dealing'": Vivian Gornick, *Fierce
       Attachments: A Memoir* (New York: Farrar, Straus & Giroux,
       2005), 6.

141   "I'm flying": Ibid., 103.

141   "She doesn't know I take": Ibid., 104.

141   "'You are what you are'": Judith Viorst, *Necessary Losses* (New
       York: Fireside Books, 1986), 56.

142   "I had always wondered": Dani Shapiro, "Not a Pretty Story,"
       in *Maybe Baby: 28 Writers Tell the Truth About Skepticism,
       Infertility, Baby Lust, Ambivalence, and How They Made the*

Biggest Decision of Their Lives, ed. Lori Leibovich, 118 (New York: HarperCollins, 2007).

142   "On a *soul* level it seemed impossible": Ibid., 119.

143   "Understand this": Ibid., 127.

145   "This emptiness turns the unmothered": Hope Edelman, *Motherless Daughters* (New York: Delta, 1994), 170.

145   "to feel loved and less alone": Kerry Cohen, *Loose Girl: A Memoir of Promiscuity* (New York: Hyperion Books, 2008), 3.

145   "is the story of any girl": Ibid., 2.

145   "self-injury represents": Karen Conterio and Wendy Lader, *Bodily Harm* (New York: Hyperion Books, 1998), 20.

146   In her groundbreaking book: Kim Chernin, *The Hungry Self: Women, Eating, and Identity* (New York: Harper & Row, 1985).

146   "As children we have": Geneen Roth, *When Food Is Love: The Relationship between Eating and Intimacy* (New York: Plume, 1992), 24.

147   "It is not possible": Ibid., 25.

147   "to absorb her healing spirit": Evelyn S. Bassoff, *Mothering Ourselves: Help and Healing for Adult Daughters* (New York: Plume, 1992), 44.

147   "For some, alcohol": Ibid., 51–52.

148   "Your mother was a sadist": Kathryn Harrison, *The Mother Knot: A Memoir* (New York: Random House, 2004), 28.

148   "Anyway, doesn't sadism imply": Ibid., 30.

148   "Remade her": Ibid., 41.

148   "Who would I be without": Ibid., 45.

149   "It impels us to do again": Viorst, *Necessary Losses,* 77.

150   "If a child is told": Richard C. Schwartz, *Internal Family Systems Therapy* (New York: Guilford Press, 1995), 52.

150   a "theft" of self-esteem: Ibid., 52–53.

150   "These burdened young parts": Ibid., 53.

151   Psychologists Cindy Hazan: Cindy Hazan and Philip Shaver, "Romantic Love Conceptualized as an Attachment Process," *Journal of Personality and Social Psychology* 52, no. 3 (1987): 511–24.

152   psychologist Kim Barthlomew proposed: Kim Bartholomew and
        Philip R. Shaver, "Methods of Assessing Adult Attachment: Do
        They Converge?" in *Attachment Theory and Close Relationships,*
        ed. Jeffry A. Simpson and W. Steven Rholes, 30–32 (New York:
        Guilford Press, 1998).

152   "characterized by intimacy": "Peer Attachment Prototypes,"
        http://www.sfu.ca/psych/faculty/bartholomew/research/
        attachment/prototypes.htm, p. 1.

152   "both across time": Kim Bartholomew and Leonard M.
        Horowitz, "Attachment Styles Among Young Adults: A Test
        of a Four-Category Model," *Journal of Personality and Social
        Psychology* 61, no. 2 (1991): 226–44.

153   While the preoccupied daughter: Kim Bartholomew, "Avoidance
        of Intimacy: An Attachment Perspective," *Journal of Social and
        Personal Relations* 7 (1990): 163.

153   "Puctuated by emotional extremes": "Peer Attachment
        Prototypes," Ibid.

153   Bartholomew's innovation: Eva C. Klohnen and Oliver P. John,
        "Models of Attachment: A Theory-Based Prototype Approach,"
        in Simpson and Rholes, *Attachment Theory,* 116–18.

153   "experience pervasive": Kim Bartholomew, "Avoidance of
        Intimacy": An Attachment Perspective," *Journal of Social and
        Personal Relationships* 7, no. 2 (1990), 164.

154   "A way of maintaining": Ibid., 164–65.

154   "as cool (or cold and arrogant: Ibid., 4.

154   "the approach to and quality of": "Peer Attachement Prototypes," 4.

154   "their adoption of a detached stance": Ibid., 5.

156   "that acts and responds": Clarissa Pinkola Estés, *Women
        Who Run with the Wolves: Myths and Stories of the Wild
        Woman Archetype* (New York: Ballantine Books, 1997),
        186.

157   the "ambivalent" mother: Ibid., 186–88.

157   a "collapsed mother": Ibid., 188–90.

157   The "child-mother": Ibid., 191–93.

158   "truly destructive mothering": Ibid., 194.

158   "the remedy is gaining mothering": Ibid., 193.

163 "When a child doesn't receive": Françoise Bourzat in discussion with the author, October 2008.

165 By making sense of our childhood: Daniel J. Siegel and Mary Hartzell, *Parenting from the Inside Out: How a Deeper Self-Understanding Can Help You Raise Children Who Thrive* (New York: Penguin Group / Jeremy P. Tarcher, 2004), 122–53.

166 "as soon as my mother looked": Julia Blackburn, *The Three of Us: A Family Story* (New York: Pantheon Books, 2008), 43.

166 "I wonder if she sat down": Ibid., 41.

Six: Turning the Wheel

Page

172 "Perhaps more than anything": Susan Maushart, *The Mask of Motherhood: How Becoming a Mother Changes Our Lives and Why We Never Talk About It* (New York: Penguin Books, 1999), 10.

172 "No one mentions the psychic": Ibid., 11.

175 "When unloved daughters embark": Françoise Bourzat in discussion with the author, October 2008.

178 "reorganized around the child": Diana Diamond and Kimberly McLauchlin Kotov, "The Representational World of the Mother in Attachment and Psychoanalytic Theory: A Review and Critique," in *The Inner World of the Mother,* ed. Dale Mendell and Patsy Turrini, 119 (Madison, CT: Psychosocial Press, 2003).

179 "there is a rapid growth": Daniel N. Stern, *The Motherhood Constellation: A Unified View of Parent-Infant Psychotherapy* (New York: Basic Books, 1990), 22–23.

179 "mothers intuitively protect": Ibid., 23.

179 Ruth F. Lax, Ph.D., has detailed: Ruth F. Lax, "Motherhood Is an Ebb and Flow—It Lasts a Lifetime—The Vicissitudes of Mother's Interaction with her 'Fantasy Child,'" in Mendell and Turrini, *Inner World,* 169–85.

179 "fixed representational world": Stern, *Motherhood Constellation,* 24.

179 "The new mother must give up": Ibid., 25.

180 "the motherhood constellation": Stern, Ibid., 28–29.

186   "It was nothing I wanted": Susan Collins, *The Children Are
       Watching: Ten Skills for Leading the Next Generation to Success*
       (Barrytown, NY: Barrytown, 1995), 247.

187   "Being a parent gives us": Daniel J. Siegel and Mary Hartzell,
       *Parenting from the Inside Out: How a Deeper Self-Understanding
       Can Help You Raise Children Who Thrive* (New York: Penguin
       Group / Jeremy P. Tarcher, 2004), 248.

193   "barriers to empathy": Martha Manning, *The Common Thread:
       Mothers and Daughters: The Bond We Never Outgrow* (New York:
       Quill, 2002), 141–54.

193   "one of the greatest" : Ibid., 142.

194   "Disruptions in Service": Ibid., 141–54.

194   "An essential part": Ibid., 145.

194   "Motherhood tests every inch": Ibid., 148.

194   "so burdened by her own": Ibid., 149.

194   "emphasize their daughters' failures": Ibid., 150.

195   "this isn't a one-time decision": Marilyn Lyga in discussion with
       the author, December 2008.

Selected Bibliography

Ainsworth, Mary, Mary Blehar, Everett Walters, and Sally Wall. *Patterns of Attachment: A Psychological Study of the Strange Situation*. Hillsdale, NJ: Lawrence Erlbaum Associates, 1978.

Allen, Sarah M., and Alan J. Hawkins. "Maternal Gatekeeping: Mothers' Beliefs and Behaviors That Inhabit Father Involvement in Family Work." *Journal of Marriage and the Family* 6, no. 1 (February 1999): 199–212.

Apter, Terri. *Altered Loves: Mothers and Daughters During Adolescence*. New York: St. Martin's Press, 1990.

———. *The Sister Knot: Why We Fight, Why We're Jealous, and Why We'll Love Each Other No Matter What*. New York: W. W. Norton, 2007.

Bank, Stephen P., and Michael D. Kahn. *The Sibling Bond*. New York: Basic Books, 1997.

Barash, Susan Shapiro. *Tripping the Prom Queen: The Truth About Women and Rivalry*. New York: St. Martin's Press, 2006.

Bartholomew, Kim. "Avoidance of Intimacy: An Attachment Perspective." *Journal of Social and Personal Relations* 7 (1990): 163.

Bartholomew, Kim, and Leonard M. Horowitz. "Attachment Styles among Young Adults: A Test of a Four-Category Model." *Journal of Personality and Social Psychology* 61, no. 2 (1991): 226–44.

Bassoff, Evelyn S. *Mothering Ourselves: Help and Healing for Adult Daughters.* New York: Plume, 1992.

———. *Mothers and Daughters: Loving and Letting Go.* New York: Plume, 1988.

Black, Kathryn. *Mothering Without a Map: The Search for the Good Mother Within.* New York: Penguin Books, 2004.

Blackburn, Julia. *The Three of Us: A Family Story.* New York: Pantheon Books, 2008.

Boer, Frits, and Judy Dunn, eds. *Children's Sibling Relationships.* Hillsdale, NJ: Laurence Erlbaum Associates, 1992.

Brenner, Marie. *Apples and Oranges: My Brother and Me, Lost and Found.* New York: Farrar, Straus & Giroux / Sarah Crichton Books, 2008.

Bryant, Brenda K., and Susan B. Crockenberg. "Correlates and Dimensions of Prosocial Behavior: A Study of Female Siblings with their Mothers." *Child Development* 51, no. 2 (June 1980): 529–44.

Chernin, Kim. *The Hungry Self: Women, Eating, and Identity.* New York: Harper & Row, 1985.

Chesler, Phyllis. *Woman's Inhumanity to Woman.* New York: Plume, 2003.

Chodorow, Nancy J. *The Reproduction of Mothering: Psychoanalysis and the Sociology of Gender.* Berkeley: University of California Press, 1998.

Cicirelli, Victor G. *Sibling Relationships Across the Life Span.* New York: Plenum Press, 1995.

Cohen, Kerry. *Loose Girl: A Memoir of Promiscuity.* New York: Hyperion Books, 2008.

Cohn, Jeffrey F., and Edward Z. Tronick. "Mother-Infant Face-to-Face

Interaction: Influence Is Bidirectional and Unrelated to Periodic Cycles in Either Partner's Behavior." *Developmental Psychology* 24, no. 3 (1988): 386–92.

———. "Three-Month-Old Infants' Reaction to Simulated Maternal Depression." *Child Development* 54 (1983): 185–95.

Collins, Susan. *Our Children Are Watching: Ten Skills for Leading the Next Generation to Success.* Barrytown, NY: Barrytown, 1995.

Conterio, Karen, and Wendy Lader. *Bodily Harm.* New York: Hyperion Books, 1998.

Cozolino Louis. *The Neuroscience of Human Relationships: Attachment and the Developing Social Brain.* New York: W. W. Norton, 2006.

De Luccie, Mary F. "Mothers: Influential Agents in Father-Child Relations." *Genetic, Social, and General Psychology Monographs* 122 (1996): 287–307.

Devlin, Rachel. *Relative Intimacy: Fathers, Daughters, and Postwar American Culture.* Chapel Hill: University of North Carolina Press, 2005.

Dillard, Annie. *An American Childhood.* New York: Harper & Row, 1987.

Douglas, Susan J., and Meredith W. Michaels. *The Mommy Myth: The Idealization of Motherhood and How It Has Undermined All Women.* New York: Free Press, 2004.

Dunn, Judy. *Sisters and Brothers: The Developing Child.* Cambridge, MA: Harvard University Press, 1985.

———. *Young Children's Close Relationships: Beyond Attachment.* Newbury Park, CA: Sage Publications, 1993.

Dunn, Judy, and Robert Plomin. *Separate Lives: Why Children Are So Different.* New York: Basic Books, 1990.

Edelman, Hope. *Motherless Daughters: The Legacy of Loss.* New York: Delta, 1994.

———. *Motherless Mothers: How Mother Loss Shapes the Parents We Become.* New York: HarperCollins, 2006.

Edwards, Rosalind, Lucy Hadfield, Helen Lucey, and Melanie Mauthner. *Sibling Identity and Relationship.* New York: Routledge, 2006.

Eichenbaum, Luise, and Susie Orbach. *Between Women: Love, Envy, and Competition in Women's Friendships.* New York: Penguin Books, 1987.

Estés, Clarissa Pinkola. *Women Who Run with the Wolves: Myths and Stories of the Wild Woman Archetype.* New York: Ballantine Books, 1997.

Evenson, Ranae J., and Robin W. Simon. "Clarifying the Relationship between Parenthood and Depression." *Journal of Health and Social Behavior* 46 (December 2005): 341–58.

Fenchel, Gerd H., ed. *The Mother-Daughter Relationship Echoes Through Time.* Lanham, MD: Rowman & Littlefield, 1998.

Fincham, Frank D., and Thomas N. Bradbury, eds. *The Psychology of Marriage: Basic Issues and Applications.* New York: Guilford Press, 1990.

Fingerman, Karen L. *Mothers and Their Adult Daughters: Mixed Emotions, Enduring Bonds.* Amherst, NY: Prometheus Books, 2003.

Fivush, Robyn. "Exploring Sex Differences in the Emotional Content of Mother-Child Conversations about the Pas.." *Sex Roles* 20, nos. 11/12 (1989): 675–91.

Flax, Jane. "The Conflict between Nurturance and Autonomy in Mother-Daughter Relationships and Within Feminism." *Feminist Studies* 4, no. 2 (June 1978): 171–89.

Fraiberg, S., E. Adelson, and V. Shapiro. "Ghosts in the Nursery: A Psychoanalytic Approach to the Problem of Impaired Mother-Infant

Relationships." *Journal of the American Academy of Child Psychiatry* 14 (1975): 387–422.

Frayley, R. Chris, and Philip R. Shaver. "Adult Romantic Attatchment: Theoretical Developments, Emerging Controversies, and Unanswered Questions." *Review of General Psychology* 4, no. 2 (2000): 132–54.

Friday, Nancy. *Jealousy.* New York: M. M. Evans, 1997.

———. *My Mother/My Self.* New York: Delacorte Press, 1977.

Fromm, Erich. *The Art of Loving: An Enquiry into the Nature of Love.* New York: Harper Colophon, 1962.

Fuller, Alexandra. *Don't Let's Go to the Dogs Tonight.* New York: Random House, 2001.

Furman, Wyndol, B. Bradford Brown, and Candice Fiering, eds. *The Development of Romantic Relationships in Adolescence.* Cambridge: Cambridge University Press, 1999.

Gilligan, Carol. *In a Different Voice: Psychological Theory and Women's Development.* Cambridge, MA: Harvard University Press, 1993.

Gornick, Vivian. *Fierce Attachments: A Memoir.* New York: Farrar, Straus & Giroux, 2005.

Harrison, Kathryn. *The Mother Knot: A Memoir.* New York: Random House, 2005.

Hazan, Cindy, and Philip Shaver. "Romantic Love Conceptualized as an Attachment Process." *Journal of Personality and Social Psychology* 52, no. 3 (1987): 511–24.

Hrdy, Sarah Blaffer. *Mother Nature: Maternal Instincts and How They Shape the Human Species.* New York: Ballantine Books, 1999.

Hyde, Janet Shibley. "The Gender Similarities Hypothesis." *American Psychologist* 60, no. 6 (September 2005): 581–92.

Karr, Mary. *The Liar's Club: A Memoir.* New York: Penguin Books, 2005.

Katzev, Aphra, Rebecca Warner, and Alan Acock. "Girls or Boys? Relationship of Child Gender to Marital Instability." *Journal of Marriage and the Family* 56 (1994): 89–100.

Klagsbrun, Francine. *Mixed Feelings: Love, Hate, Rivalry, and Reconciliation Among Brothers and Sisters.* New York: Bantam Books, 1992.

Lamb, Michael E. *The Role of the Father in Child Development.* Hoboken, NJ: John Wiley & Sons, 2004.

Leder, Jane Mersky. *Brothers and Sisters: How They Shape Our Lives.* New York: St. Martin's Press, 1991.

Leibovich, Lori, ed. *Maybe Baby: 28 Writers Tell the Truth About Skepticism, Infertility, Baby Lust, Childlessness, Ambivalence, and How They Made the Biggest Decision of Their Lives.* New York: Harper-Collins, 2007.

Leonard, Linda Schierse. *The Wounded Woman: Healing the Father-Daughter Relationship.* Boston: Shambhala, 1998.

Lerner, Harriet. *The Mother Dance.* New York: HarperCollins, 1998.

Lewis, Thomas, Fari Amini, and Richard Lannon. *A General Theory of Love.* New York: Vintage, 2000.

Manning, Martha. *The Common Thread: Mothers and Daughters: The Bond We Never Outgrow.* New York: Quill, 2002.

Marsiglio, William. "Contemporary Scholarship on Fatherhood: Culture, Identity, and Conduct." *Journal of Family Issues* 14, no. 4 (December 1993): 486–509.

Matthias, Barbara. *Between Sisters: Secret Rivals, Intimate Friends.* New York: Delacorte Press, 1992.

Maushart, Susan. *The Mask of Motherhood: How Becoming a Mother Changes Our Lives and Why We Never Talk About It.* New York: Penguin Books, 1999.

Mauthner, Melanie L. *Sistering: Power and Change in Female Relationships.* London: Macmillan / Palgrave, 2005.

McClure, Erin B. "A Meta-Analytic Review of Sex differences in Facial Expression Processing and Their Development in Infants, Children, and Adolescents." *Psychological Bulletin* 126, no. 3 (2000): 424–50.

Mendell, Dale, and Patsy Turrini. *The Inner World of the Mother.* Madison, CT: Psychosocial Press, 2003.

Merrell, Susan Scarf. *The Accidental Bond: The Power of Sibling Relationships.* New York: Times Books, 1995.

Miller, Alice. *The Drama of the Gifted Child: The Search for the True Self.* New York: HarperPerennial, 1997.

Millman, Marcia. *The Perfect Sister: What Draws Us Together. What Drives Us Apart.* New York: Harcourt, 2004.

Mintz, Stephen. *Huck's Raft: A History of American Childhood.* Cambridge, MA: Harvard University Press / Belknap Press, 2004.

Morgan, Philip, Diane Lye, and Gretchen Condran. "Sons, Daughters, and the Risk of Marital Disruption." *American Journal of Sociology* 94, no. 1 (1988): 110–29.

Nielsen, Linda. *Embracing the Father: How to Build the Relationship You've Always Wanted with Your Dad.* New York: McGraw-Hill, 2004.

Parker, Roszika. *Mother Love/Mother Hate: The Power of Maternal Ambivalence.* New York: Basic Books, 1995.

Pollack, William. *Real Boys: Rescuing Our Sons from the Myths of Boyhood.* New York: Henry Holt, 1998.

Rich, Adrienne. *Of Woman Born: Motherhood as Experience and Institution.* New York: W. W. Norton, 1986.

Robb, Christina. *This Changes Everything: The Relational Revolution in Psychology.* New York: Picador, 2007.

Roiphe, Anne. *Fruitful: A Real Mother in the Modern World.* Boston: Houghton Mifflin, 1996.

Roth, Geneen. *When Food Is Love: The Relationship Between Eating and Intimacy.* New York: Plume, 1992.

Rubenstein, Carin. *The Sacrificial Mother: Escaping the Trap of Self-Denial.* New York: Hyperion Books, 1998.

Ryff, Carol D., and Marsha Mailick. *The Parental Experience in Midlife.* Chicago: University of Chicago Press, 1996.

Salovey, Peter, ed. *The Psychology of Jealousy and Envy.* New York: Guilford Press, 1991.

Scharfe, Elaine, and Kim Bartholomew. "Reliability and Stability of Adult Attachment Patterns." *Personal Relationships,* 1 (1994), 23–43.

Schwartz, Richard C. *Internal Family Systems Therapy.* New York: Guilford Press, 1995.

Sharpe, Sue. *Fathers and Daughters.* London: Routledge, 1994.

Siegel, Daniel J. *The Developing Mind: How Relationship and the Brain Interact to Shape Who We Are.* New York: Guilford Press, 1999.

Siegel, Daniel J., and Mary Hartzell. *Parenting from the Inside Out: How a Deeper Self-Understanding Can Help You Raise Children Who Thrive.* New York: Penguin Group / Jeremy P. Tarcher, 2004.

Simpson, Jeffry A., and W. Steven Rholes. *Attachment Theory and Close Relationships.* New York: Guilford Press, 1998.

Snyderman, Nancy, and Peg Streep. *Girl in the Mirror: Mothers and Daughters in the Years of Adolescence.* New York: Hyperion Books, 2002.

Sonnenberg, Susanna. *Her Last Death: A Memoir.* New York: Scribner, 2008.

Sorce, James F., Robert N. Emde, Joseph Campos, and Mary D. Klinnert. "Maternal Emotional Signaling: Its Effects on the Visual Cliff Behavior of 1-year-olds." *Developmental Psychology* 21, no. 1 (1985): 195–200.

Stark, Vikki. *My Sister, My Self: Understanding the Sibling Relationships That Shape Our Lives, Our Loves, and Ourselves.* New York: McGraw-Hill, 2007.

Steinberg, Laurence, with Wendy Steinberg. *Crossing Paths: How Your Child's Adolescence Triggers Your Own Crisis.* New York: Simon & Schuster, 1994.

Stern, Daniel N. *The Interpersonal World of the Infant: A View from Psychoanalysis and Developmental Psychology.* New York: Basic Books, 2000.

———. *The Motherhood Constellation: A Unified View of Parent-Infant Psychotherapy.* New York: Basic Books, 1995.

Stern, Daniel N., and Nadia Bruschweiler-Stern. *The Birth of a Mother: How the Motherhood Experience Changes You Forever.* New York: Basic Books, 1998.

Tannen, Deborah. *You're Wearing That? Understanding Mothers and Daughters in Conversation.* New York: Ballantine Books, 2006.

Thomas, Lewis, Fari Amini, and Richard Lannon. *A General Theory of Love.* New York: Vintage, 2000.

Thurer, Shari L. *The Myths of Motherhood: How Culture Reinvents the Good Mother.* Boston: Houghton Mifflin, 1994.

Tronick, Edward Z. "Emotions and Emotional Communication in Infants," *American Psychologist* 44, no. 2 (February 1, 1989): 112–19.

van Mens-Verhulst, Janneke, Karlein Schreurs, and Liesbeth Woertman, eds. *Daughtering and Mothering: Female Subjectivity Reanalyzed.* London: Routledge, 1993.

Viorst, Judith. *Necessary Losses.* New York: Fireside Books, 1986.

Volling, Brenda L., Nancy L. McElwain, Paul C. Notaro, and Carla Herrera. "Parents' Emotional Availability and Infant Emotional Competence: Infant Attachment and Emerging Self-Regulation." *Journal of Family Psychology* 16, no. 4 (2002): 447–65.

Walls, Jeannette. *The Glass Castle.* New York: Scribner, 2005.

Walters, Marianne, Betty Carter, Peggy Papp, and Olga Silverstein. *The Invisible Web: Gender Patterns in Family Relationships.* New York: Guilford Press, 1988.

Walters, Suzanna Dannuta. *Lives Together/Worlds Apart: Mothers and Daughters in Popular Culture.* Berkeley: University of California Press, 1992.

Warner, Marina. *From the Beast to the Blonde: On Fairy Tales and Their Tellers.* New York: Farrar, Straus & Giroux, 1994.

Weinberg, M. Katherine, Edward Z. Tronick, Jeffrey F. Cohn, and Karen L. Olson. "Gender Differences in Emotional Expressivity and Self-Regulation During Early Infancy."*Developmental Psychology* 35 (1999): 175–88.

Whitehead, Barbara Dafoe. *The Divorce Culture: Rethinking Our Commitments to Marriage and Family.* New York: Vintage, 1998.

Zax, Barbara, and Stephan Poulter. *Mending the Broken Bough: Restoring the Promise of the Mother-Daughter Relationship.* New York: Berkley Books, 1998.

Index